Life at the Limit

Life at the Limit

Tony Duffield

© TD 2023
Tony Duffield

The right of Tony Duffield to be identified as the author of this work
has been assessed by him in accordance with
The Copyright, Designs and Patents Act 1988

Cover picture by Mick Robinson

First published 2025
by
BENTNOSE PUBLICATIONS
Polegate, Sussex

ISBN 978-1-0369-0724-2

For information and sales:
https://bentnosepublications.wordpress.com

Designed and typeset in 12/16 Baskerville by J. D. Smedley 2024

IN MEMORY OF OUR GOOD FRIEND DOUGLAS

To Norman and Gerry Wood,
without whose influence
we may never have discovered
the joys of motorcycling.

Contents

Introduction

I SUPPOSE I always knew one day I would actually have to sit down and write this book. I guess you could say we were a pretty lawless bunch back then, growing up as we did throughout an era when big noisy British motorcycles were king. It was the era of post World War II world. Many younger parents were ex-service personnel, veterans only recently demobbed from duty and wartime service. Some parents had even fought in both world wars. It was a time of hard work and poverty with few comforts. This was the era of Rock 'n Roll and Teddy Boys, soon to be followed by the leather-clad 'Ton-Up Boys', transport cafés and coffee bars, the Café Racers, the jukebox and record races. A decade or so on came Rockers, Mods, scooters and the Mini, miniskirts and the pill. The freedom of the open road with minimal traffic at a time when most young people still lived at home, when everything closed down at eleven o'clock at night, when the police were patrolling empty roads after midnight, stopping anyone still out and noting down their details—a time when you had to get up at some seemingly unearthly hour in the morning to be at work.

However, it was also a time when the few police cars around the area were relatively slow. The local village 'Bobby' cycled or pounded the beat on foot, but beware, as the local cop knew most on his patch and was not above paying a visit to your father or administering his own form of justice down a dark alley in the form of a backhander or two. A time when drinking and driving was normal and the test of whether you were fit to drive or not depended on if you could walk a straight line down the centre of the road unaided. When there was no helmet or seat belt laws (seat belts were fitted to very few cars back then) and Bank Holiday brawls with the Mods at the seaside towns filled the newspapers and became the norm.

It was a time of freedom when if you were fortunate to have access to a vehicle a short trip to the next town or village seemed like an exciting holiday excursion to London. If you had a powerful bike you could roam free and felt like you were king of the road. An era that was about the power of your wrist on the twist grip and the wind in your hair, a time when you could buy four gallons of petrol for less than £1 and still get change.

When we were out riding we rode hard and fast. We partied wildly and courted danger but we accepted the risks. Our aim was simple, to have as much fun as possible. The threat of death was never far away and was a constant companion. We lost a few along the way but it was the death of our good friend Douglas at just thirty years old in his sleep from natural causes that hit home the most. His death seemed so unfair and futile. After the funeral we all discussed the group's previous exploits in a local bar. It was decided that pen be put to paper and our story should be recorded, at least for us as a group, even if for no one else.

'Grasscut' (Nick Goble), provoked by others, decided that as I had a good memory for long-term facts and I could, in his words, tell a good story, I should be given the unenviable task of writing it all down. Over the years and on many occasions, Grass has constantly badgered and hounded me to get on with it, so it is mainly down to his influence that this story is at last in print.

It is the story of a wild and somewhat lawless band of bikers from the late 1960s and throughout the decade of the 1970s. A story of passion for fast motorcycles, partying, extraordinary comradeship and the thrill of high speed.

A story based on truth and fact.

So finally this is their story. I hope it makes good reading.

Cricket

'WHACK' went the bat as it hit the ball.

"Quick, run".

A general pounding of feet on the hard ground.

"Two runs".

The youngest boy retrieved the ball and threw it back to the bowler standing by the old pram axle stuck in the ground that served as the bowler's stump.

Thud, thud, thud, as the bowler in his short grey Wellington boots started his run.

"Out!"

"Was not".

"Was".

Some disagreement ensued. The neighbour's son standing behind the wicket in his white shorts cast his vote.

The others agreed, "Out".

The eldest boy, in a huff, threw down the bat, which was almost immediately picked up by the youngest boy who then took his place at the wicket.

The ball was returned to the bowler.

"Ready?"

The bowler paused, standing stiff for a moment and listening.

"What's up?"

There it was again.

The game stopped briefly.

"It's them," he shouted, "I can hear them".

In the distance was a low rumble. For a moment it dulled but then came back louder this time.

The boys listened for a moment then the batsman threw down the bat.

As one the three brothers began to run, the neighbour's son a short distance behind.

The noise increased from the low rumble to a definite roar.

From the back garden they ran round the side of the house.

The left of the single concrete path was bedecked with tall yellow flowers, on the right lay a large lawn.

Ahead was a small wall with a closed gate that led directly into the road.

Reaching the gate the young boys knew better than to go any further into the road.

The roaring increased dramatically until it reached a deafening crescendo.

The young boys jumped up and down with excitement, waving fanatically.

In almost a blur two 650 Triumph motorcycles flashed by, side by side, at full throttle. The sound was ear shattering, both of the helmetless riders lying flat across the bike petrol tanks in a race, their hair blowing in the breeze.

In an instant they were gone, past open fields and the main farmyard, the sound tailing off. A slight whiff of exhaust smoke hung in the air. In the distance the sound of gear changing could be heard as the bikes were forced to change down to negotiate a tight left hand bend just short of the farmhouse and then onward again, before eventually fading away.

Thrilled, the three young brothers decided there and then that when they got older they too would ride big and powerful motorcycles just like their uncles, and to this day all three of us do.

CHAPTER ONE

Growing up

I WAS born seven years after the end or World War II and my two brothers within the next three years. Life was really quite tough for many families and some wartime rationing was still in place on some foods. I am told that I had a ration book for the first few years of my life.

Our father Len had been born in the East End of London where his family had a wholesale/retail bakery business in East Ham. The family business sold bread and cakes over much of London as well as from their own shop at 44 High Street South. Our dad's first driving experiences occurred there as an under-age teenager when he would drive one of the firm's delivery vans home across the Woolwich Ferry after a delivery round wearing his brother's cap to try to make himself look older while his brother slept in the back of the van.

There were four children in the family, two girls and two boys of which our dad was the youngest. He had a boyhood friend called George. Dad and his friend roamed the area getting into all kinds of mischief. If George was not around, dad liked nothing better than to cycle down to the Queen Victoria and Albert Docks where he would sit for hours watching the ships coming and going or discharging and loading cargo at the other docks or when at home, being an avid reader, he would read books.

In 1939 war was declared and after a while dad and George decided to join up. George was aeroplane crazy—the two boys had once gone to the Hendon Air Display together. Therefore, George applied to be enlisted into the Royal Air Force while our father applied to join the Army. George was accepted for Royal Air Force Volunteer Reserve (RAFVR) duty but our dad was turned down for Army service as the recruiting sergeant thought he looked too young and told him to "Come back sonny when you're old enough", despite dad being actually eighteen years old. Not to be perturbed he went down to the Local Defence Volunteer post and enlisted into what later became known as the Home Guard for home defence instead.

It was in this role that dad got his first taste of action as it was on Saturday afternoon in September 1940 that massed formations of German planes attacked the London docks near his home. Our dad happened to be in the cinema at Forest Gate when bombs started to fall, so he ran all the way back to East Ham to Home Guard HQ under the town hall in the middle of an air raid. This was the start of the London blitz where Londoners faced bombing on most nights for around eight months. Many people were killed and many more injured during this terrible time.

In 1941 dad was called up into the regular army and so left the Home Guard. He was sent to Gloucester after his basic training and was later posted abroad to see action. His brother Ronald was already serving with the Royal Berkshire Regiment and his sister Doris joined the Royal Navy (WRENS). On his first night at the Gloucester camp dad had been placed on camp guard duty. On entering the guard room he had seen his brother's name at the top of the board. His brother had been in charge of the guard the night before, his regiment having just left. Sadly, dad was never to see his brother again. For the next five years dad was posted all round the world it seems learning as much about the Black Market as he did about fighting.

In late 1944 a German V2 rocket, the first ballistic missile, fell on the East Ham street where they lived and blew the front out of the family home. It also destroyed the home of dad's boyhood friend George, the blast from which George's mother was to die of her injuries. In early 1945, when home on leave, dad learned that his brother Ron had been killed in Burma whilst fighting the Japanese. More bad news was to come as dad's great friend George's Lancaster bomber had received a direct hit on a raid over France on the run up to D Day with the loss of the entire crew. Sadly our father went along to his own demolished home where he managed to at least retrieve his bomb damaged collection of Just William books from the rubble.

Faced with the appalling events of this time dad's parents decided to leave London for good and so bought a newsagent, tobacconist and off-licence business in a small village in the south east of England near the sea. His parents sent dad a letter as he was still serving abroad on active Army service requesting that he join them there when he was demobbed; and so it was that on a sunny day in 1946 our father first stepped from a steam train at a station in a little Sussex village that he had never heard of until a few months before. The same little village where he was to meet and marry a local farmer's daughter. A little village where he was to spend the rest of his life.

For the first three or four years of my life we lived in rented accommodation, but in 1956 our grandfather (our dad's father) died and his business was sold. Dad inherited some money from his father's estate and so our parents purchased our own house on a country lane to the north of our village. Our mother's family owned a mainly dairy farm further along this same lane and her and her brothers and sisters were born in the farmhouse, as was I and both of my brothers and many of my cousins as well. I can vividly remember the day we moved house, when all our furniture and belongings were loaded onto a tractor and trailer which then set off to our new home. Our grandad (mother's father) had taken over this farm from his father as had his father before him. It had been in the family since the late 1800's.

Our mother was one of seven children, four girls and three boys. Our uncles all worked on the land for their father for much of their lives. All three were very fit and active and all played football for the local team. I remember that it was an occasion of much family pride when all went to the village recreation ground to see all of our mother's brothers play for the same team in the same match. Later, Eric the elder brother, went to work on local building sites leaving the farm work to the two younger boys, although he still provided holiday and emergency relief work when needed.

Farming was hard, physical and labour intensive work. There was no such things as power tools back then on the farm so everything had to be done by hand or by primitive agricultural machinery; indeed electricity had only finally come to the farm and farmhouse after the war had finished. Drills and grinders had to be hand cranked and with no welding available most repairs meant that jobs were carried out by hand drilling holes and nut and bolting them back together. Trees were cut down and chopped up using axes and huge crosscut hand saws operated by two people. Nothing was wasted, wartime mentality prevailed. The wartime slogan of 'Make do and Mend' had cut deep and was still the order of the day. All spare wood was stacked and stored and all decent metal was stored in the large tool shed for future use. Used nails and screws were straightened and re-used. With much still on ration, if you could get it you could not afford it. Many materials were still in short supply. This wartime mentality filtered down to us and I still store such materials now for re-use if practical. The staple footwear of a farmer is his Wellington boots. Even as children we wore them rain or shine. They are easy to peel on or off, require no lacing up, are waterproof and treading in God knows what are perfect for the job in hand. When extra labour was needed such as at harvest times and herding cattle through the village to graze on more distant grasslands our grandfather would enlist the assistance of the whole family to do the job. These days are remembered fondly by us all as happy and carefree times.

It was our two younger uncles that we looked up to the most and looking back almost hero-worshipped. Both had that young, almost tearaway attitude to life. The brothers were in their own ways as different as chalk and cheese. Norman, the elder of the two, was the steadier and did not drink or smoke. He was a perfectionist and he always prided himself with doing a good job at whatever he was doing..

Gerry, on the other hand, was equally as capable but would prefer to do a quick, functional job rather than seek perfection. Gerry was partial to a good drinking session on occasions and also enjoyed smoking cigarettes. He was the wilder of the two being a number of years younger than Norman. Both owned Triumph 650 motorcycles and in a shed at the farm they had an early Triumph 500 Speed Twin with a sidecar fitted. The sidecar body had been removed and replaced with a large wooden box for small jobs around the farm. On occasions our uncles would put us in the sidecar box and blast around the farmyard, sliding sideways on the slippery cow shit on the concrete yard or rip across the fields to move an electric cattle fence. All very exciting stuff to us three young and impressionable boys.

Gerry's era was that of the 'Ton Up Boy', laying flat across the tank trying to wring the last mile an hour from his roaring steed. He would roar through the village, much to the annoyance of some locals and the odd police officer, race to the pubs and dances as well as go to motorcycle race meetings. On one occasion a member of the public complained to our grandmother that

Gerry laid his bike over so far as he swept into the High Street that he almost hit his head on the metal Keep Left sign. After this, whenever Gerry saw that upright citizens were watching him he would rev the bike harder, lay it over further and go even closer to the sign.

Late one evening our grandmother received a phone call at the farmhouse from a lady stating that Gerry had gone through a hedge outside her house on his motorcycle and he was the worse for wear from the effects of alcohol. Our grandparents got in the car and drove down and loaded up the drunken offender and brought him home to sleep it off. On another day he was pursued by a motorcycle cop on a Speed Twin, but Gerry's 650 T110 was the quicker. He built up a lead on the cop, raced home and quickly put the bike in the shed and rushed indoors. Then he sat in the farmhouse kitchen drinking tea watching the cop go up and down the road looking for him.

Prior to buying his beloved Triumph Tiger T110 Gerry had previously owned an AJS single cylinder 500. It was on this motorcycle on the route home from seeing his girlfriend Gerry received his first and ultimate claim to fame when he ran down the vicar of a local village and sent him spinning down the road on his backside after the vicar had tried to make a late dash across the road in front of him.

Norman would also speak of his exploits on his old Norton single as well as later on the Triumph twin. When riding the Norton he would race along flat out, shut down the throttle and with the engine on overrun would retard the manual ignition timing fully so that the bike would backfire repeatedly and shoot flame out of the end of his open 'Brooklands Can' exhaust. This was particularly impressive at night.

When the brothers got married and settled down this did not stop their exploits. They simply fitted sidecars to their machines to accommodate the family and continued to ride them hard, on occasions lifting the sidecar wheel into the air on left-hand bends, cutting corners and riding with the sidecar wheel over the pavement to get the edge over an opponent or drifting the outfit around a couple of solo motorcycles on wet roads on right-hand bends to take the lead.

As I was getting nearer my legal riding age myself, I would spend many hours at the farm during milking discussing with Gerry his earlier exploits. There was something in this whole way of life that appealed to me immensely; the speed, the freedom of the open road, the power of a large and noisy motorcycle, the ability to go anywhere you wanted when you wanted to and the whole almost outlaw image on the edge of society. This whole way of life I found to be very exciting and I guess it had not only that effect on me but on my brothers also.

CHAPTER TWO

Learning the ropes

ALL the children in the village went to our local village school until we were eleven years old. We all knew each other and got on pretty well. After undergoing our eleven-plus exams we were split up with the brainiest members of our year going on to grammar school and the rest of us to the local secondary modern school. It was going to that school that came as something of a nasty shock to some of us, as our classmates from the village junior school were generally our friends. We were suddenly learning alongside pupils from the surrounding district who were bussed in daily from the more outside areas. Amongst these pupils were a number of bullies and petty thugs that saw it as their duty to pick on those they thought of as weaker than themselves or more placid. These people, along with one other who had recently moved into the area, had the ability to make one's school life a total misery while at school which already had a bad bullying problem.

The school bully is basically a coward, generally not so tough on his own, but usually needs a group of friends or hangers-on around him to back him up. This is usually the case with all bullies and not just at school. If the school bully hits you and you do not retaliate you soon find that his hangers-on will bully you also. This was the case for myself for the first three years at that school. The fear of if you fight back they will all set upon you and beat you up stops you from defending yourself. During the fourth and final year at secondary school one particular bully pushed me fairly hard and I lashed out from instinct and hit him back with some force. His little band of hoodlums all backed off and none of them ever tried to hit me again. I realised at this point that even if you are afraid always take on the bully of the pack, for even if you go down fighting it is better than being a coward. It is a fact that in many situations the aggressor is all mouth and will often back off if confronted or clobbered, so you may not have a real fight on your hands after all. I resigned myself at this point to never take any crap from anyone ever again and then we left school for good, but this leads me to another future occurrence.

Although I had decided the fact that I was eventually going to get myself a big Triumph twin motorcycle, there was a small problem of having to get my riding test passed. At that time a rider was permitted to ride a motorcycle first on L plates not exceeding 250cc as a solo motorcycle or bigger machines if they were permanently fitted with a sidecar. My cousin John had a fairly stylish used 125cc Honda twin for sale of the type that were flooding the country from Japan back then; so I worked hard and put every penny I earned towards the purchase price of £60 figuring that it would be a nice bike to at least learn on. We already had old motorbikes which we had ridden around the fields so I was not a complete novice. When the time came I duly handed over the cash and took possession of this gleaming red steed. It really was my pride and joy.

I rode my motorbike as often as I could. This was the Mods and Rockers era. At school everyone would ask you if you were either a Mod or a Rocker. Pretty much you were one or the other, although there was the odd flaky character that was a bit of a hippy. By then most at school identified as Mods with only a few Rockers, perhaps ten per cent of the intake, but it is a fact that many that dressed as, and called themselves Mods, never owned a scooter at all, choosing instead to catch a bus into town and pose around the streets in all their gear. One evening I rode out to a neighbouring village youth club and parked my bike outside the library opposite. When I came out later a number of scooters had parked nearby and a group of about five or six Mods were around my bike. I noticed that one scooter was pretty fancy and recognised it as one owned by a Mod known as Bresco. His scooter had an expensive paint job and had a number of tuning parts fitted. Other local Mods looked up to Bresco as they thought him and his scooter to be pretty cool. As I approached I noticed that one Mod was crouching down and tampering with my bike. I was absolutely livid and stormed over to them in a rage. In a loud and angry voice I confronted them. "If that bike does not start you are in trouble". Bresco turned and sneered at me, but did nothing. However, the crouching Mod jumped up and asked me what the hell I was going to do about it and struck me in the face. I was carrying my crash helmet, so I let him have it straight over the head with all my might. He went straight down. Bresco, this self-styled head man of the pack backed off and the other Mods parted. Bresco was not known as a particularly hard case— merely a figurehead. I rescued my bike, which luckily fired up straight away and I quickly rode away. Luckily I had caught them before they had done any damage. More proof, if you need it, that if you stand up and confront an aggressor, all too often they will back down and think twice before crossing you again in the future.

I had a friend from my schooldays also named John, and he owned a battered BSA 250 C12 with a leopard skin seat cover and dropped Ace handlebars. John's family owned a smallholding. I took to riding around the local area with him. One evening when out, I misjudged the second of a double bend and went into a hedge. John gave me a good ribbing about that, but around a week later the boot was on the other foot. We had ridden to a country pub called the Fullers Arms and John had taken a mate called Bob along. On the way home we stormed across the reservoir road and John tore into a forty-five degree left bend at the top. When we left the pub Bob had lit a cigarette and anyone who rides a bike knows that because of the airflow a lit cigarette will burn to nothing in a very short space of time. Generally people that do this, do it because it may look cool, rather than for a practical factor. I could see that John was going too fast to make the curve. As he threw the bike in, everything grounded in a shower of sparks and they were off the bike. The BSA and John went sliding down the road while Bob was thrown into the air and landed heavily. His lit cigarette disintegrated into a load of sparks on the road, so now we were even. This time the joke was on John.

After a while John introduced me to a couple of his mates, Eric and Mick, who lived in the seaside town of Seaford about ten miles further along the coast. In the summer of 1968 on August Bank Holiday weekend there was a motorcycle show held at the Hotel Metropole on Brighton's seafront. Myself, Mick and Eric and my brother Tel riding on Mick's pillion, went along to the show on our bikes. I guess we were still a bit green on the Mods and Rockers front back then regarding any possible threat. When we left the hotel after the show we mounted our bikes and rode back along Brighton seafront. Suddenly we were confronted by hordes of Mods, hundreds of the buggers, all yelling and screaming abuse and being held back by a police cordon. When we arrived back at home we were all covered in green phlegm where the gangs of Mods had spat all over us; but then, looking back, we were probably lucky to get off that lightly that day.

One evening we decided to ride over to the Top Rank ice rink at Brighton to go ice skating, so myself, Mick and Eric rode over on our bikes. Eric owned a couple of bikes, one was a pretty immaculate Velocette 350 Viper. The silencer was rotted out on the Velo when Eric got hold of it, so he had bought another silencer that was quite loud. Fearing that the law may take a more than passing interest in his noisy bike Eric decided to try to quieten it down a bit and so purchased a quantity of wire wool and proceeded to stuff it into the silencer. Eric rode the bike around for a few days and all seemed fine. He was happy with the result, so we all set off for the ice rink as previously arranged. A good evening was had by all and we came out and set off home. The weather had turned nasty, conditions were atrocious. The winds were gale force and torrential rain was falling with some flooding. We left Brighton and had to lean into the wind on the straights to stay upright. As we rode along the top of Telscombe Cliffs taking a battering from the downpour, Eric's silencer caught fire and lots of red hot shards of burning wire were flying right across the road. The fire in the silencer continued with the same results until all of the wire had burnt itself out and the Viper was back to its noisy self again, but what an awful ride home it was that night. We were totally drenched.

One summer morning I was out riding the local country roads and passed through a small historic old smugglers' village. I was hardly clear of the village when there was a terrific roar from behind and a bright red Ducati motorcycle flew past. I could see from behind that he was running an open megaphone silencer. The rider sped smoothly through a series of bends, dropped over the hill and was gone. I was fascinated by the speed and absolute smoothness of the rider. If I had but known it, then this was my first encounter with the legendary Roger 'Dilly' Dumbrell, a local legend in his own lifetime and the man everyone wanted to beat. His name was a household word in local bike folklore. His exploits on the road and run-ins with the police and courts were the stuff of legend.

Mick was a trainee mechanic and worked in a small garage in the afore-mentioned smugglers' village. As he worked in the area, Mick would often drink in one of the village pubs with some of the locals. His favourite drinking hole was the bar in the Market Inn, which is reported to have an upstairs room with seven doors in that one room. This was where in the old days of smuggling the contraband could be rowed up the river at the dead of night and hidden around the village. The smugglers would hold their meetings in that one room. If the customs men had burst through one door the smugglers would have bolted out of the other six and fled. One day I rode into the village and stopped at Mick's garage for fuel. Mick was not working that day, but a young lad (with black frizzy hair) who was on petrol pump duty came out to serve me with petrol. He could not have been older than fourteen years old. He filled my tank and I paid him. As he turned to walk away he said, "You think you are quick on that bike, but really you're just a wanker". He was quick on his feet and nipped off back inside laughing. I was horrified. Who the hell was that cheeky bloody kid? When I saw Mick I asked him about the kid. Mick told me they called him Sprogg and he was the bane of their working lives with his constant cheek. The boys at the garage had got so fed up with Sprogg that they chased him down, dragged him inside, removed his trousers and gave his testicles a liberal coating with a handful of grease. When the cheek had not stopped they went even further. There was a girl that Sprogg fancied that used to ride on the back seat of the local bus. Sprogg used to cycle behind the bus in the narrow streets waving to her so the garage boys greased the brake blocks on his pedal cycle and he ran into the back of the bus. This seemed to quieten him down a bit, at least for a little while.

A few months on, and my motorcycle test passed, I found a Triumph 500 Speed Twin, similar in looks, if not in outright cubic capacity to our uncle's bikes for £30 in a neighbouring village. The bike was a bit older than I would have preferred, but it was in good shape and good mechanical order. I was overwhelmed. I finally had the big Triumph twin of the type that I had wanted since that day as a young boy. I started hanging around the village and drank in the Smugglers Bar as well. For a small smugglers' village it had a good youth club held once a week in the village hall and it was new ground with fresh people and was free of Mods. Always a bonus! I soon came across other bikers from the area, one had the modern equivalent of my own bike. He was known as 'Kiddie' and he was a few years older than myself. He had just bought a brand new Triumph Daytona 500, the latest twin carburettor version of my old Speed Twin. There was Geoff and his mate Tim. Then there was Johnny whose family ran the local youth hostel. Den a mechanic who worked in a garage in another village further out, a quietly spoken, gentle giant of a man of few words, but a very fast rider. Then there was Sam, a local antique dealer in the village. A year or two on there was Tank who was Sprogg's elder brother; he was so named because of his stocky build. Then there was a guy with a Triumph 350 Tiger 90 whose name now escapes me, and last but not least there was Snout.

Snout came from Litlington, a small village a couple of miles out, and had just sold his Honda 160 twin and bought a 1960 Triumph 650 Bonneville with a duplex frame. Triumph only made this particular model for a year or two so Bonnevilles of this period are now quite rare. Snout was a real character. He worked for a turf farm cutting turf each day. He had long ginger collar length hair that was thick and rough to the touch. It was like coconut matting. He was around six feet six inches tall and never wore a leather jacket or jeans, but instead usually dressed in a dark olive green suit type jacket with black trousers and white shirt, a tie and ordinary polished shoes. He was called 'Snout' because of the shape of his nose and he called everyone 'Young Laddie'. It was his favourite saying and it was always 'Young Laddie' this and 'Young Laddie' that. Working on the land as he did, he was a tough physical specimen. When he hit the dance floor at discos he would fan his fingers out on both hands and drop both middle fingers a couple of inches and throw himself around the floor with much gusto despite his sizeable bulk. I can still vividly picture him throwing himself around the village hall dance floor to Yellow River by Christie jerking his hands back and forth as he danced, his long ginger hair flailing and all of the girls trying to keep up with him. Some sight, as he towered over them all.

One night I left the village with Kiddie and we were getting a bit of a lick on gunning our 500 Triumphs when both filaments of his headlamp blew plunging him into total darkness so he had to follow me to his home. It was soon to become apparent that these country boys were fast riders and I was struggling to keep up. Some of them rode smaller Japanese bikes which were pretty quick and they rode them hard. Soon some of my younger mates from my home village came of riding age and they also began to ride with us. There was Pud, short for Pudding, as he was a little on the plump side when he was a kid, but was now slimmer, and Mad Mongol so named as his party piece was to throw one leg over the saddle of his Honda 250 CB72 and roar along the centre of the road weaving in and out of the cat's eyes while riding side saddle. Someone had made a mention of it saying it was like seeing Genghis Khan and the Mad Mongol hordes on the rampage. Then there was my brother Tel and Bog Wright, who got that name after his mum made him a sleeping bag out of an old eiderdown or duvet. When Tel saw it rolled up he suggested that the bag looked like a bog roll (toilet roll) and the name then stuck.

After a brief and unsuccessful episode with a Tiger Cub, Tel had given up on British bikes and later bought a Suzuki.

When we were out riding as a pack it was obvious that my Speed Twin was totally outclassed. A Suzuki T200 Invader was as fast as my 500 Triumph. Oh, sure the Triumph had the edge on a long straight, but as you had to ease up slightly for any corner, Geoff on his Suzuki 200, would ride around the outside of you with his lighter more agile bike. Kiddie's modern Triumph had an extra ten miles an hour over mine, but it was still lacking. A Suzuki Super Six 250 was now as fast as a Triumph 650 Thunderbird. Around this time I got a job at the nearby Birds Eye factory which paid good money for shift work. I blew up the Speed Twin engine trying to stay with the others. Now, with some decent money coming in I had my engine completely rebuilt by a tuning specialist with many hot parts fitted at great expense. Eventually, once run in, I was able to see 105mph on the clock—fifteen miles an hour faster than before and now on a par with Kiddie's Triumph. The problem was the extra power made the bike unreliable and it was always breaking down—as was Kiddie's much newer bike. It was with sad reflection that we eventually decided that there may be some truth in the old saying, "If you can't beat them, join them". Admitting defeat was a sad day for us as I felt I may have in some small way let my uncles down, and Kiddie up to this point had always owned British bikes, mainly BSA or Triumphs. Things were changing, no longer were British bikes competitive with Japanese. You could not hold a British bike flat out for mile after mile without it breaking down or blowing up, but with a Japanese bike you could and it still would not leak oil at the end of it. At this time you could walk into any café or disco and pick out which bikers rode British and which rode Japanese. The British bike owners always had at least one oily shoe. Those infamous words uttered by the Managing Director of Triumph Motorcycles, Edward Turner, addressing the British bike industry, when he said, "We have nothing to fear from the Japanese, they are just manufacturers of mopeds and scooters", was to become the death knell of the whole British motorcycle industry.

CHAPTER THREE

The Litlington TT

IT was great fun hanging out over the village with a bunch of like-minded souls. We used to meet in the Market Square where our bikes would be lined up in a row. Most nights we would head out on rides and other times we would just sit and talk or maybe go in the Smugglers for a beer or two. On Fridays the village youth club sometimes held a disco. On the left of the square was an old fashioned traditional butcher's shop. The butcher had a horse and trap, and at the local annual village fair he would drive around the field selling his meat and sausages. The butcher prided himself on quality and won awards for his popular sausages. Outside his shop stood a disabled charity box about three feet high in the shape of a child in leg irons. The box was chained to the support of his shop blind. If we roared into the village as a pack he would rush out, unlock his charity box and hurriedly drag it into his shop and lock the door. He obviously thought we were nothing but a load of no good yobs.

It was here in the village that I first met 'Dilly' Dumbrell in person, living as he did nearby. He was probably five or six years older than me, as were two of the other riders. Dilly loved all motorcycles and over the years had many different makes, models and sizes of bikes. He lived on a country road a mile or two from the farm cottage where his father owned the farm. Nearly opposite his cottage in Milton Street was a small flint built farm building about the size of a normal garage, affectionately known as 'The Shed'. This was where Dilly kept his bikes and his tools to fettle them. He was a perfectionist and was constantly cleaning, polishing and tuning his bike or bikes to get the best out of them. In the centre of the shed was a low home-made workbench which he would run his bike up onto to work on it, with a bigger work bench right across the back wall that held a vice and some of his tools. Dilly did not drink and he just liked to ride, so if he turned up at the village you knew there was a tear-up going on. He was fast and super smooth. He would sweep through the country lanes at high speed with a grace and perfection that I had never seen before on the road, his style similar to that of many times champion and famous motorcycle racer Mike Hailwood. Not an inch of him was in the airstream more than needed to be. There was an old song that was sometimes played on the radio called Poetry in Motion, which described Dilly's riding style perfectly. When people saw him ride for the first time, they were quite frankly gob-smacked. Many years later an older biker said to me that he had been to several Isle of Man TT race weeks before he had met Dilly and seen him ride, but he was still utterly amazed by the man's grace, style and speed.

Simon and Roger were two good friends, both sensible and re-spectable motorcyclists. They had recently bought two new matching maroon and silver Triumph T120 Bonnevilles. Out for a ride they arrived at Alfriston and stopped at the Smugglers for a lunchtime drink. They were just finishing their drinks when Dilly and his pack came howling through the village en route to Dilly's shed and disappeared. Simon commented on the fact that the boys were in a hurry as they picked up their helmets to leave. Mounting their bikes they went through the normal rigmarole of starting a British bike; ignition on, fuel on, tickle both carbu-rettors to flood the fuel through, adjust chokes, pull in clutch and use kickstart to rock engine over to compression stroke. Just as they did this there was a loud screech of brakes. A police car skidded to a halt beside Simon. The policeman nearest him shouted, "Move and you're nicked!" Startled, Simon overbalanced and almost fell over with the bike as he hovered unsteadily on one foot—his other foot high on the kickstart, being about to be thrust down to kick the engine into life. The cops exited the car and accused them of being the tearaways. Their whole appearance and demeanour was not that of yobs or reckless riders. Eventually after protesting their innocence, common sense prevailed, and the cops cleared off in the opposite direction from which they had come.

One afternoon Dilly and the group had been out on a fast run. The group were a number of quick riders who were really competitive. Although the run was a fairly quick one, Dilly's bike was slightly off-tune and he was not happy with its flat-out performance, and so it was that the pack ended up back at the shed. As soon as they arrived, Dilly opened the double doors and ran his bike up onto the small workbench and pulled the doors closed. The group were inside just having a chat when there was a sudden loud squeal of tyres outside. It was the police. Two officers burst into the shed in an aggressive manner. "Have you been out on your bikes?" demanded the first one. The other cop, hot on his heels, backing up his fellow officer, "Have you just come from racing through the village?" "Not us", retorted Dilly with a smile, "We have been here all the time". Unconvinced the first cop strode over and put his hand firmly on the bike's exhaust. He leapt back with a loud yell of pain. "Oh, sorry" said Dilly, almost by way of apology, "I should have told you that I have just been running it up." As the disgruntled cops got back in their car to drive away, a roar of laughter could be heard erupting from within the walls of the shed.

Today was his lucky day. Dilly had heard of a 500 Manx Norton race bike for sale at a good price. He had done a bit of track practice in his time, but circuit racing was not his cup of tea.

Riding at speed on the road was his forte, where he could just jump on his bike at a whim and ride to his heart's content as and when he wished. To go racing you needed some form of race transport to carry bike, tools, spares and equipment, and at the time Dilly did not have a car licence. Motorcycles were his life and he had no time for cars, not even the slightest inclination ever to get a licence. He had no intention of keeping the Manx Norton either; but he saw it was a nice machine that he could sell on, perhaps for a good profit. So he purchased the Manx Norton, which was duly delivered to the shed. The bike was wheeled onto the bench and got the full Dilly treatment. Tank and seat off, oils changed, new spark plug, valve clearances checked and adjusted, new fork oil and new chain fitted. Petrol tank and seat were replaced—the bike was ready to rock and roll. Fully satisfied Dilly retired to his farm cottage for his evening meal.

Soon motorcycles could be heard in the distance as one by one the group arrived to see the iconic machine. They all walked over to the shed together and when the doors were opened stood back and stared in awe at the gleaming motorcycle. "Got to start it Dill", was the general mood of the group. "Go on, fire the fucker up". Willing hands helped as the bike was manhandled from the bench and wheeled out into the evening sunshine. A gallon or two of petrol was poured into the fuel tank. Second gear selected, bike pulled backwards and rocked to compression, kill switch off and Dilly donned his helmet and gloves, clutch in. A couple of lads started pushing. Dilly threw his backside down hard into the racing seat and the engine fired instantly. The noise from that open megaphone was loud and sweet, but deafening and there was a whiff of Castrol R racing oil drifting in the air. Braaabbaaa, braaabbaa... superb!

Dilly, blipping the throttle set off steadily up the road. Luckily the street was a quiet country road as this was a proper thoroughbred race bike with an open race pipe and was in no way road legal. As the group stood at the roadside waiting to see some action Dilly's father appeared from a field with his dog, crossed the road, opened a gate opposite and disappeared into that field. The Norton could be heard in the distance, its rider blipping the throttle at the end of the road to bring the engine up to normal running temperature. Suddenly the revs went up and with a terrific roar like thunder the Norton started its run, faster and faster, the rider changing up through the gearbox. Down the hill and then it could be heard rushing into the bend just up the road when impending disaster... a flock of sheep had suddenly appeared in the field near the gate. Then bike and rider appeared accelerating hard out of the bend, Dilly gunning the Norton hard down the straight. With that the flock of sheep were coming out of the gate onto the wide road verge. Dilly and the Norton flew past, still hard on the throttle, and disappeared around the next bend. The sheep jumped high in the air in blind panic and stampeded back into the field from where they had just come from. A red faced Mr. Dumbrell came running out of the field. He was really angry and shook his stick. "what the... who the bloody hell was that?" "It was your son Mr. Dumbrell," came the reply. "My God, he will kill his bloody self", a sudden look of sadness in the elderly farmer's eyes.

Dilly rode into the village. There was a run coming off. The bikes were lined up. Den, Kiddie and Dilly were all of a similar age, the rest were younger. These elder three were very fast riders, as was Geoff who was my age. Johnny had not arrived but had said he would be there. The group had a circuit that started and finished at the shed. It was a timed circuit of about ten miles and on public roads. Most of the circuit was on open speed limits but a short stretch of about a mile or so was in a 30 miles per hour speed limit in Seaford. On the shed wall was a blackboard where the name of each rider was chalked up with the size of his machine, e.g.; 125, 250, 350, 500 and over. A rider would be flagged away with a handkerchief while someone else timed him with a stopwatch. When he returned his time was checked and the fastest time for that class was chalked onto the board where it remained until someone else beat it. This was known as the Local TT or Litlington TT. Johnny was after the record for the 125cc class when he crashed. This was not a completely unheard of scenario, as riders rode hard to try to beat another's TT class record. The group were all hanging around at the shed when Johnny was out for his class record and they could hear his bike coming on its return. They heard the bike, having turned into the lane and flat out down the hill. On the final left hand bend before the shed Johnny had dropped the Suzuki, which spun around and hit a telegraph pole on the corner, destroying the rear mudguard which was part of the pressed steel frame. Johnny had been looking for another bike of reasonable cubic capacity for a while, and as Dilly had several, he bought a nice raced up Montesa 250 Impala Sport from him. The Montesa was a very quick and under-rated bike of that era. Being a single cylinder two-stroke the engine was narrow and fast with excellent ground clearance on corners. It had a racing tank and seat, clip on handlebars and a Yamaha racing front brake—in short it was a cracking looking bike. The worst thing about it, if there was one, was that it was still a petrol/oil mix system at a time when most two-strokes had moved on to an oil pump Posilube type system. Johnny now owned and loved the Montesa and thoroughly enjoyed riding it. This same bike in other hands was to prove extremely successful on the race tracks, but more about that later.

So still waiting for Johnny the pack decided to spur him on into coming out to play. As previously stated, Johnny's family ran the local Youth Hostel. The YHA building wall was right on the edge of the road. The road narrowed dramatically at this point and went through a type of cutting with the hostel right on the edge of the road on the left side and a high bank with high trees on the right. There was one window overlooking the road and that was Johnny's room. Johnny had previously told the boys that if he was laying on his bed, the window open, and a vehicle flew through the cutting at speed his curtain actually blew into the room. With this in mind the group left the village in the direction of the hostel, gathering speed as they went. Closing on the hostel together, they changed down a gear and gave it all they had. As they flew through the cutting, past the hostel dropping down over the first hill of High 'n Over, they backed off. Turning around between the two bends at the bottom they rode slowly back. Johnny in his room had got the message. Down went the bike mag. "Get that bloody bike out boy. Let's ride."

Some amusing things happened when we were hanging around the village. In the 1960s the fashion had been to wear tight drain-pipe jeans with a large turn up at the bottom, with your hair in a quiff and greased back with Brylcreem, and your black leather jacket on. This was the Rocker look. Very few people wore motor-cycle boots at this time as they were expensive, probably around two week's wages, or even more for some folk.

Geoff had started his Suzuki. He turned around in the road and went to put his foot down but his kickstart had gone up his trouser leg. He struggled to get his foot down, but couldn't, and went down in an un-ceremonious heap on the tarmac, pinned down by his own bike.

On another occasion we were leaving the village to go to a disco when Snout said to keep the noise down and ride steadily as we had already supped a few beers. He kicked his Bonneville into life and with a terrific roar took off like a scalded cat and literally tore out of the village. "Bloody hell, what did he say?" yelled Pud over the din as the pack took off after Snout. Arriving at the disco Pud questioned Snout about his actions. "You told us all to take it easy and keep the noise down, and then you took off like a madman from the village". A rather flustered Snout replied, "The throttle stuck open, young laddie".

One night we all set off from the village to head for Seaford's fish and chip shop. I was riding on Pud's pillion seat. We took off but failed to even make the first tight left-hand bend, shooting across the road, we took out a section of wooden picket fencing around a cottage, which collapsed under us. The bike fell on top of it. "Quick, quick," urged Pud, as we picked the bike up and set off after the others as quickly as we could. Luckily, nothing was coming the other way.

Geoff lived on top of a hill near a water tower in a company house as his dad worked for the Water Board. Geoff had traded his Suzuki 200 in for a nice new blue Suzuki T250J. These were a lovely looking bike and very quick for a 250 at that time showing 100mph on the speedo on a flat road. To get this speed on a British bike you would have to own a 650cc or even bigger capacity motorcycle in standard trim, depending on the make and model. I also bought one of the T250Js, and now it is one of the bikes that I wished I had kept for posterity, but back then you had to sell your bike in order to finance the next one. Geoff ran in the engine of his new bike for a few hundred miles and then one evening he set off through the country lanes towards the village. Sprogg the cheeky kid from the garage used to cycle to the village and ride around the Market Square cheeking everyone and generally being a right pain in the arse. On the night in question, Geoff was on his way over and Sprogg was in the village. Geoff turned off left and gunned his new bike down the straight which led further on to a tight right-hander that swept around a bend where Plonk Barn jutted out into the road. A man was walking his dog along the straight and frantically tried to wave Geoff down. Members of the public would often do this when you were out riding, as they were appalled at our speed and the standard gesture was to stick your fingers up to them. Geoff cannot remember if that was his response at the time, but whatever he kept the power on and swept on into a right-hander before the bend with the barn on it. Suddenly, oh shit. A fully grown tree had fallen across the road. Geoff was going too fast to stop. He was still doing around 60mph when he hit the tree trunk and somersaulted over the handlebars and flew into the branches. As he was climbing out of the shrubbery in a dishevelled state the dog walker came running up and gasped, "Didn't you see me waving at you? I was trying to warn you that there was a tree down across the road". "No, I didn't see fuck all" said Geoff, now somewhat pissed off. Later when Geoff spoke to Sprogg, he told him he had been in the village and heard the bike coming at speed from across the river and then it suddenly and abruptly stopped, and then there was nothing but silence.

Kiddie, Dilly and Den had been out on a long ride and they were racing back to the village. These three older riders were really competitive and none would give way, which led to some really close riding. Hurtling back from the coast, they took the road inland. Kiddie had the lead with Dilly next and then Den. Den was experiencing a gear selection problem on his Suzuki. Like many mechanics who work on other people's vehicles all the time, they may perhaps tend to skimp on their own mechanical maintenance. On one Sunday morning, whilst riding hard, Den's bike had holed a piston and he had gone home. He was out on the bike again in the afternoon. When someone asked how he had fixed the two-stroke machine so quickly, the man of a few words simply said, "I put a nut and bolt through it, boy". Now that's what you call an emergency repair.

Shortly after they turned off the coast road this day, they headed towards the village. Riding hard they climbed up a fairly long steep gradient right to the top of the South Downs, from where you could see for miles around. After you crested the hill the road plunged dramatically and steeply downhill for a fair distance before leading into a fast right-hand curve of High 'n Over. Then it was hard on the brakes and into a tight left-hand hairpin bend before a quick squirt on the throttle as a hundred yards on was a tight right-hander followed by an equally tight left with an adverse camber and an awkward manhole cover right on the racing line as it climbed up the short but very steep hill and swept onwards past the YHA where Johnny lived and down towards the village. This whole section was nicknamed by some as 'the switchback', after a twisty turny up and down fairground ride. Incredible speeds could be reached down this hill and if you crested the first initial brow fast, man and machine literally took off. It took a brave man to keep that throttle open and fly over the top, as for a second or two, it was completely blind as you then took the plunge down into obscurity down the hill. It was likely that the road would be clear as you could see any vehicles in front of you as you sped up the long gradient from the Seaford coast road but you could not be 100 per cent sure. I know of one incident where someone had parked a van just down from the brow near the dew pond which caused a bad accident.

On this occasion though, our three daredevils had a clear road and they flew over the crest of the hill with fistfuls of throttle on tap, flying through the air, men and machines together took the plunge into obscurity. Kiddie held the lead, picking up speed as he glimpsed 90mph on the clock. Suddenly Dilly swept past him and then Den took the pair of them, but as he shifted into sixth, he missed the gear. When he found the gear, it was second or third and it locked the rear wheel solid. Smoke poured from the rear tyre and the rear of the bike skidded out to the left. Thinking he was off, Kiddie and Dilly backed hurriedly off their throttles and took instant avoiding action—but Den simply pulled in the clutch, got the whole lot under control, and finding the Suzuki nicely lined for the fast right-hand curve, put the power on hard and cleared off. When they arrived back at the village, Kiddie shook his head in amazement and remarked that he had never seen so much smoke come off a motorcycle tyre in his life. Den, always the quiet gentle giant said nothing, but just grinned. This was just typical of the man.

CHAPTER FOUR

Crazy riders

WHEN I first left school I got a job as a trainee butcher in a small local supermarket. It was not my first choice, but it was employment offered to me and it paid more than double the salary of an apprentice motor mechanic, which was what I really wanted to do. Growing up, I wanted to be a farmer, but our grandmother had given my brothers and I a lecture telling us that farming was extremely hard work, having to be on hand all hours, seven days a week; and sometimes up to twenty-four hours a day. There was precious little money in it for all the toil and hard labour, and if the farmer was lucky enough to own his own land, that was his only real asset as there was not a great deal left of his income for anything else after bills and suppliers were all paid. So farming was out as a career and I went for an apprenticeship at a large motor garage in town, but with a large influx of applicants I was turned down, which salary wise did me a large favour. One morning our mother came home from a shopping trip and told me of a position in the local butchery department that was up for grabs, so I went along and got the job.

All was fine for a few years, and I guess you would say at least I was learning a trade, so I tolerated the job. Although we got time off in the week I hated working Saturdays and we were also expected to go into work on the Good Friday when the rest of the shop was closed to prepare meat for the busy Easter bank holiday weekend ahead. This really pissed me off as there was aways some good motorcycle racing on that day at our nearest race track Brands Hatch. To make matters worse, Saturday was the weekly clean up day, when all meat was removed from the refrigerator and the fridge scrubbed down from top to bottom. The wooden racks along the sides were removed and I had to take them outside and scrub them thoroughly in all weathers. The whole of our meat department was washed down and sanitised.

When the local lads started riding with us, I would sometimes be out in the summer sunshine on a Saturday scrubbing down the dreaded meat racks, and I could hear the motorcycles of Pud, the Mad Mongol and Bog Wright out roaming the streets—I hated working there. I could identify each by its sound and often had a fair idea where they would be going, so when Geoff told me one night that they were looking for someone to operate lathes and milling machines in the engineering works where he was employed and they were willing to train you up I went along and took the job. At the engineering shop the wages were better and the hours were eight thirty till five thirty on a five-day week, with overtime weekend work paid at time and a third only if you wanted it. This was perfect and I learned valuable skills while there, which I still use to this day.

At this time my 500 Speed Twin was not being too reliable and there were spells when it was off the road undergoing repair. If this happened Geoff would offer to drop in on his way to work to pick me up on his bike, to give me a lift to work. To say that Geoff was a crazy bastard when riding his bike would be a serious understatement. At this time our mother still got up early in the morning and went off to do a small milk delivery round for her uncle. After she had finished her milk round she would drop into the farmhouse for a cup of tea with her mother—our grand-mother. Outside the farmhouse on the road was a drain, and water from that drain always ran right across the road, so in the winter it sometimes froze solid. As Geoff picked me up on his bike my mother warned us of the danger that there was a strip of ice from the drain right across the road about eighteen inches wide outside my grandmother's farmhouse, and to be careful. Geoff set off at a cracking pace as we left my home on this frosty morning. I thought he was pushing it a bit as he took the left-hander just past the old farmyard and outside a small scrapyard. I was thinking that he would be shutting down for the icy strip as we flew down the hill towards the farmhouse, but Geoff showed no sign of backing off. He kept the throttle nailed. Holy shit! We hit the ice and the bike skidded sideways—on our right was a six feet high wooden fence and we were sliding at it sideways on. Suddenly, as we were about to skid off the edge of the road, both wheels gripped and we were in a straight line again. It was a miracle that we were still on the bike. Geoff had not even flinched, and had kept the throttle on throughout, as if nothing had happened. I hung on for grim death for the rest of the trip, arriving at work a nervous wreck. I sure as hell did not need a laxative that morning.

A few months on the Triumph was off the road again so I had no choice but to ride on Geoff's pillion again. I figured that at least it was warm this time and the roads were dry. It was a Thursday morning, Geoff arrived and we set off for work in his normal manner, whizzing down the road past the old farm and into scrapyard corner. As we went into the left-hander everything grounded and we were off, the bike skidding down the road on its side with us skidding along behind on our arses. We picked the bike up, kicked the footrest straight and continued to work a little battered, bruised and a little worse for wear. I was getting decidedly unnerved by Geoff's riding habits, but I was getting my bike back on Tuesday, so I told myself I would have to brave it till then. On the Friday our boss asked if we could both work on Saturday as the company had a big contract to fulfil, so we agreed. On Saturday morning we set off as normal, but this time Geoff took a different route through the country lanes. Coming out of the end of the lane onto the main road, Geoff gunned the bike and we cranked through a series of bends towards the market town of Hailsham where we worked. Approaching the town limit we hurtled into the bend by the cemetery. This bend could be deceptive in as much as it tightened up on itself as you came into it. We failed to make it and down we went again. That was twice in three days the bastard had thrown me down the road. This time I did not get off so lightly as my leg got stuck under the bike and it tore skin and flesh from my kneecap. I was in much pain at work and all weekend and decided enough was enough and I would not go back on Geoff's bike again. I got up early on Monday morning, limped to the bus stop and got the bus in to work. After an uncomfortable day at work I hobbled up to the bus stop to catch the bus back home. At this time there was still no helmet law for motorcyclists. Geoff arrived at the bus stop and pulled up, telling me to not be such a cock and get on. He gestured over his shoulder to the back seat. I told him in no uncertain terms to fuck off. Skidding down the road twice on my arse in three days was just too much, so just piss off. Geoff opened the throttle and with a smirk and a grin he sped away. I had learned a hard lesson, and I have never rode pillion to Geoff since.

It was all happening at the village, Dilly, Den and a couple of others were out on a run through country lanes. Den was holding the lead from Dilly. As Den was hurtling around a fast left-hand curve, the cow parsley on the bank slapping his leg, Den suddenly came across a large branch sticking out from the hedge towards him. Cranking hard and with Dilly trying to ride around the outside of him there was little room to manoeuvre. The end of the branch came at Den like a spear; it went under the belt of his

Belstaff jacket and tore through his jacket pocket before snapping off. Den continued the race. Much bullshit was talked in the local pubs and bars thereafter about the day that Den rode back to the village after a tear up 'with a tree in his pocket'.

Sprogg, the cheeky young kid from the garage, had got a new part-time job in a motorcycle shop a few miles away in a nearby town. After he had been there for just a few months he bought an old 600cc side valve Norton with a sidecar fitted from the shop owner. This motorcycle combination had been languishing at the back of the workshop in a grubby state for some years ever since it had been taken in part-exchange for a motorcycle. It was duly delivered to Sprogg's home, where he immediately set about stripping off the sidecar body and fitting just a platform made from an old door to the sidecar chassis. At first the compression was a bit much for Sprogg and he struggled to start it. On occasions his dad or his brother Tank would start it for him, but Sprogg soon got the hang of it and it was not long before he was tearing around the fields with his brothers and sister hanging on to the sidecar platform, power sliding sideways on the grass field or ripping across mud and grassland with the sidecar wheel high in the air.

Kiddie, out on his bike for a blast on a Saturday morning, dropped in to Eric Kennard's motorcycle dealership and Sprogg was there working. Eric was old school and had been in the trade for donkey's years. He was close to retirement age. The proprietor always wore a three-quarter length grey shop coat but had the curious habit of standing and scratching his testicles while he was talking to customers. Jeff, the head mechanic and Sprogg were busy servicing and preparing a Triumph 650 Bonneville with a Watsonian sports sidecar for a customer who had just bought it. The outfit fully serviced and valeted—the new owner arrived to collect it. Eric walked around, briefing the customer on the used machine and the finer points of how to control and ride a combination as opposed to a solo motorcycle. The satisfied owner donned his helmet and gloves, mounted the bike, kick-started it and took off up the road. The outfit's steering was shaking its head, the handlebars were veering from side to side. The rider shut off in a panic, the outfit, veering to the right, crossed the white line in the centre of the road, almost colliding with a car travelling in the opposite direction, which hooted loudly and took evasive action to avoid him. "Fucking wanker," remarked Sprogg loudly as the new owner got the bike under some sort of control and rode slowly and gingerly away in the distance, only to re-appear half an hour later to demand his money back. Eric had gone to lunch; the customer had a flaming row with Jeff the mechanic, insisting that the outfit was faulty, dangerous and a death trap. Kennards motorcycle shop was surrounded on three sides by a large gravel car park. Jeff was stating that there was nothing wrong with the motorcycle outfit and that riding a com-bination was completely different to riding a solo machine. The new owner was shouting back that the machine had a mind of its own. Sprogg and Kiddie stood watching the hostile exchange of words until Sprogg had had enough. He leapt on the bike, kicked it into life and revved it up. He told the owner there was fuck all wrong with the outfit and that he needed to stop pussy-footing around and get to grips with the machine. He then took off with a fistful of throttle. Tearing up the car park he drifted into a fast curve round to the right, then flicked it to the left, picked up the sidecar wheel and rode back with it three feet in the air. He then put in another lap, similar to the first. He rode back to the waiting group and skidded to a halt on the gravel, cut the motor and told the customer, "There's fuck all wrong with that!" A fifteen-year-old kid had just shown them how to ride an outfit. The unsure owner got back on the outfit and rode it away again with it all still shaking its head despite Jeff having cranked the steering damper down an extra third of a turn. Hopefully the new owner would in the end get the hang of it.

Leaving school that summer Sprogg got a full-time job at Kennards bike shop. A local motorcycle cop would sometimes drop into the shop for a chat. In the following harsh winter the bike cop's visits became more regular as he would come in for a warm coffee and to warm himself next to the waste oil-burning stove. The next summer Sprogg had his sixteenth birthday. The law on learner motorcyclists had now changed. At sixteen years old a learner could now ride a moped of less than fifty cc engine capacity. As a result of the new law many manufacturers began building sports mopeds. All of the Japanese manufacturers brought out such models as did the Italians, Malaguti and Garelli amongst them. Of all the sports mopeds the Garelli Rekord was probably the fastest, seeing close to seventy mph on the speedo, flat across the tank, downhill and with the wind behind you. The problem with most of the mopeds and particulary the Garelli Rekord was that to get the extra speed the motor was highly revving and more stressed, and so became less reliable. Probably the most reliable sports fifty was the Honda SS50, simply because it was a four-stroke—although it was slower than the two-strokes. Sprogg, of course, bought a Garelli Rekord. He ran the motor in and then rode it hard wherever he went. Then he dropped in at the shed one day and announced to Dilly and the gang that he was going for the fifty cc local TT record. Stop watch at the ready Sprogg was flagged away. He rode hard all the way around the circuit, being flat across the tank most of the way. When he got to the short stretch of road that went through the thirty mph he did not back off and kept the throttle wide open. Suddenly there was a police siren from behind and a motorcycle cop overtook him and flagged him down. It was Mick the bike cop that came into

Kennards. Sprogg thought it would be quite alright as he knew the cop, so he said, "Hello, Mick", in a cheery manner. The bike cop replied, "Oh, its you. You were doing sixty-five down there in the thirty mph limit". "Look, can't we forget this Mick?" suggested Sprogg, but the cop refused, got his book out and booked him for speeding. "Oh, you bastard", muttered Sprogg as he was handed the notice to produce his documents. When it came to the court the case got into the local paper. Recounting the matter many years on, Sprogg recalled that his street credentials went through the roof with his former school friends when they read in the paper that he had been nicked for sixty-five mph in a thirty mph limit on a Garelli moped of all things.

CHAPTER FIVE

Highlight capers

AROUND this time we heard of a café in the nearby seaside town of Eastbourne, where many of the local bikers hung out, known as the Highlight Café. Fairly late one summer's evening we rode down there. It was getting dark and the place was heaving. A row of motorcycles about a hundred yards long lined up right across the front of the lit up café and beyond on both sides. The jukebox was belting out *Born to be Wild* by Steppenwolf. Three pinball tables at the back of the café in an alcove on the left wall were in constant use with enthusiastic players going at them like men possessed, all of the tables banging and clanging. Loud conversations were going on, the participants raising their voices to be heard over the jukebox volume. Groups of leather-clad bikers hung around outside chatting, laughing and checking out the different motorcycles. The café had a good atmosphere, it was a happening place. I liked the Highlight from that very first night. The café was run by a friendly Greek Cypriot couple, affectionately known as Sid and Doris, who always gave the bikers a warm welcome. The café stayed open all the time and throngs of bikers were still buying food, but there was no sitting for an hour over a cold coffee as the café was not that large and seating was always at a premium. Sid would close up only when the cash register finally stopped ringing for the night.

We began to frequent the joint three or four times a week, as well as still going over to the village or sometimes ride out to country pubs such as the Black Horse which was in the same local area where Kiddie lived. We would go to parties and village discos, of which there were many in the area back then. It was commonplace at the time for most people to drink and drive and no one thought anything of it although it was a criminal offence. A couple of Eastbourne cinemas decided to maximise their profits by adding an extra late sitting and so started what they called late night cinema with a programme kicking off at ten p.m. on a Friday and Saturday evening. The form was to find a suitable pub for a couple of pints and then ride into Eastbourne to the cinema, taking care where you parked your bike, well away from any Mod hangout because they would push your bike over, or even worse. These late sittings could be, shall we say, a little boisterous on occasions as the viewers were often slightly oiled, which usually kept the cinema managers on edge and on their toes. I remember on one occasion we watched *Easy Rider* with Peter Fonda and Denis Hopper, and another time *On Any Sunday*—a good bike film starring Steve McQueen, both at late night cinema sittings. Cinema over, it was a quick dash down the Highlight for a meal if Sid and Doris were still open—if not it was fish and chips on Seaside as the enterprising owner of The Dolphin chippy now stayed open late. This was, and still is, the best chippy in town. After one late night viewing we roared down to the Highlight and Sid had just closed up. There were ten of us. Sid came out and asked how many wanted meals. "Eight", came back the reply, so the door was duly opened, the lights turned up, the pinball tables and the jukebox switched back on and pumped with cash, hammered out *Spirit in the Sky* by Norman Greenbaum along with such timeless motorcycle classics as *Leader of the Pack* by the Shangri Las, *Terry* by Twinkle and of course the most played record in the Highlight of that era *Born to be Wild*, the epitaph of many a biker blared from the jukebox speakers. Whenever I hear that track or pass by the shop that was once the old café, I think of that song and the good days of the Highlight... the two were inseparable like a hand in a glove.

After a few visits to the Highlight we began to notice that the café would periodically empty for ten minutes or so, and then everyone would come flooding back in again. These periods seemed to correspond with a tall lanky chap called Chris finishing his meal, picking up his gloves and crash helmet and walking out of the door. The next time it happened, when everyone got up we followed to see what the action was all about. Chris owned an immaculate 1968 cherry and silver Triumph T120 650 Bonneville and he ran the Red Bus Disco in a local nightclub and an outside disco. The bike was fitted with a couple of swept up straight through dragstack pipes which had recently come on the market, and god did they make that bike bark. It soon became obvious that Chris followed a set routine. He would start his bike and ride slowly up the road to a large garage forecourt where he would sit for a few minutes warming his engine up. The garage was closed at night-time. When ready, Chris would throttle up and start his run towards the café and waiting crowd. He rode close to the edge of the road around 18 inches or so from the kerb. Changing into second gear he gave the bike some serious stick and then would suddenly throttle back. Timing it to perfection to catch the engine over-run and with the fork springs compressing, he would hit the camber where a side road emerged, whacking the throttle wide open. As the fork springs unloaded their tension the front wheel instantly went airborne and the bike stood up near vertical. Chris stormed past the café with the bike on the rear wheel. He would keep the front pointing skywards for a hundred yards or so, finally dropping the wheel down only to negotiate a curve leading to a railway bridge. It was a brilliant performance of skill and timing and Chris had perfected it to a fine art. I now have a bike identical to Chris's Bonneville. It is a heavy bike for one with only around 47 horsepower at the engine sprocket, and even now I am still not a hundred percent sure quite how he managed it.

One evening Chris gave a performance of a lifetime. He had ridden up to the garage forecourt as normal and was sitting waiting, warming his motor up, when a group of four Mods rode past on scooters. Once again Chris's timing was spot on. He let the Mods pass and then let rip. He hit the emerging camber and up went the front wheel vertically. As Chris overtook the scooters on the back wheel, the second Mod in line, alerted by the noise of the Bonneville's revving engine looked hastily around. By being distracted, his scooter hit the kerb and he fell off. The two following scooters were unable to avoid their fallen friend and both fell off trying. A huge cheer erupted from the crowd watching from the café, followed by a succession of catcalls and insults. That was one hell of a performance that neither Chris or the bikers at the Highlight would forget in a hurry.

Smed was a grandfather figure at the Highlight and always seemed to be there. He was a few years older than most of the general clientele of the café, more a sort of father figure to some of the youngsters. He was balding slightly and was a little overweight. Smed was constantly ribbed by the others but would always come back with his own form of sarcasm. He was a printer by trade and also served as an RAC/ACU instructor and examiner, teaching mainly young motorcyclists how to ride bikes. Smed also ran a weekly motorcycle maintenance evening at a local youth club which was extremely popular. On top of this Smed would often help struggling or poor motorcyclists to repair or maintain their machines, often at his lock-up garage and in his own time and for free. Smed loved motorcycles and was a popular and highly respected man. To this day many motorcyclists will still honestly state that they owe their first interest in motorcycles to Smed and his unfailing and devoted generosity to help them.

With a huge crash and the sound of breaking glass the door flew open. A group of around twenty Mods burst into the café.

They had come looking for trouble and were tooled up; their leader was brandishing a large adjustable wrench which he was about to bring down heavily onto the jukebox, when he was intercepted. The Mods had misjudged badly as that night there was a higher than average amount of particularly hard bikers in the café. A terrific scrap ensued within the café itself. Although initially surprised the Rockers and Greasers within waded into the Mods. Led by a huge biker known as Big Jim they disarmed and battered the Mods—giving them a really good pasting. Several Mods were knocked unconscious within the café. Big Jim was a bouncer at the same nightclub where Chris ran his Red Bus disco. He was also a sidecar racer on the local circuits, an action man, a real tough guy. The fight lost, some of the Mods tried to flee but were chased down and caught and beaten by Big Jim and the pursuing band of bikers. Very few escaped. One was knocked out cold and was left hanging unconscious on the iron railings from the neck of his Crombie coat opposite the Rose and Crown pub. This attack was probably for the abuse and embarrassment suffered by the Mods who fell from their scooters outside the café as Chris had pulled his usual stunt a few weeks before. The Mods on the rampage that night learned a valuable lesson as this was the first and only time that the Mods had ever tried to invade the Highlight Café as they had come off a very poor second.

Another chap who frequented the Highlight Café regularly was a biker known universally as 'Manure'. This label came about as this unfortunate fellow's surname happened to rhyme with the word manure. Like Chris, Manure was a 'wheelie king', he could and did regularly point the front wheel of his Suzuki Hustler skywards for a couple of hundred yards or more. A Suzuki T250 Hustler was a light and sporty two-stroke with a good power band that would lift the front wheel easily, especially when carrying a pillion passenger. Manure would use this to its full advantage, and his displays were often awe-inspiring. As previously stated, when I owned the Triumph, I got a job at the local Birds Eye frozen food factory. For a young chap the rate of pay and conditions were excellent at Birds Eye and I used some of these extra earnings to pay for an expert to rebuild the Speed Twin engine with hot parts in order to produce extra power and therefore higher speeds. When I started at Birds Eye, I was initially moved around the different departments as needed. When I was placed to work on the Arctic Roll production line, who did I find working there but Manure. The two of us became good friends, and we still are to this day.

Working on the line with Manure was good fun, with a bit of banter often going on between us. His normal place on the line was on the end of the ovens. As the long sponges came along the production line on greaseproof paper it was his job to stack them into wire mesh trays. As the trays filled up he stacked them onto trolleys. When the trolleys were full, he pulled them across the tiled floor with a loading hook to the next part of the line where a layer of jam was put in and they were then filled with ice cream. On this particular day it was time for Manure's meal break and I had to cover his job while he was absent. All went well for half an hour or so, and then just as he came back from lunch, I was pulling a stack of trays along with the hook when one of the trolley wheels dropped into a gap where a quarry tile had broken and the whole stack of sponges went flying across the floor. Manure fell about laughing and called me all the names under the sun; that was until the line foreman told me to continue to carry on with the job I was doing and made Manure clear up the mess that I had made. Manure was furious, but I thought it was really funny as the joke was now on him.

We were on shift work, and being on the early shift we finished at two p.m. it was a lovely sunny day, and with the Triumph motor away at the engine rebuilders, Manure offered to give me a lift home. He promised to take it easy and not to pull any wheelies on his bike as I did not have a helmet with me. There was still no helmet law in place even then. I thought it would be safe enough, as it was thirty and forty mph speed limits all the way from Birds Eye to my house, but how wrong could I have been. As we took a large roundabout within a forty mph limit, Manure cranked the bike over, everything decked and we were off. When you have, or see a spill like this, things seem to happen in slow motion, and I still have a clear memory of skidding down the road on my backside behind Manure and his bike, which was emitting sparks from its underside, while all the time sliding and trying to keep my head from hitting the road surface. This was beginning to become something of a habit. One which I could definitely do without.

CHAPTER SIX

"You're just Café Racers"

ABOUT this time I bought an old, fair sized van. The van often became used as a breakdown recovery vehicle for the mainly unreliable British motorcycles of the day, along with a usual collection of crashed motorcycles. I got hold of some plastic milk crates, and when our parents threw out some old furniture I saved the cushions, which with the milk crates turned upside-down were used as temporary seating in the back of the van. The old van became affectionately known as 'the truck'. Over the years there were several similar such 'trucks', but the ones most favoured were the models with sliding doors, and a strong roof rack often came in useful. On most summer days we preferred to drive with the front doors hooked back and the cab open to the elements. These trucks also became transport for the walking wounded and drunks as well as transport for the film crew to film our antics and a chuck wagon to carry supplies and camping gear on camping trips

It was a lovely summer's day and a whole load of us had gone out to a country tea haunt. Most were on their bikes, but as I still hadn't got the Triumph engine back I was driving the truck with a couple of passengers and we had met the rest there. We were on our way back through the country lanes when the bikes caught up with us, near to the smallest church in the country. As we neared the church driveway entrance I moved over to the left to give the bikes plenty of room to pass. As I did so I saw a large group of motorcycles hurtling down Lullington hill coming towards us in the opposite direction. As I pulled over, Snout, who was leading our group of bikes went to overtake on his Bonneville when he suddenly saw the other group coming at him head-on at speed, up to three abreast. Snout braked hard, but a rider called 'Blue' clipped the back of Snout's bike and went down in the road. Everything then happened so fast. Several bikes bunched up and went down and the bikes flying down the hill ploughed into the carnage. I remember catching a glimpse of one of the leaders of the other group as the accident happened— he was a rider known as 'Robbo' who I had seen a few times at the Highlight. Blue's Honda was fitted with a race fairing and with one leg stuck under his machine, Blue could do no more than cringe and try to tuck behind his fairing as he lay there help- less in the road. Robbo hit Blue's bike, riding clean over the front wheel and smashing Blue's fairing to pieces. He rode completely over Blue's prone body before stopping further on. Several other bikes from Robbo's pack ploughed into the wreckage; bikes were going everywhere. In a bid to escape, one of our riders, Mad Mongol rode up the bank, but a flying motorcycle from the other group collided with his machine and snapped the kickstart clean off with the end of its shaft still in it. It was total carnage, but by sheer good fortune all injuries were slight.

Blue had quite a reputation; he was constantly hounded by the police and had extra pages stapled into his licence to take all the endorsements handed out by the courts. After one accident his girlfriend ended up in a coma from which she never recovered and he ended up with a glass eye. Quite a wild character he was to meet an early and untimely death. Blue was a digger driver for a main firm of civil engineering contractors. One dark winter's evening Blue and his contractor gang were working alongside a main road near the Kent border. With darkness upon them and his gang rushing to complete work in a hole and finish up for the day, Blue decided to park his JCB digger over a trench with its headlights on so that the workers could see what they were doing. Blue jumped down from his cab, and grabbing a shovel leapt into the hole. A lorry came around the corner and hit the rear bucket of the JCB, pushing it into the hole. Blue was crushed by his own digger and died instantly; and so ended the life of this somewhat wild and unorthodox, but fun, character.

The cops arrived at the multiple pile up in force and arranged to interview everyone at their home addresses at a later date. They dished out a handful of tickets for the riders to produce their documents within a five day period at a nearby police station. As the handful of tickets looked similar to a fanned out hand of playing cards we decided to have a mass run to the cop shop, which we later did. We completely overwhelmed the desk sergeant at the station with paperwork. While we were in the process of sorting out the documentation a motorcycle speed cop came out to prepare for his shift. He asked what we were all riding and came outside to take a look at our bikes. Looking at Snout's Bonneville, he said, "Listen, I have got a 650 Triumph Saint and I am on duty in ten minutes. I'll bet you £5 that my Saint is quicker than your Bonneville". We all knew that this was total rubbish as a police Saint carried a lower gearing ratio than standard Triumph models to make it more town friendly and cope with carrying the extra weight of the police crap of the day. Back then the police bikes had to carry a heavy radio telephone in a cutaway on the petrol tank, which could not be used on the move. The bike cop had to physically stop by the roadside to call into his base, similar to making a telephone call. This was a great asset to anyone being pursued by a bike speed cop and a huge disadvantage to him. To add even more to the weight of the bike it was fitted with a big heavy fairing, built more to keep the weather off the rider rather than for speed. Add to that the panniers with all the first aid kit and the rest of the garbage that they had to carry.

The police radio telephone itself used to give off a sharp, loud and repetitive three blip signal when the set was switched on, so as a bike came along a road we would all stand and whistle in time with the three blip signal just to wind him up. Also there was no such thing as an available database to find the owner of any given vehicle. A registration clerk in an office somewhere would have to sift through many files of paper records for hours on end in an effort to try to track down a single offender, so that it was hardly at all practical.

As we donned our helmets and gloves the speed cop appeared and we all took off. I was gutted that day that I had to ride pillion again. The bike cop out front opened up the police Saint and was pulling seventy mph in the thirty limit; our pack of bikes were with him all the way. When we left the town limits and he got on the dual carriageway he wound the Saint up to its flat out speed of ninety to ninety-five mph. Snout gunned his Bonnie and was right on the cop's tail with the rest of the pack behind him, but no one had the guts to overtake the cop. It sure was a sight to see, our bikes bunched up on the tail of the speed cop. Snout had an extra unused, but available, fifteen to twenty miles an hour over the police bike. This carried on for a few miles and then with a wave of his hand the cop turned off and accelerated away. He had been a good sport. This was typical of some cops back then. As motorcycle enthusiasts themselves the odd few actively enjoyed a run or pursuit, that is until they lost, then boy they would have your guts for garters, but, hey, it was all part of the fun and of living a relatively carefree and wild lifestyle.

During and after World War II many people, sick of war, had thrown caution to the wind and the resounding result in the post war years was a huge baby boom. The only music available then on radio and vinyl records as you grew up was the same music your parents listened to. That all changed with the advent of

Rock 'n Roll in the 1950s and with the coming about of the sharp dressed, if sometimes violent Teddy Boys. Youngsters of the day suddenly had their own brand of music and a different image that they could follow. Slowly, after wartime depredation times started to get a little better until the end of the fifties many people started to find that they had an extra pound or two in their pocket at the end of a week's hard labour. Some chose to invest these extra funds in a secondhand motorcycle or a used car. For many it was the first vehicle that they had ever owned. Not having much money, some motorcyclists began to tune or modify their machines to get the most from them. This was the era of the magic 'Ton', the mystical 100mph barrier that everyone strove to beat. These lads became known as the 'Ton-Up Boys'. In their quest for more speed they saved up and bought newer and faster machinery. This led to a large increase in motorcycle sales and this was a huge boom to the British bike industry, although worrying signs were already on the horizon in respect of Japan's motorcycle producers.

Jukeboxes had first come to Britain from America in the late 1940s and began to be installed in pubs in the 1950s. By the 1960s they were commonplace in most bars and transport cafés. The Ton-Up Boys and Teds were well aware of the American diner scene with its jukeboxes, hot rodders and bike outlaws from films and newsreels. There was the 1952 classic film *The Wild One* starring Marlon Brando and Lee Marvin, banned in Britain, but there were no USA type diners in Britain. The Ton-Up boys therefore started to visit the transport cafés where the lorry drivers hung out for their meal breaks, providing of course, that the café had the all-important jukebox. This was a welcome boost in trade for the café owners who made the most of it by staying open late and putting up with bits of boisterous behaviour. The tables and seating was screwed to the floor in many cafés and the teaspoons were often chained to the counter.

The Ton-Up Boys modified their bikes to look like those of their heroes on the race track as well as tuning them for maximum speed; riders such as world champion Geoff Duke, Derek Minter, John Hartle, Bob McIntyre and the up-and-coming Mike Hailwood. There were actually relatively few British motorcycles overall that could crack the magic ton barrier in standard trim. Among the most well-known was the BSA 500 Gold Star, 650 Rocket Gold Star, the Velocette 500 Venom and Thruxton, a number of models from Norton including the 600 Dominator 99, 650SS and 750 Atlas, along with a smattering of models from Triumph— one being the infamous 650 Bonneville named after a Triumph speed record set at Bonneville Salt Flats, Utah, in 1954. The first Triumph 650 Bonneville rolled off the production line in late 1958, but the first ones were not sold and registered until early 1959. Last, but not least, was the range of several Vincent 1000cc v-twin models. It took at least a decent 500cc bike back then to achieve the elusive figure of 100mph while lying prone across the petrol tank, so the phrase of 'tune your bike, not your speedo' became the saying of the day. The Ton-Up Boys would race from café to café and so the truck drivers would rib them, "You're not real racers, you're just Café Racers", and so the phrase was born. The boys and their bikes had, by accident of circumstance become part of a movement known as Café Racers, their bikes being of similar style to that of the track racers. The newspapers sensationalised their exploits. With first page headlines such as 'Dicing with Death' and 'Suicide Squad' they created an era, a legend, a moment in history that will live on and far outlive the Rockers themselves. Rocker cafés such as the Ace Café on London's North Circular Road, The Busy Bee at Watford and Johnsons near Death Hill and Brands Hatch, became world famous. With record races being the order of the day, the newspaper reporters and photographers would frequent these cafés. A record race involved a Rocker donning his bike gear, walking to the jukebox and putting on a record. He would then rush to his bike, start it and race around a given road circuit to try to get back before the record finished. There were many casualties on record runs and Death Hill achieved its name for that very reason. One evening a well-known reporter with his photographer arrived at Johnsons Café; he wanted to see a 'Chicken Run'. A 'Chicken Run' was where two Rockers would start at opposite ends of a given stretch of road and roar towards each other, swerving away only at the last possible moment. On this particular evening the reporter and photographer went from group to group offering them a fiver to see some action. Finally, a couple of likely lads stepped forward— they would take the money and show him a chicken run, they said. Taking the cash the two walked over to some bikes. The news crew followed. At the last moment the lads walked on past the bikes around the back of the café where there was a wire mesh compound with a dozen hens in it. "There," they said, "is your chicken run". The whole crowd at the café erupted into loud and spontaneous applause and laughter.

Modern thinking has placed T. E. Lawrence, of *Lawrence of Arabia* fame, as probably the first ever Ton-Up Boy

This is most likely because Lawrence had a reputation as a speed freak. He would constantly ride at speeds of up to, and a little over, 100mph across the tank of his hand-built Brough Superior SS100, which in the 1930s cost as much as a house to buy, so very few people could ever afford one. Many bikes and most cars at that time were pretty slow affairs in comparison with a Brough Superior. In 1935 Lawrence was thrown from his beloved Brough just a few hundred yards from his cottage Clouds Hill, whilst trying to avoid two boys cycling, although conspiracy theories abound that he may have been assassinated.

He died from head injuries six days later in the hospital at the nearby Bovington army camp. This great hero of the desert was buried in the small cemetery at the nearby village of Moreton, just a few hundred yards from the church where his funeral was held and a fairly short ride from his cottage.

Around the end of the 1950s the Ton-Up Boys began to be known as Rockers. There is some speculation as to how or where this came about, but it would seem that apart from these young tearaways being addicted to Rock and Roll music belting out on the café jukeboxes it also had something to do with the rocker arms and the thump, thump, thump vibration of the big British four-stroke single cylinder motorcycles that were the preference to try to top the magic ton. This period corresponded with motorcycle boots being more often worn with white sea boot socks turned down over the top in what we now generally associate with the traditional Rocker image of the day, along with Brylcreem and the all-important quiff hairstyle in the same style as Teddy Boys before them. Previously you wore what you had and many motorcyclists wore hobnail type work boots or even turned down Wellington boots. Real leather motorcycle boots were expensive and could cost the equivalent of three or four weeks take home pay for a teenager. I eventually bought my first pair of bike boots from a mail order catalogue run by a friend, paying a few shillings a week until they were paid for. Prior to the arrival of the Ton-Up Boy scene, riders used to wear a Mackintosh or army greatcoat bought from army surplus stores along with a collar and tie and often worn with ordinary leather shoes and sometimes a flat cap.

About the same time as the Rocker made an appearance a small group of youngsters in London, fed up with the lifestyles and clothes of the period, decided to create their own scene and their own style of clothing. They chose some items from the styles of continental Europe and began to dress smartly in gear they

51

thought modern and swish. They called themselves Modernists and as the movement grew the name was soon shortened to Mods. Big, noisy, greasy motorcycles were not for them so they looked for a cleaner form of transport, one which would keep their fancy clothes relatively clean. Before long they came up with the mainly Italian scooters from Lambretta and Vespa. Italian businessmen and women had for some time been using scooters for general everyday transport, including going to and fro for work. The scooter legshields and engine covers kept clothes relatively clean and dry, and a windscreen was sometimes fitted for extra weather protection. As the Mods movement grew high street outlets began to cash in on the new craze and sell and mass produce Mod clothing and Mod numbers swelled. They also had their own brand of music, and bands like The Who made their name and their millions from identifying themselves with the Mod movement. The Mods and their girls thought they looked pretty cool. Some festooned their scooters with loads of mirrors and spotlights, none of which worked, and some had Bresco-style fancy paint jobs. A tuner called Ancilotti began to manufacture parts for racing which he claimed would take a highly tuned scooter to 100mph. Clearly if this was the case the engine would not last very long. Early on some scooters were fitted with a chrome rear carrier some with a spare wheel attached and the girls thought it looked great to lean right back against it. Later, proper back rests were being sold as an accessory with an upholstered pad which the girls used lay right back on, but in reality all this did was to lighten the front wheel of the scooter dramatically, already unpredictable on uneven roads because of its small wheels and made it even more inherently unstable. Sometimes a whippy car aerial was fitted to the rear of the scooter. At the time the oil company, Esso, was running a sales campaign and the slogan was 'Put a tiger in your tank'. Esso garages were dishing out free tie-on tiger tails with gallons of petrol and some Mods tied these on their scooter or aerials. Mods took to wearing khaki parkas over their clothes for some protection against the weather and to help keep their clothes clean. Although they thought they looked good, we thought they were a bunch of sissies. We could never understand how anyone could actually think they looked tough or cool on a bike built for Italian women to go shopping on.

It is a fact that most Rockers were manual workers of some kind or other, who were used to getting their hands dirty, be it in heavy industry, factories, garages, labourers of some kind on the land, whereas most Mods worked in banks, offices, as shop assistants or as message boys; trades in which their form of employment left them relatively clean and tidy.

Bank Holiday brawls with the Mods in seaside towns were still active at this time. It became common knowledge that there was going to be a large Mod gathering at Margate over the August bank holiday weekend that year, so half a dozen or so of us decided to go along, more out of curiosity than a zest for violence. The first clashes with the Mods had started early in 1964 in Southend and continued on the beaches of Brighton in August that same year. The Mods and Rockers cult film *Quadrophenia* is a fairly accurate, but dramatised account, of what happened that summer, now commonly remembered as the 'Battle of Brighton', particularly if you view it against the original footage shot at the time. It later transpired that much of the violence was stirred up by newspaper reporters, who, desperate for headline stories, went to the Rockers and told them, "A tenner is yours if you attack those mods over there," and then did the same with the Mods.

We arrived at Margate and there was not a single Mod in sight, so we parked down a side street on the extreme fringes of the town. Carefully and with some trepidation we had a look around. We then came across a large group of Rockers marching up the road.

There was probably a couple of hundred of us, feeling pretty safe we marched up the road like an invading army. More Rockers were joining us all the time, small groups appearing out of side streets. Nearing the town centre, ten or twelve Mods passed across the road we were on, looked in our direction and ran. A shout of "Mods" rang out from the front of our pack and the whole of our group broke into a run, turning to the left after the Mods. Around the corner were masses of Mods waiting for us. It was an ambush. As we turned back from where we had come there was an at least equal group, if not more, charging into us from behind. We were heavily outnumbered. Scuffles broke out as the Rockers fought to escape the massed numbers of Mods who were trying to crush us. Bottles and other missiles were being thrown. We were being hemmed in, when we came across an alley and bolted down it, hoping that it was not a dead end. We were lucky, it came out in another street and we made good our escape. We made our way to higher ground and sat down on a grassy hillock a good distance away, from where we had a good view all around and could see if anyone was heading in our direction. We were fairly safe here for the moment.

From our vantage point we saw a group of about a dozen Teddy Boys getting into a matt black, long wheelbase double wheeled Ford Transit van. They were cruising around the town to check out the action. They had done a couple of laps of the town when the Mods set up an ambush for them. There was a railway bridge where the road sloped down to get under it. It was here that the Mods struck. They had hoarded a fair amount of bricks, large stones, bottles and other missiles, and as the Transit passed under the bridge they let the Teds have it. A hail of bricks were thrown through every window of the van. There were loud screams and swearing shouted at the top of voices from inside the vehicle as blind panic ensued. The Mods closed in closer still and beat and kicked the van as it tried to escape. The hail of missiles continued, there was not a window, light or straight panel left on the van as it finally sped away. At this point we decided that discretion may be the better part of valour and so beat a hasty retreat in the direction of home. All in all it had been a very lucky escape.

In the early 1960s the Rockers far outnumbered the Mods. Many old Rockers remember fondly good school friends who bought scooters and became Mods. The two groups remained friends locally after leaving school and beyond. They would go to youth clubs, coffee bars and share a pint or two together, but as time went on the Mods numbers increased dramatically. The rivalry between the two groups increased on a national level. The Mods hated us and we hated them. You could not park your bike in or near a Mod area because the chances of it getting vandalised were high, so we would respond in kind. On the British motor-cycle you had to turn on fuel and ignition, then 'tickle' the car-burettor until the fuel flooded out to prime the engine and maybe apply some choke if cold. Then with two or three resounding kicks, with any luck, your bike may start. Only then could you ride away. The Mods would watch and wait until you started going through this starting procedure and then strike. Those Rockers now in possession of the new incoming Japanese imports would give one quick kick and away; or some like the new Hondas had electric starters, so could speed off quickly. Although the British bikes were at a disadvantage here, they really excelled on the open roads, where the Mods were easily chased down and dealt with, often with a swift kick into the scooters side panel to send them spinning down the road on their backsides.

As previously stated, many Mods were Mods only for the cloth-ing and the image and never owned a scooter. The scooterists probably made up only a third of all Mods in the movement.

By the beginning of the 1970s the Mod movement had run its course. The original Modernists had become completely dis-illusioned with the whole scene. The movement which they had started to be individualists had been hijacked, taken over and watered down by the big clothing and shopping empires for the sake of profit and other individuals making a fast buck or two. Later in the 1980s Paul Weller of the Jam pop group made an attempt to resurrect the scooter scene which was only partly successful. The riders were not Mods but called themselves Scooter Boys and followed the Weller brand of music. Sadly the heady days of the swinging sixties were over and with it the quiff hairstyles. We now grew our hair long and they called us Greasers. British bikes were on the wane in favour of the more refined imports from Japan. The legend of the Mods and Rockers would pass into British folklore. We were not sorry to see the back of our sworn enemies, the Mods, but on the horizon another dark cloud was looming as another group, more violent than the Mods, was on its way. They came ready dressed for violence and disorder; they were derived from the football hooligans and they called themselves Skinheads.

CHAPTER SEVEN

The Skinhead curse

THE first clash between our group and the Skinheads came about one night when I was not present. Back in the pre-credit card or bank card days everyone was paid in cash at the end or the working week. The vast majority of young people did not have a bank account and lived very much hand to mouth. Generally on a Friday afternoon or Saturday morning, workers were handed a small brown pay packet with their wages inside, in cash, minus the National Insurance contribution and Income Tax stoppages listed on the outside of the envelope. As a young person still living at home you would then part with an agreed portion of your weekly income to your parents for your keep, which went towards the bills and running of the general household. After everything was paid this did not leave an awful lot for the worker or wage-earner, him or herself. As a result you had to be careful with your money to make it stretch to next pay day. Things like riding your motorcycle or having the odd meal at the Highlight; or a few pints in the pubs did not cost too much, but if you had a great weekend with too many beers and bought too many rounds of drinks when pissed, then you could get through your disposable cash very quickly, with the result that you had to stay in for the rest of the week until the next pay day. Sometimes your parents might lend you a quid or two to see you through, but this was not always the case. In all groups there will always be people who will drink all the time that drinks are forthcoming, but will leave to go to the toilet when it was their turn to buy a round; and ours was no exception. It was one of the nights that I was grounded through lack of funds that the Skinheads chose to strike.

Our local youth club held weekly discos, and one week a young and particularly cheeky local Skinhead ran lippy to a Greaser from a neighbouring town who in turn gave him a clip around the ear. The next week a number of our band attended the weekly disco as usual. They began to notice that the disco was beginning to fill up with Skinheads; a number of them from outside of the local area. It was clear that something was afoot and all hell was going to kick off soon—so they decided to leave and go to the a pub in the High Street for a few drinks. So Snout, Pud, Mad Mongol, Bog and others, together with a number of girls, made their way to the pub. After an hour or two the coast seemed clear, so they finished their drinks and left the pub. Further up the High Street they were surrounded and ambushed by the waiting Skinheads. The Skinheads were led by a particularly nasty and violent individual from Eastbourne who had a fearsome reputation. He was the front man for the group, the leader, a thug and the main agitator that led them on. Whereas the Mods existed for their love of fashionable clothing, music and their scooters, the Skinheads existed only to meter out extreme violence or 'aggro' as they called it. They wore big 'bovver boots' purely to kick the crap out of their victims, or to stamp on their heads and limbs whilst victims were down on the ground. Nor were they fussy about who they beat senseless—any victim would do, but rival groups, that stood out by different forms of dress or way of life, like us, were particularly at risk of their aggression. With the Mods, violence had come about between our groups almost by accident, merely as a clash or cultures, but Skinheads existed purely for the creation of total disorder and extreme violence. A decade or more before, a fight had been almost gentlemanly in comparison; normally between two people— and if one got the better of the other and put him down, then the fight was won and over. It would only continue if your opponent got up for more, until he was put down for good. It was the scuffles on the beaches with the Mods that had led to the massed running battles that involved large numbers of people fighting and throwing missiles over a large front.

On this particular night our band of bikers was trapped, surrounded and grossly outnumbered, hemmed in by the marauding Skinheads who were throwing bottles and wielding sticks and planks of wood with three or four four-inch nails driven through them. Pud was whacked across the back with one such plank with a nail in it. It perforated his leather jacket and drove deep into the flesh on his back. The bikers took quite a beating. Finally as the fury of the Skinhead attack began to ease, they managed to force a way out and to escape. They turned up later at my house, battered and bruised. Pud took his jacket off. There was a clear hole where the nail had penetrated the leather and a blood stain where blood had worked into the lining of the jacket measuring about six inches across. Despite his injuries Pud declined to go to hospital for treatment. Luckily for him the wound did not fester and healed up well of its own accord.

A few weeks later another situation arose in another nearby town. There were reports of a large battle that took place in the local shopping centre between bikers from a couple of neighbouring towns and local Skinheads. This time the Skinheads did not have it all their own way as the numbers on both sides were fairly even. The mass fight was over a scuffle with a girl at a nearby barbecue the week before. When the Greasers arrived in town the Skinheads rushed around contacting friends and followers to try to meet the threat with massed numbers. One of the Skinheads had a van so some of them drove to a nearby building site and stole a number of fencing stakes to use as weapons. The two rival factions lined up opposite each other in the precinct and charged into each other. The Skinheads were armed with the fencing stakes, but so fearsome was the Greasers' attack upon their ranks that many of the younger Skinheads dropped their fencing stakes and ran away when the action started. The stakes were then eagerly snatched up by the bikers and used to batter the remaining Skinheads. There were quite a few injuries afflicted, including a broken leg, and when the matter came to court three or four of the combatants were jailed for charges regarding affray and violent disorder.

Some months on some of our gang had been to the beach. They decided to stop at the Wimpy Bar in town for a meal or a burger. Having eaten they returned to their motorcycles, donned their helmets and gloves and started their machines. Snout's Triumph Bonneville did not want to start, but the noise of the other bikes alerted a group of Skinheads in a nearby coffee bar. The Skinheads came out of the coffee bar and legged it down the road in a large group, jeering. From past experience all knew this was not a good situation. The prime time to attack was when the British biker was trying to start his machine. If the others were to take off quickly he would be left extremely vulnerable to attack by the marauding Mods or Skinheads. Snout's bike fired up and all took off. Pud looked back and saw that Snout had not pulled away. On a café racer type of motorcycle, fitted with rearsets the right-hand footrest had to be lifted up to miss the kickstart during the starting procedure, then put down again to start to ride away. This is what had delayed Snout. Seeing the danger, Pud spun his bike around and went back. As he pulled up, Snout stamped the Bonneville into gear and took off. Seizing the opportunity the Skinheads pounced, and dragging Pud from his bike gave him a thorough kicking in the road. This was textbook tactic of both Mods and Skinheads. Some things still had not changed.

CHAPTER EIGHT

Strange new friends

A LOVELY summer's afternoon, and I was at home working on my Speed Twin, fitting the rebuilt engine, fresh from the tuners. There was the loud roar of a big Triumph coming up the road and Snout duly arrived. He sat chatting for a while and then made me an offer I could not refuse. "Take the Bonny out for a spin 'Young Laddie' and see what you can get out of it". It was a hot day and I was wearing a part-buttoned shirt with an open neck. My sleeves were rolled up nearly to the shoulder. Without further delay I mounted the Bonny and leapt on the kickstart. As I took off down the road it occurred to me that maybe it would have been wiser to wear a helmet—but then this was near the end of the Rocker era, there was still no helmet law, and everyone took risks. Most of us actively enjoyed being part of the outlaw image. I pulled out onto the main road. The 650 Bonneville had much more power than my own 500, it was a dream to ride. Keeping an eye open for the cops, I wound the bike up through the gears until my streaming eyes felt like they were going to be torn from their sockets; my flapping shirt was whipping me and was being torn from my back. I glanced down at the clocks and saw the speedo was reading between 105 and 110mph. The bike had a bit more to give if I had pushed it, but the adverse affect of the elements and wind pressure on my unprotected body meant I was getting one hell of an incompatible battering at that speed without a jacket, so reluctantly I backed off and eventually turned the bike around to head back. I was well impressed, I had cracked the magic ton for the very first time. Triumph in their ultimate wisdom, had seen fit to number some of their models to the speed that they were supposed to do in miles per hour. The 350cc Tiger or T90 should do ninety mph, the 500cc T100 or Tiger 100 should really do 100mph and the single carburettor 650cc Tiger 110 or T110 had a stated speed of 110mph. The Bonneville which had the benefit of twin carburettors was a T120 and so should do, in theory, in standard trim push 120mph, but, in reality, allowing for the average speedo error of the day, around ten per cent or so, around 110mph was a more realistic true figure, although the speedometer may well read 120mph at the time. This was my first experience of riding a Triumph Bonneville, and the experience stuck in my mind over the years. I had really wanted a Bonneville, but the 'on the road' price of a new Bonny was then £348 and my salary at the time meant I could not afford one. Riding this bike and clocking up my first ton had left a big impression on me, but I was to wait another twenty-five or thirty years until I eventually came across a Bonneville by accident, going cheap, that needed restoration. Only then was I able to add such a model to my collection. What was that saying about looking back through rose tinted glasses?

The Highlight Café was not the only biker cafe in the local area. There was another late night cafe with a jukebox, which like the Highlight stayed open late all the time that its customers were spending money. It was the Steering Wheel in a small market town, and it was directly opposite the railway station. The Steering Wheel was run by a couple who were believed to be Polish, and although full blown cooked meals were not available at night, a range of low cost snacks along with tea, coffee, soft drinks and a few pastries were. Several of the more popular sandwiches that were available at the Wheel were the infamous delicacy, the skinless sausage sandwich, which consisted of four sausages served between two slices of bread and—a throw-back from the wartime austerity, the fried Spam sandwich, which contained slices of fried luncheon meat. The sausage sandwiches particularly, were universally known by us as the thumbprint sandwiches, as a couple of thumb-prints were generally visible in the bread where it had been held down when cut. These were not dirty marks, merely imprints. These snacks may not seem much now, but in the 1960s and 70s expectations were much lower, and to the hungry biker they tasted delicious. The clientele at the Steering Wheel was more varied than the Highlight, incorporating a greater variety of the local night time population, along with a fair number of motorcyclists. We would attend the Steering Wheel on occasions after the pubs shut. The flooring at the Wheel was made up of linoleum tiles which looked like as if at some point someone had acquired a whole load of random and different coloured floor tile samples and laid them in no particular order. The atmosphere there was completely different from the Highlight and it had a couple of darker corners favoured by courting couples, but it could nevertheless be a bustling, busy and sometimes popular place. Like the Highlight, the jukebox boomed out continuously.

Our youngest brother, Martin had now become of motorcycle riding age. For a few years now Mart had been begging lifts on the pillion of both mine and my other brother Tel's bikes or on the rear seats of our friends' motorcycles whenever possible and had so become something of an honorary member of the group. Mart had been very lucky, as he narrowly missed having the new moped law enforced on him by less than a month. Owing to the large number of accidents and deaths related to novice learner motorcyclists riding up to 250cc machines, the British government had decided to limit all 16-year-old motorcyclists to mopeds of under 50cc capacity. Mart had just squeaked in before the enforcement date and being a fan of the Ducati motorcycle marque had bought himself a Ducati. Sadly the Ducati suffered, as all Italian motorcycles did, with the problem of poor Italian electrics. One day Pud grabbed hold of Mart and tried to wrestle him to the ground. Mart wriggled, twisted and squirmed in a mad effort to get away from Pud and prevent him from putting him down. Pud gasped out, "My God, you are like a wriggling worm, you are, trying to hang on to you". And so it was that from that day the name stuck and Mart became known as 'Worm' for ever more—as indeed he still is to this day.

A new housing estate had been built in our village and among the newcomers that moved in were two families that were related and bore the same surname. The two families lived in adjoining houses and most of the siblings were around the same age as us. Like ourselves, some of them shared a common passion for motorcycles and as a result began to hang around with us. Their parents were very accommodating and welcomed us all into their homes, and so the number in our group grew. Indeed it was not long before Pud and Bog Wright began dating two of the sisters. These families were known to us as the Warbs. Most parents preferred their offspring to go and meet up with their friends out-side of the family home. The Warb family homes, like ours, were a bikers' open house, not always it has to be said, to the joy of the neighbours.

There was another person, a rather strange character, who had moved onto the new estate with his elderly parents. He rode a light blue Triumph Tina T10 scooter, a ninety-eight cc two-stroke with automatic transmission. An absolute piece of unreliable junk that typified the total demise of the British motorcycle industry. This chap really was an odd looking character. He had a long, thin face with a pointed chin, and what made him look even stranger, was that his mother cut his hair in what was known as a pudding basin cut—a haircut where an empty upturned pudding basin was placed on your head and your hair cut around it with a dead straight fringe. The unfortunate fellow furthermore possessed an open faced helmet with a green tinted bubble visor clipped onto the front of it with studs. His abnormally long chin stuck out from under the bottom of his bubble visor, by at least several inches and the green visor tint made him look positively ill. We nicknamed him Herman, after Herman Munster in the American horror series 'The Munsters', and whenever we were grouped outside our house and he went by in a cloud of smoke, the standing crowd would all cheer loudly.

After a few weeks or so, Herman came along, and we all cheered as usual, so he stopped. He spoke slowly, but purposefully in an unusual voice—he had some strange mannerisms, "Aw, hello you old buggers, what are you up to?" He then went on chatting mainly about the scooter being unreliable and that he was going to buy a motorbike. It became apparent from what he had said that his parents had him late in life and that he had experienced a good education at a boarding school. In some ways he was very clever but in others he was seriously lacking and decidedly odd. He was what the old country boys in the local farming villages would call, 'Thruppence short of a shilling' meaning in laymans terms that someone was not perhaps the full ticket. He told us that he worked at the Dental Board in town where he was an office boy delivering paper files between departments on a trolley. Then as quickly as he arrived he was gone. It later transpired that he had no friends to speak of and so spent much of his time indoors playing his record collection, which was substantial and actually included some good stuff. One of Herman's pastimes at home was to play darts in his room. As a result he was a surprisingly good and accurate darts player, although, like everything else, his technique was really odd and left a lot to be desired. For some reason he would hurl darts with some force, as if he was throwing a javelin, which left the dartboard pockmarked from the weight of impact.

For a few weeks we saw no more of Herman, and then one evening he just turned up at our house, out of the blue, with a sparkling new blue Honda. From that point on he attached himself more and more to the group and turned up frequently. There were no hard and fast rules regarding who could or could not ride with us. We were a pretty easy going bunch and basically felt anyone with a love of motorcycles could not be all bad. We rode hard and fast, but stragglers such as Herman usually knew our destination and would sometimes arrive up to some time later. If anyone who did not fit in or caused problems had turned up they would have been told in no uncertain terms to fuck off. In a way, although Herman was a total embarrassment at times, we felt sorry for him. He was actually a pretty reasonable guy underneath, albeit with some strange habits and as a result he became the butt of many a person's jokes. If you saw Herman walking down the street behind a fence or hedge, his head went up and down by about 12 inches as he walked, so we would duck into a doorway and as his head dropped down behind the fence we would loudly shout "Herman, Herman" and his head would suddenly shoot up over the top of the fence looking for us. If he could not see us he would run to the end of the fence and look around it. He was constantly baited all the time. Many years later he was killed in a horrific and tragic accident. There was not one of us that did not feel a twinge of sadness at hearing of his passing.

Although Herman was tall he was very skinny and wiry, and when he lost his temper he could be immensely strong and powerful, with a very strong vice-like grip. We were about to find out just how quick his temper could be. One night we were in the Highlight which was crammed full to bursting point as usual.

When Herman happened to glance away, our brother Tel leant over and tipped sugar into Herman's Coca-Cola. After a few seconds the Coke erupted over the top of the glass like a volcano, onto the table then directly into Herman's lap. Herman did not know what Tel had done, but as king of practical jokes and sarcasm, it was a fair bet that Tel was involved. Herman did no more than leap to his feet in a blind rage and with a shout of, "Wahay, wahay… you fucking bastard", he punched Tel straight in the mouth. Tel jumped up and retaliated, punching Herman back equally hard. The two really went for it there and then inside the cafe, exchanging blow after blow over the table before we managed to get the fight outside. Once outside, Herman soon realised that he was out of his depth and backed down. This was the scenario that we were to see many times during the few years that Herman rode with us—he would totally lose his rag and lash out without thinking, thereby getting himself into trouble with a tougher opponent who was not always someone prepared to back off and eventually cool it. We broke the fight up and Herman calmed down, but Tel gave him a stern warning regarding any possible future occurrence. As Tel turned away, Herman verbally retaliated, "Hey, don't get grizzly with me… Grizzly", and from that day on Tel has universally been known by that nickname he gained that day - "Grizzly".

Bog Wright worked at an engineering works and during his lunch hour he got hold of a piece of three-quarter inch wide flat steel out of the scrap bin and bent it into a U-shape. He then got a large nut and bolt and cut the head off the bolt, welding the bolt head to one side of the U-shaped piece of flat steel. He welded the nut with the stem of the bolt still on it to the other side of the U-shaped flat. That night he took it to the Highlight and passed it discretely to Smed. When the rest of us arrived with Herman, Smed came out of the cafe wearing the nut and bolt around his neck. With the U-shape flat hidden under his hair it looked for all intents and purposes as if Smed had a nut and bolt right through his neck. He took Herman off perfectly, "Aw hello you old buggers". Everyone fell about laughing and even Herman saw the funny side and then told Smed to fuck off. After much merriment in the cafe, with various people trying on the nut and bolt, it was put on Herman, but he struggled and would not wear it. When we went to leave someone had inflated a Durex condom to a large balloon size and tied it to the grab rail of Herman's new bike. "Aw, what's that?" asked Herman, prodding the offending object. An amused biker came over with a lighted cigarette and burst the condom."Is it chewing gum?" questioned Herman, "it's all sticky". Another bright biker stepped up and replied. "Yes, it's Wrigleys New Form", combining the type of condom with the name of a well-known chewing gum company. There was another loud roar of laughter.

At this time our next door neighbours moved out and the house was put up for sale. Our mother was formerly a fully trained hairdresser before becoming a housewife. She kept her hand in by hairdressing her family and friends, who would sometimes ask if she could take on a relative or friend of their own, which she sometimes did. On this occasion, one of her lady clients she had met in this manner, informed our mother that her daughter and husband were interested in buying next door. The husband, she said, had something of a strange but wild sense of humour and he was, as she put it, 'something of a card'.

A few days later some of us were working on a bike in the back garden, when there was a loud knock on the upstairs bedroom window next door. We looked up to see a hand making gestures from under the curtain. We were horrified. Who was this person that dared to make rude gestures at us in our garden? We were soon to find out. The daughter and husband had duly purchased the empty property. He was, we heard, an undertaker from London, who ran a branch of a large family business and wanted a country retreat to get away from the rat race and the pressures of what could be a somewhat grizzly job. If we had but known it, this was the start of a whole new era of fun and excitement. Our new neighbour was to throw himself wholeheartedly into the atmosphere of the group. There was never a dull moment when he was around. Within a short space of time he was to become affectionately known by all as 'Dick the Undertaker'. Looking back now I wonder if he may have had an ulterior motive hanging around and drinking with a wild group of bikers; he may have just had a good eye for business.

A few weeks on and our parents decided to go away for the weekend to attend a friend's special wedding anniversary. This was unheard of, as they never went away, but it sure was a hell of an excuse for a good party. The party went off really well. A new record was at number one in the charts at that time. It was the single *Rock and Roll - Part One*, and on the flip side was part two, recorded by Gary Glitter. During the course of the party this record got played over and over again throughout the evening by the drunken hordes, owing in part to our seriously lacking record collection. Later, many revellers were feeling hungry so Kiddie volunteered to ride to a fish and chip shop which did not close until midnight. The chippy was some distance away and Kiddie took off at speed to ride hard to get there in time to purchase our large order before closing time, so bets were placed whether or not he could make it in time, but he did.

Throughout the evening we had been lacing Herman's drinks with spirits. Herman did not drink much, and so became very drunk. We stuffed the pockets of his Belstaff jacket with empty beer cans and condoms and sent him on his way home. We watched from a window as he left, staggering from fence to lamp

69

post. Later, as things quietened down, we piled into Bob's van and drove down to Herman's house to see if he got home ok. We were all singing, drinking and banging on the sides of the van. We threw our empties on his lawn, then we drove away. In the morning Herman's parents remarked to him that he must have been late as they did not hear him come in, but then neighbours began to knock to complain about the noise and drunken behaviour, pointing out the number of empty cans on the lawn.

The party continued on until about three o'clock in the morning, when the party-goers, somewhat worse for wear, finally ended up crashing out at pretty much where they were.

It was a late start on Sunday morning, most still being worse for wear, but a number of full English breakfasts were eventually cooked which most managed to eat. While we sat all around the large table we suddenly noticed the top of a police helmet appear from behind a bush outside our house. The helmet ducked down again only to re-appear several times before the top of a bush suddenly parted and there was the face of our new neighbour wearing a genuine police helmet. He had made off with the helmet as a student, when it was knocked from a policeman's head during the Grosvenor Square Vietnam anti-war riots of the 1960s. From that time on our new neighbour made himself more and more an honorary member of our group. Dick the Undertaker had only just moved into the house next door with his lovely wife Jill and their two young children. Jill's mother lived with them in the property full-time. She kept house for the family when they were not there or were living in their London apartment. The couple became our neighbours most weekends as well as holidays. Dick was great fun to be around. He had a wicked and infectious, if not strange sense of humour. He was fairly tall but thin. He could take off actor Kenneth Williams perfectly and even looked a bit like him. Jill, for her part, was very friendly and happy to go along with most things that her husband got involved in and her mother just tolerated Dick and his wild ways. Living in the house permanently and being in her latter years, there were chores that the mother-in-law could not manage, and so she would sometimes ask us to help. It was not unusual, therefore, to see a biker in a leather jacket and motorcycle boots trudging up and down her lawn behind a coughing and spluttering lawn-mower or putting her rubbish bins out for her.

On one occasion, when Dick and his family arrived from London for their weekend relaxation period, he invited myself and my brother Worm to go out to a pub with him for a few drinks and then on to an Indian restaurant. Being country boys we had never tried Indian food before and so were somewhat intrigued. We went to the pub in Dick's car and sunk a couple of pints each before moving on to town to an Indian of Dick's choice. Being unfamiliar with the food Dick did the ordering. He ordered spicy tandoori chicken and pints of lager all round. The service was very slow so Dick kept ordering more and more lager while we waited. He began to get quite tipsy and began to har-angue the waiters in his best Kenneth Williams' voice as they scurried past to and from the kitchen. "Come along now. Hurry up now. Come along". He repeated this over and over again until our food finally arrived. By this time he was quite drunk. The food was very spicy and hot, probably as a result of winding up the waiters and we had to drink still more lagers as we were sweating profusely. We paid the bill, left and went back to the car, by which time it was dark. Looking back Dick was quite unfit to drive, but we were all well pissed by that time. Back in the car, Dick fired it up and took off up the road where he made a right turn into a one-way street going the wrong way. We tried to warn him, but he was singing. On our right three policemen had stopped a coach, and they spun around in amazement as we went past.

The car was an automatic and Dick floored it; the auto box kicked down and we sped down the straight road and across several junctions. The end of the road was coming up fast and we shouted a warning, but it was too late. We went straight over the traffic island and with a loud bang completely flattened the Keep Left sign. By this point Dick seemed to get it together and we continued our way homeward sticking more or less to the speed limits until we came to a large roundabout on the outskirts of town. As we negotiated the roundabout there was a police car sitting up a side road on our left. Dick hooted at the police and pointed a finger at them, but to our surprise they did nothing at all and we carried on home. In the morning we spoke to Dick regarding the incident but it seemed that he had little, if not any, recollection of it all, but we had a very lucky escape that night.

Dick's sense of humour knew no bounds. He had a love of classic cars and would own several at a time. One weekend he arrived in a big old black Austin 16. The car had running boards and it soon became known as his 'gangster car'. "Come on lads", he said, "let's hit the road", so about six of us piled in it and set off to cruise the local roads in the dark. Dick spotted a pedestrian and coasted up slowly next to him. He then called out of the window to the chap and asked directions to the town that we were already in. The chap was trying to tell him but Dick slowly let up the clutch and the car moved off at walking pace. The chap was walking alongside and Dick pointed forward, "This way," he asked. After about a hundred yards or so the chap gave up with a final shout of "You're mad", and we drove away. Next he found an older woman walking her dog and pulled the same stunt again. "Can you tell me the way to...". "You're in it", came the reply. "Sorry," said Dick with a hand to his ear as he let up the clutch. "I said you're in it, you are in it," she shouted, keeping pace with the car. "Is this the way?" asked Dick pointing ahead and gently increased the speed. The woman and her dog broke into a trot to keep pace with us. Our speed crept up until both the woman and the dog were sprinting alongside the car with her shouting, "You're in it, you're in it" and we drove away. Our next victim was the local bully, an obnoxious character once a Mod but now a Skinhead, so we ducked down as Dick pulled the same stunt again. The Skinhead pointed back the way we had come from, so Dick turned round and went back before returning and calling out the window loudly, "You lied to me", whereupon we all popped up and yelled abuse and told the Skinhead what a complete tosser he was. Similar such forays with Dick soon became the norm as we were never quite sure what he or his sense of humour would come up with next.

Dick joined CAMRA (The Campaign for Real Ale). He researched all the CAMRA pubs in the area, and with us, his resident band of bikers in tow, he visited more than a few along with his dutiful wife Jill. This usually led to many a boozy night as many of us drank more of the strong amber brew than we probably should have done, and so suffered the hangover effects in the morning. These excursions are remembered fondly and as very happy times by most.

CHAPTER NINE

A snowy encounter

BY this time we were spending more time at the Black Horse, the village pub just down the road from the farm cottage were Kiddie lived. A woman called Margaret had recently taken over the pub as landlady. She either welcomed or tolerated us, probably for the amount of money that we put over the bar, so it became another regular haunt. As with all pubs, especially in the villages, there were usually a few real local characters who visited these places regularly. The Black Horse was no exception. The villagers were quite friendly and made us feel welcome.

One cold winter's evening we were all sitting around the roaring log fire at the Horse when Dick the Undertaker and wife Jill arrived and joined us for a drink, and the joking increased drastically. There was a notorious motorcycle cop in our area who was universally known as TT—simply as these were his initials and not for his interest in the Isle of Man TT racing. TT spent much of his time chasing down speeding motorcyclists and car drivers, a challenge that he did with much gusto; and he actively enjoyed it, so he was not particularly well liked. TT was not all bad, however, as he regularly gave up his spare time to teach mainly youngsters to ride motorcycles on the RAC/ACU training scheme, a scheme that he did purely on a voluntary basis. As a result he knew most of the motorcyclists in the area. So there we were, the undertaker and his wife and the band of Greasers, when who walked in but TT. He strolled over to the bar, got a beer and then came over for a chat, sitting down and joining our group. At first we felt more than a bit uncomfortable in his company, but

TT soon made it clear that he was off duty that night, the beer was flowing and the chat was purely because of his love of motorcycling and not his role as a speed cop. However, it certainly was a strange cross section of society that night, and led to a very unusual evening indeed; but later we all agreed you could never trust a copper.

It was when out riding with Dilly, Kiddie and Geoff and the rest of the pack that we first encountered Fred, a short chap of good character and a cracking sense of humour—along with a lot to say for himself. Fred was the same age as Dilly, Kiddie and Den, so a few years older than some of us. Like them Fred was a very fast rider. Fred had race-prepared his Suzuki Super Six to go racing, but had then got married and with a child on the way his racing debut had been delayed, at least for the time being. He had a habit of starting wild antics and could even turn a simple bar billiards match in a pub into a near riot. His sense of humour was infectious.

Fred had the first full face crash helmet that I had ever seen. It was an American Bell helmet. Full face helmets were just becoming available in Great Britain at that time. Bell helmets were expensive and not many people could afford them, so lesser mortals had to settle for the cheaper brands on the British market, the most popular being made by Owens of Bow and so branded Bowbilt Helmets. Fred, by his very nature, set himself up for a good ribbing, and so became a constant target of everyone's jokes; one of the most well known being that he was so slow that he had dead flies on the back of his crash helmet where he caught them by surprise when he out-braked them.

About this time Robbo from the Highlight, who had earlier been involved in the big bike pile-up, also started riding with the group. After a while he brought along a friend of his, a fellow motorcyclist known as Maz. Maz was the son of an English mother and a Polish war veteran father who had stayed on in Britain after World War II rather than return to his native homeland which was now under Russian control. Maz's real name was Mario, but as nobody could pronounce his Polish surname he was universally known (by a shortened version) as Maz. He was a quiet but likeable well spoken fellow who would simply just smile at the constant ribbing that he would often receive.

One day Fred was working at the home of a middle-aged chap when he noticed in the garage a comparatively rare Honda CB77 305cc in immaculate condition. Speaking to the owner he enquired about the bike and was told it had not been used for years and he was thinking of selling it. Fred tentatively asked as to what the asking price may be, and was told by the owner that he wanted £50 for the bike. Fred could not believe his luck and duly parted with the cash and collected the bike. He spent the best part of Saturday getting the bike up, running and serviced. Unable to get insurance, road tax or MOT test at the weekend he decided to risk the consequences and on the Sunday morning rode over to Dilly's shed where he found Maz already there. Dilly was well impressed with Fred's bargain and suggested they road test the bike, so the three of them set off on their bikes in the direction of the coast. Fred found that the Honda must have had a pampered life, the motor being choked up, meaning that it would not rev out or go over seventy mph. By holding the throttle hard against the stop in every gear it slowly began to free up and rev more freely until over ninety mph was visible on the speedo. The three bikes passed through a seaside town. Leaving the town they opened up, increasing their speed when they encountered a motorcycle cop travelling in the opposite direction. Being a motorcyclist himself the cop took more than a fleeting interest in Fred's unusual Honda. Fred panicked, edged forward next to Dilly and gestured over his shoulder looking back at the bike cop as he turned around. The three bikes took off at high speed heading for a tight, twisty road where their smaller agile bikes would have the advantage. The speed cop, now alerted, set off in hot pursuit on his Norton Commando. Riding flat out across their fuel tanks they could see the cop was gaining on them, so given the opportunity at a road junction they hastily split up and went separate ways. Fred flew through a series of corners at high speed, constantly glancing back to see if he was still being pursued. In essence he was racing against himself. He spotted a pub on a bend up ahead and made for it. He raced through the car park entrance, startling the outside drinkers at the tables, only to realise that the car park surface was loose gravel, sending the Honda into a broad sideways slide as he disappeared around the back of the pub in a cloud of dust.

Meanwhile the cop set his sights on Dilly. Maz on the slowest bike was soon overhauled and passed in the cop's quest to home in on his prey; so Maz quickly did a U-turn heading back in the direction they had come from and then set a rapid course for home. Dilly came to a long straight and with the Norton's extra power the cop chased down Dilly on his slower bike. Realising he was done for, Dilly pulled over and took his helmet off. He knew the speed cop, who was absolutely livid. "It's you, it's you," he ranted. "Don't tell me there's nothing bigger than a two and a half amongst you?" He went on, "Look at my bike, just look, we have to verify any damage to our machines". He pointed to the bottom of his fairing where it hung in shreds of fibreglass on both sides and then to his boots with both of the toes scuffed from gravel rash. The Norton was steaming. Once he'd calmed down the cop threw Dilly a lifeline, "You all come along to the local cop shop tonight for a good dressing down at seven o'clock or you are nicked," he threatened. Dilly got home and contacted the others who were understandably wary about trusting a speed cop, but they all finally agreed to make the appointment. Fred took his normal road bike and also lent Maz his old jacket which was covered in motorcycle badges. The cop read them the riot act, ranting and raving about the idiocy of their riding and worked himself into a frenzy. He started pushing Maz around shouting, "Look at you in your bloody jacket, what do you think you are, a Hell's Angel? Fred was beside himself, trying not to laugh as it was his jacket. The cop turned his back, strode over to the window, looking out. He turned back suddenly, "OK, who is the clever bugger that has swapped bikes?"

Sadly summer came to an end, winter was setting in. Hard frosts made an unwelcome appearance. On the evening of Christmas Eve a dozen or so of us, including Pud, Bog, Spud, Grizzly, Geoff and the Mad Mongol, decided to ride out into the countryside to a quiet pub called the Yew Tree. As we neared the pub, slowly at first, and as if it hardly meant it, snowflakes began to fall. We arrived at the pub and went in. As usual there was a roaring log fire in the hearth and the bar was warm. The Yew Tree was run by an ex-policeman, now an ageing chap who had been the village bobby until retirement from the police force some years earlier. Now the landlord of a local pub 'out in the sticks', accessible only via narrow country lanes, he was known as Pop. He was quite a jolly fellow, friendly and likeable and he would often position himself to one side or the other of the roaring fire with a drink, constantly poking the logs on the fire with his wooden walking stick.

After a few drinks and much merriment, Spud went out to use the outside toilet and came rushing back in announcing that two inches of snow had fallen. With that the pub emptied and a colossal snowball fight took place outside. After some time we returned to the bar with frozen hands and fingers for more beers and a warm up. The drinking continued for several more hours before we decided to leave. We knew that Kiddie would be at his local the Black Horse for a Christmas Eve drinking session, so we decided to go there to meet up with him. We opened the pub door to leave and stepped back in amazement. It was a real winter wonderland, and an extra two more inches of snow had fallen. The snow was now over four inches deep and it was so quiet, there was not a sound. We brushed the snow from our bikes and fired them up, then set off gingerly for the Black Horse. Disaster struck almost immediately as Geoff, with Grizzly riding pillion, slid off slowly into a hedge on the first right-hand bend, dropping the bike and splitting the crotch of Grizzly's trousers. They remounted and we set off again, only for a rider called Mick to break his frozen throttle cable on his BSA. Given the conditions he had no choice but to pull off the outer cable cover and with the inner cable wrapped firmly around his gloved hand, we gently continued on our way with Mick holding his ape hanger handle-bars with only his left hand and manipulating the throttle care-fully with his right.

I was next off, with Pud's girlfriend Terri on the back. Terri was riding on my pillion as Pud had not yet passed his motorcycle test. We had gently rounded a corner and slid off gracefully into a snowdrift. I picked up the bike. Everyone was laughing as Terri was on her back trying to get up and slip sliding around, so I cupped my hands and shovelled snow over her. This was all slow speed stuff with a soft landing so no damage had been done to either bikes or riders, save for the stitchwork needed on Grizzly's trousers. After yet another start we continued on our way slowly through the snowy lanes under trees, their boughs laden heavily with snow, with our headlights picking out the falling snowflakes. I marvelled to myself while riding along in the arctic conditions how every snowflake seems to come at you head on, only to swerve around you at the last moment, or such is the impression it gave. Eventually we approached the end of the lane where it joined the main road. Across the main road and clearly visible were the welcoming lights of the Black Horse, shining like a beacon through the blizzard. There was no traffic on the main road so with some hesitance we crossed over, pulling up under the pub's glaring outside lights. On entering Kiddie spun round with a shout of "Hello you bastards". He was drinking with a rider called Leery who had recently sold his BSA to buy a speedway bike. Leery had been helping out at the local speedway track throughout the summer season and had decided that was the way he wanted to go. Later he was to go on to become a very successful professional league rider and eventually manager of the local speedway team.

On entering the pub Grizzly noticed a group of women sniggering at the torn crotch of his trousers. "Oh shit, my nuts are hanging out", he gasped, somewhat embarrassed, so taking one of his leather gauntlet gloves from inside his crash helmet, he wedged it sideways inside the gusset to cover his manhood, a pose he had to maintain for the rest of our time in the pub.

Another drink, another warm-up in front of the pub's fire, and myself and Mad Mongol decided to ride to the local chalk pit just up the road. Leery fired up my bike and started riding sideways speedway style round and round the pub car park. The snow had stopped falling and everything still had that strange muffled silence. After recovering my bike from Leery's grasp we set off to the chalk pit, where we raced around its banked snowy walls until we got bored and rode back to the Black Horse. It transpired that Kiddie had picked up the now bikeless Leery from his home three miles away and now had to take him home. Kiddie was slightly the worse for wear from the affects of alcohol. Given the snowy conditions we were making bets on whether he would make it or not. The pub was now closing so we all set off home with Kiddie and Leery leading and pulling away from us into the gloom. The next day we had to ask if they had made it safely 'without tasting the tarmac', which they did.

Christmas day started with a lie-in followed by a cooked breakfast. After this was a general opening of presents and a surprise visit by the Warbs. There was then a general exodus to the pub for lunchtime drinks. The Black Horse was only open two hours on Christmas Day, after which we descended upon the Warbs' family homes for drinks and another snowball fight. Later we all decided it had been the best Christmas ever.

CHAPTER TEN

Under the paintwork

BRANDS HATCH was our nearest road racing circuit. The road to it took you through shortcuts through narrow and twisty country lanes, the distance being a mere 40 miles. It seems incredible now, but back in the days of the British bikes, we would start preparing our bikes a week or so before in an all out effort to make as sure as possible that they would make it there and back without breaking down. Within our group it was always a hotly contested ride and the nearer you got to the circuit there were more bikes on the road, with their riders also hell bent on high speed full throttle tear up. On most of these forays, at least one or two of the group's bikes would expire at the roadside, either in desperate need of some fettling, more serious attention or an ultimate engine blow up. On occasions there were crashes or slide-offs, some of which would need to be recovered by a van—as did some of the more major mechanical problems.

So the week before would often start with your spare time being taken up with an oil or spark plug change, sometimes along with a set of points. Ignition timing was meticulously adjusted, as were the tappet clearances, in fact anything that could give you a slight edge over the others or a little more reliability. Drive chains were often removed and boiled in Linklife (an evil smelling concoction which looked like a mixture of graphite grease and candle wax) and came with a tin with a handle. The trick was always to keep an old chain handy, disconnecting the split link on your bike's chain and hooking up the old chain to it. You then pulled the bikes chain around until you got to the split link, after which you removed the bike chain and washed it thoroughly in paraffin or petrol, leaving the old chain on the bike. After washing the bike chain you hung it up to dry with a piece of wire. You placed the tin of Linklife on a camping stove and put the chain into it, letting it bubble away for twenty minutes or so in the greasy brew. I know of some who took the opportunity when their parents were out to do this on the kitchen stove, but it stunk the whole house out and you risked getting a backhander from your angry father when your parents got home. Also the handle on the tin the mixture came in was not very secure and often led to spillage or splashing. Once well simmered you lifted the hot chain out of the tin by the wire and hung it up to drip dry back into the tin. Once the grease mixture had cooled off and set, you refitted the link, pulled the chain around, removed the old one, reconnected the split link and adjusted the newer chain accordingly. All nuts and bolts on the bike were checked for general tightness. Brakes and tyre pressures were checked and adjusted and the whole bike was degreased, washed and often polished. Only then were you ready to roll. Neglect your bike maintenance at your own peril was the order of the day.

I remember my first trip to Brands Hatch, watching in amazement as Mike Hailwood on the legendary Honda screaming six cylinder RC166 took on the two-stroke Yamahas of Phil Read and Bill Ivy. Mike Hailwood, many times world champion, an incredible rider in his own right, who many years on was to sadly lose his life along with that of his daughter in a car crash, while taking his children to get fish and chips.

When race day arrived a dozen or so of us would meet and set off, riding hard in the direction of Brands Hatch. We would always make a race of it, there and back. On this occasion we had passed through Tonbridge when there was a sudden and terrific roar. A Norvin 1000 flew past, its rider wearing an old-fashioned 'pudding basin' style helmet with goggles. He gave us a large grin as he passed by. The road was a little damp so we were reluctant to use too much throttle. The Norvin was a Vincent 1000cc V-twin engine mounted in a Norton 'Featherbed' frame, a fast engine in an excellent handling frame and fitted with Norton Roadholder forks. All the best options of the period. The Norvin entered a downhill right-hand curve. On the left was a wood yard. Suddenly the front wheel of the Norvin broke away, pitching its rider from the saddle. He skidded down the road face down and into the wood yard and disappeared under a fir tree with only his legs visible sticking out under it. The Norvin was spinning around in the road and we struggled to avoid it. We stopped, rushed back to pick up the bike and see if the rider was OK. He had hit a partly buried water stop tap cover with his pelvis as he slid along the ground in the wood yard ripping it out of the ground, so he had some serious skin scuffing with bruising already beginning to show. Once we were satisfied he was reasonably alright we left and continued on our way.

After an excellent day's racing we left the circuit, formed up and set off at high speed towards home and the Black Horse. As was customary the last one to arrive back at the pub was to fund the others a round of drinks. This would always lead to a hotly contested, all out race. Back on our side of Tunbridge Wells, Kiddie, who was normally up near the head of the pack began to slow and his bike developed a misfire—a carburettor had worked loose. Try as he might he could not maintain the pace and began to fall back, only to be overtaken by the slower riders. On the route home lay the second country lane short cut, Argos Hill. By the time Kiddie reached the turn off, the pack were no-where to be seen. Riding hard he entered the short cut, throwing his bike enthusiastically through the narrow twisty lane, when he suddenly encountered a car coming at him in the opposite direction. In his hurry he had over-committed himself. Unable to avoid the car by staying on the road he went through the hedge on the left and ended up in some bushes. The car driver was furious. Kiddie, somewhat winded, crawled from the undergrowth to face an angry tirade, "What the bloody hell... you idiot... I just ran into your bloody mates down the road". "What?", questioned Kiddie quickly, "How far ahead were they, the bastards?" The car driver, still seething, confirmed the group had been a mile or so further on when he had come across them. Dragging his bike from the dense shrubbery, Kiddie snatched a screwdriver from the tool kit, tightened the carburettor, kicked the footrest straight and fired up the bike. Giving it a fistful of revs he took off with the motorist still shouting abuse after him. Kiddie rode as hard as he dared but was unable to make up ground and so arrived at the Black Horse after the others to a tremendous cheer from the car park. For once, Kiddie, the man who was so used to getting a free beer bought for him on such occasions, had to put his hand in his pocket and buy a full round of drinks for all. It really was a blow to pride, and one he would not be allowed to forget in a hurry.

It was around this time, after a few high speed 'get offs', mainly on country roads, that a few of the group came up with an idea. The majority of the police patrolled the main A roads, so we tended to ride on the smaller B and country roads, where we could often race each other (out of sight of the law). Currently our motorcycles were a mixed array of varied machines consisting of different makes, models and engine sizes—some British, some Japanese with the odd Italian steed for good measure. "What if," Dilly had suggested, "we all bought one of the new range of speedy 125cc motorcycles currently on the market from Japan?" That way, he reasoned, we would all be evenly matched up with perhaps eighty mph on tap for country road scratching.

Travelling slower, but competitively, he felt could be safer, lead to less serious injuries should there be an accident or two, but with just as much fun. To most of us the plan was flawed for several reasons. Firstly, the majority of us could only afford one mode of transport, that being our current motorcycle which had to be a universal jack of all trades, suitable for all occasions. Sunday or evening tear-ups were one thing, but further distances and faster roads called for a higher capacity engine and a bigger more comfortable all round machine. Secondly, most of us preferred a bigger more manly bike, and thirdly, we figured out that if we hit something bloody hard it made no difference what the hell you were riding. It was this latter prophecy that eventually was to prove fatally correct.

So it was that the plan was put into action, but with just four of the group deciding to swap their current machines for new 125cc Japanese offerings—these being Dilly, Fred, Robbo and Maz. There is no doubt that once run in these machines definitely led to some very close and exciting racing, not only amongst those four, but with others in the group, on roads more favourable to smaller, more agile, machines. It soon transpired that most of these riders used all means possible to gain any advantage, even reverting to the old 'pudding basin' style of helmets with goggles to get two inches lower on the petrol tank. This stance led to one of Fred's favourite sayings, "I was so low I was under the fucking paintwork." This was a quote which he was to use so often over the years.

Cricket: The author, his brothers and a neighbour enjoying a game of cricket in the garden.

The author, age 16, on his Honda C92. In the 1960s we rode in what we had. In this case it was secondhand, 30 bob (£1.50), Black Prince riding gear and Wellington boots.

Photo by Gerry Wood

The author's Triumph Speed Twin.

Photo: Norman Harris

The early years: Dilly outside his flint-built motorcycle shed.

Photo: Mick Robinson

Dilly's crashed Kawasaki 250 Samurai.   Photo: Beckett Newspapers

The infamous Montesa Impala Sports.   Photo: Mick Robinson

Ready for departure to the Trans-Atlantic Motorcycle Racing Series.

Cooking the grub at the Oulton Park racing circuit.

Maz was our first casualty.

Smed and his Kawasaki Z1.
Photo: Beckett Newspapers

Protestors at The Black Horse.

Photo: Beckett Newspapers

Rockers outside Eastbourne's Highlight Café in the 1960s.

NOTE: A decade spans the gap between photos above and below. In the 1960s the bikes were mainly British. Brycreem and quiffs were commonplace. By the middle of the 1970s we wore our hair long, the bkes were predominantly Japanese and the Mods and Skinheads called us Greasers.

Highlight greasers outside the Habibe in Eastbourne's South Street on the opening night of the Habibe Motorcycle Club which soon became known as Eastbourne Wheels. *Photos: Beckett Newspapers*

Kiddie leads the pack on a run across the marshes.   *Photo: Mick Robinson*

The boys and girls of the Wallis Centre, East Grinstead.
Photo: Nicholas "Steph" Stephanakis (Youth Leader)

Kiddie in action on his Suzuki GT750.

The gang at The Black Horse.

Photo: Dick the Undertaker

CHAPTER ELEVEN

Fun and antics

MARGARET, the landlady of the Black Horse seemed to be losing interest in the pub trade and was spending more and more time away from the premises. She had hired a selection of different bar staff as the months went by to hold the fort in her absence. Most of these temporary bar staff were quite amicable, but a few not so much so.

On a cold and frosty winter's night we would often ride to the pub individually where we would meet up, sit and warm ourselves around the log fire, drinking and joking amongst ourselves. The weekday nights being quiet we decided to bring a portable tape recorder and stage an oral account of the local TT with fast action commentary, impersonated interviews of certain well known local characters along the route (often those with distinctive mannerisms) and also imitate the sounds of the bikes taking part. This made for some highly amusing playback relished by ourselves, but not always with the bar staff. On one particular chilly night a barman called Charles complained bitterly with regards to Worm's loud rendition of a Ducati on full song across the 'switchback', which he referred to as, "all too much and a total fiasco". From then on the tape player was discretely ditched rather than possibly cause further problems for us at our favourite local drinking hole.

With spring on its way and the evenings drawing out, yet another barman appeared—a large, loud and bombastic fellow who had an air about him that he always felt he was in the right.

He decided he was going to hold a treasure hunt from the pub, and badgered everyone to buy tickets from him, including us. Mostly, we felt that treasure hunts were for older people and not young tearaways like us. However the barman would not take no for an answer and continued to try to hound us into buying tickets, with the prize being a huge bottle of Scotch Whisky.

During a quiet spell Grizzly noticed Kiddie slide discretely up to the bar in a furtive manner and quietly purchase a ticket. This was a surprise for us all, as we had decided to a man, the event was not for us. Giving it some thought, Grizzly felt that for Kiddie to enter the event he must be damn sure of winning. So he figures that Kiddie, being employed as a truck delivery driver for a local fencing supplier, would know the local area and beyond like the back of his hand. When Kiddie went to the toilet Grizzly sneaked up to the bar and bought a ticket himself, his intention being to wrestle the bottle of Scotch from Kiddie's grasp. He said nothing.

Come the night of the treasure hunt, all the participants in their cars, along with Kiddie and Grizzly on their motorcycles—with both girlfriends riding pillion, took off from the pub with their page full of clues to items they had to find and mark off on the circuit of approximately thirty miles. Kiddie set a cracking pace but Grizzly hung on to his every move. As he had suspected, Kiddie knew just where he was going. They whizzed around the circuit solving clue after clue until the last one, which Kiddie solved in an instant. He took off back towards the pub hard on the throttle with a full house of clues while Grizzly struggled to find the last one. Finally, he got it and took off after Kiddie. There was a bright moon that night and the temperature had fallen and a late frost had begun to form. Both bikes were on full song, but the ground that needed to be covered to catch Kiddie seemed hopeless. On the final stretch of straight road to the pub Kiddie was feeling really confident, the Scotch was already in the bag, he felt. The throttle was hard against the stop when his bike began to misfire. As they flew over the bridge across the river the bike faltered, cut out and went onto one cylinder. "Bollocks," yelled Kiddie. "What's up?" asked Sandra as they coasted to a halt "Quick, get off and push, I think the bloody bike has holed a piston," snapped Kiddie. They were just half a mile from the pub. In the far distance the crackle of an exhaust note broke the stillness of the night air. "Fuck, fuck, run, run." "But why are we running?" Sandra quipped, "It's uphill," she panted. "Fuck the hill, if we don't run that fucking bastard will get the whisky." The distant exhaust note grew louder as the approaching bike rounded the final bends and opened up again, having reached the beginning of the long straight. The noise increased dramatically, Kiddie and Sandra crested the hill gasping for breath. Grizzly was on them in seconds and flew past on full throttle with his horn blaring. "Fucking bastard", screamed Kiddie after him into the darkness. The first one back with all the correct answers to the clues, was Grizzly, who claimed his prize. The luckless couple arrived pushing the dead motorcycle. Grizzly could not resist it. As Kiddie struggled the bike onto its centre stand, Grizzly picked up the huge bottle off the bar and called out to him from the pub door. "Fuck off Griz, I've had enough" came back the disgruntled reply, "Stick the Scotch up your fucking arse."

Not long after this a new landlord and landlady took over the Black Horse. The couple were used to having motorcyclists frequent their pub as they had formerly run a pub in the village of Ash in Kent, near to the infamous Johnsons rocker cafe on the A20 along from Death Hill and Brands Hatch. Arthur was a huge nearly bald man, not only tall but plump also, whereas his wife Madge was a small petite woman with dyed ginger hair and a squeaky voice. Arthur was clearly in the wrong trade, as, because of his sizeable bulk, he found every chore a real effort. Although a nice chap himself, having to go down the cellar to change over a beer barrel or similar, he found it a struggle he could do without, and so he would often complain. They brought with them a huge German Shepherd dog, which strangely enough let everyone into the pub, but if someone opened the door to leave he would run round and round behind the bar barking loudly. The dog did this every time, without fail, and Madge would state in her squeaky voice, "He don't like you going you know, he don't like you going".

Summer dawned and apart from sometimes appearing at the Black Horse for an odd weekday night drink, if they were down from London, Dick the Undertaker and his wife Jill would often turn up on a sunny Sunday lunchtime with the whole family, which consisted of their two children and Jill's mother who kept home for them. There could be up to thirty or forty bikers at the pub on Sunday lunchtime. Dick had recently bought a new Ford Granada estate car. Not only was this the family car, but the seats could be put down and the car would be used in conjunction with their funeral business for the odd pick up or whatever. On a hot summer's day the car and the pub windows were open and Dick would take the mother-in-law and the kids a drink and some crisps to the car. When the mother-in-law had finished her gin and tonic she would continually raise and lower her glass out of the sun roof and call, "Oouie, oouie" at the top of her voice for a refill, sometimes on several occasions, until Dick heard her. He would cup a hand to his ear and question loudly, "Hark, is that the cry of the lesser speckled mother-in-law?". This same sequence of events would be repeated several times during the lunchtime session each time the mother-in-law wanted another G&T.

With his excellent mastery of accents and mannerisms, Dick would take off Madge the landlady perfectly. As the dog ran around the bar barking wildly, Dick would impersonate her. "He don't like you going you know, he don't like the going of YOU". He would put the emphasis on the 'you' and state it louder than the rest.

A few days later Dick came to our house, "Are you squeamish?", he asked. I replied that I was not. "Oh, good," he said, "because I have a pick-up in town". We jumped into the Granada and there was a coffin-shaped shell in the back. Dick was dressed in shorts, t-shirt and flip-flop sandals—hardly undertaking gear I thought, but we set off into town to the morgue to pick up an old lady. On arrival Dick gestured me towards her feet, so I grabbed her by the ankles and we lifted her into the coffin. Dick thanked me and tipped the mortician. We loaded her into the car and Dick enlightened me. "They sit around all year and do nothing, then come down from London to the coast on a coach trip. A few G&Ts and a quick Knees-up Mother Brown and they are dropping like flies." He rubbed his hands enthusiastically together, "it's really good for trade". With that we set off, "Oh, that reminds me, I have to get some Mesowax to waterproof my tent with—she won't mind". said Dick as we later parked her outside Millets and went to buy the much needed substance. He set off home, dropping me off and then taking his deceased client back to London.

Dick and wife Jill arrived back at their weekend pad next door. My mother was in our kitchen. Our front door opened, and with a friendly shout, "good morning Beerile", our undertaker friend walked in. This was perfectly normal as our next door neighbours would often visit unannounced as we did with them. Our mother's real name is Beryl, but Dick had his own form of the English language. He would often distort the Queen's English to get a laugh, or for his own purposes, but this was his pet name for her. "Oh, hello", she replied and continued to prepare the vegetables, grown in our own garden, in preparation for our evening meal later on. Seeing what she was doing, Dick mused, "Oh, Beerile, I have just been straining my greens", but sometimes Dick's sense of humour was lost on her.

Not getting the laugh he wanted Dick went into our large lounge, where myself, my two brothers and a handful of our mates were. Pleasantries were exchanged. There were four biker girls sitting on the sofa. Dick walked over to our drinks cabinet. Sat on the top was a large bottle of Pernod which someone had brought to the party we had when our parents were away. Our parents paid a few shillings each week into an off-licence (drink supplier) Christmas club, and a few weeks before Christmas we put in our Christmas order. There was always more booze than we drank over the festival period which remained in the cabinet for special occasions, or until next year, as none of us drank at home. We preferred to drink at the pub. No one liked Pernod however, so it became Dick's custom on visiting to pour himself a small glass of Pernod on arrival. He then went over to the sofa, and although it was full, he would wriggle his backside into the middle of the girls sitting there and sit with his arms around them. This again was Dick's custom. He liked women and he was openly a flirt. After a while his wife Jill came around and told him that lunch was nearly ready. Dick acknowledged her but continued with his conversation. About 20 minutes later she returned with his roast dinner along with a knife and fork on a tray with the words, "If you're staying here, you might as well have your lunch here". It was not that she minded him cuddling the girls. She knew what her husband was like and trusted him, but after cooking lunch she did not want it to go to waste. Dick thanked her and she left. He looked at the meal before stating that he really did not feel like a big meal at that point, so a grateful Kiddie ate it instead.

Later our mother's sister (our auntie) dropped in to visit. Our mother introduced her to Dick. "Have you met our next door neighbour?" she asked. Our auntie's voice was unsteady. "Oh, oh, err yes, I think I have", she wavered. Dick seized her hand and kissed it. "Dear lady", he said, and stepped back. He looked her up and down, bade us all farewell and left. Our auntie cringed, "Oh, that man gives me the creeps. I feel that he is measuring me up with his eyes". This was just another part of Dick's sense of humour.

CHAPTER TWELVE

Young Kiddie

KIDDIE wandered over to the sheds of the farm cottage where he lived. In reality it was one longish corrugated iron shed, but was divided into three sections. On the left was an open coal shed where the fuel for the cottage Rayburn stove was stockpiled. On the right-hand side was the section where the lawn mower and a few rusty garden tools and implements were kept with its rickety door and rusty hinges. In the middle was a section about five feet wide where Kiddie's motorcycle was stored. From the roof of the shed hung a long length of hessian sacking which served as the only form of any door for the bike shed. Kiddie pulled back the sacking door.

"Bastard," he spat, jumping back with a start. The ginger tomcat, which had been asleep on the seat of the bike, awoke suddenly and fled, taking off at high speed. Kiddie swung a boot in the direction of the cat, but it was too quick and he missed. Kiddie's dad had come out to put some cans into the rubbish bin. "I'm gonna shoot that fucking cat one day," Kiddie complained, "look what the bastard has done to my bloody bike". He pointed out the muddy paw prints and the cat hair all over the seat. His dad laughed, "He likes the heat of the engine when you come in at night, it's cosy for him, and he is a good ratter". Kiddie's younger brother, Herb, had come out to see what all the commotion was about. "Poor Cooking Fat", he joked. "Hey, Kiddie, even the bloody cat is too quick for you". "Just piss off boy, you turd", snapped Kiddie in return. There was no love lost between the two brothers with an age difference of eleven years between the two boys. Kiddie found his brother to be an irritation, a real pain in the backside. Herb for his part never missed an opportunity to wind up his elder brother.

The boy's father, Vic, had experienced a very hard life. He had joined the British Army at age sixteen and was posted to the Royal Artillery Regiment. At that time many artillery pieces were still horse-drawn and the vast majority were still of World War I vintage. After basic training World War II had broken out, and with his regiment now mechanised he was posted to France with the British Expeditionary Force. This was the period now known as the Phoney War. When Germany invaded France his regiment was in danger of being overrun, and they were forced to retreat. Fighting a rearguard action back towards the French coast, they finally ended up trapped along with hundreds of thousands of troops on the beaches of Dunkirk, now minus all their equipment, while being shelled day and night. This was the start of Operation Dynamo, when ships of Britain's Royal Navy, along with many others from all walks of life, including lifeboats, and the infamous armada of 'Little Ships', were sent across the English Channel to Dunkirk in an attempt to lift the majority of the allied troops from the beaches. These were desperate times with thousands of casualties, and many ships were sunk. As Vic tried to get away, ship after ship that he got on was hit—five times in total. Vic finally got away on the sixth attempt and was repatriated to England after which, rested and recovered, he was put back into the line. He fought the rest of the war out with his regiment. In a final count, over 333,000 allied troops were rescued from the Dunkirk beaches—from under the German onslaught—by the crews of the Royal Navy and heroic volunteer sailors.

Post-war, and after being demobbed from military service, Vic was working as a farmhand on a farm at Ditchling in Sussex, when he ploughed up a World War II bomb which exploded, blowing up his tractor and plough. He spent a considerable time in hospital recovering from his injuries, during which his hair turned white, as a direct result of the shock of the blast. Time passed by and then more tragedy struck as his wife and the boys' mother died unexpectedly while she was still at a relatively young age. Now, having moved to another farm in East Sussex, Vic was doing his best to bring up his family, while living in a tied cottage on the farm which went with the job. Times were extremely tough for the family, as it was for many others at this time.

Visiting Kiddie at the farm cottage I noticed a row of tea towels hanging on the rail of the Rayburn to dry, but the tea towels had no centres in them. There was a hole in the middle of each big enough to kick a small football through. This was typical of post-war poverty and wartime; nothing wasted mentality. Our own mother, herself, kept a bag containing scraps of material which she used for the patching of worn garments or as cleaning cloths.

As their father worked long hours on the farm, Kiddie and his brother had to fend for themselves most of the time, including getting their own meals and doing their own washing. With no washing machine available Kiddie would wash and scrub his clothes in the kitchen sink. He would then put them into a bowl. Then he would take them outside and hang them on the washing line with water still pouring out of them. He would hang his tee-shirts upside down from the waistband and often from only one peg, which meant that most of his tee-shirts were stretched, longer one side than the other. This was not so noticeable in the winter when shirts were tucked in, or often worn with a jumper, but in the summer with his tee-shirts worn over trousers, it was highly noticeable.

One Sunday lunchtime Kiddie came into the pub wearing such a tee-shirt that was about eight inches longer on one side than the other, not only that but it had a visible peg mark on the longer side. Fred was beside himself with glee; this type of thing appealed to his sense of humour immensely. He kept going from person to person pointing it out and sniggering. "Look", he said, chuckling, "tonight we are all coming in with pegs on our tee-shirts to take the piss out of Kiddie". We all thought that this was a bit unfair, so decided not to go along with the ploy. Fred left the pub with a big smile and a thumbs up to everyone.

That evening we met at the pub, which was crowded. Part way through the evening Fred arrived and made a big entrance. "Dahdah", he called out loudly and stood in the doorway giving the big thumbs up with both hands. He had five or six clothes pegs hanging on the bottom hem of his tee-shirt. With a look of horror he exclaimed, "You bastards have set me up", after he suddenly realised that no one else had got any pegs on their tee-shirts. Kiddie spun round at the bar, where he was getting a drink, and collapsed into laughter, not realising the joke was on him. "Look at Fred, the bloody idiot, he has forgotten to take the clothes pegs off his tee-shirt". Fred's joke had backfired totally. I guess you could say the joke was on both of them equally that day.

Kevin was the son of Kiddie's next door neighbour. He had recently bought a Suzuki Invader and was learning to ride, so he had L plates fitted on his bike. Kevin was a naturally speedy rider. There were many of these popular and quick little bikes about at that time. Kevin got a job at the same company as where Kiddie worked, so the pair began to race each other to and from work each day. Setting off as usual to work one morning, Kiddie was leading on the country road as the pair crested a rise at speed, only to find a digger digging a trench across the road and a large pile of rubble and soil blocking their path. Kiddie was on a flyer and unable to stop, was left with no other option but to ride straight over the heap of rubble just as the digger bucket was coming down again. Ducking instinctively, he hit his chin on the steering damper knob as the bucking bike went over the top, which later left him with a large black bruise on his chin. Kevin managed to stop and the digger driver exited his cab yelling abuse. Kiddie instantly noticed a considerable drop in engine power after the event and so feared that some serious mechanical damage had occurred. However, a quick inspection further up the road showed that both exhaust front pipes had been squashed almost flat from underneath, meaning the exhaust gases were severely restricted, and so unable to escape. The pair arrived at work without further incident and during his lunch break Kiddie had to borrow an electric drill from a mechanic and drilled a number of holes in the flattened pipes in order to let the exhaust gases escape. The holes in the downpipes now resembled a kitchen colander. Kiddie was forced to continue to ride the bike in that state for a couple more weeks or so, until he managed to source some replacement exhaust pipes for the bike. Only later, on the way home, did the pair realise that the roadworks warning signs had been blown over by the wind, which explained why they had not seen them in the first place. Kiddie later stated that contact between his chin and the steering damper had nearly knocked him out.

"Give me a lift to the village", insisted Sprogg. "Get lost", replied Kevin, but before he could ride away Sprogg leapt onto the rear seat of the Invader. "You will have to take me now because I am not getting off", he yelled. They set off, and nearing the village they came to the hump-back bridge over the river. There was a car ahead. Although the approach road was wide enough for two cars, the bridge itself was quite narrow and only wide enough for one vehicle at time. Being a hump-back bridge it was blind until you were almost upon it. The driver of the car in front had committed himself to cross the bridge when a car came from the other direction at speed. The car in front of Kevin did an emergency stop, catching Kevin unawares, and Kevin's bike ran into the back of the car. Making the most of the momentum, and quick as a flash, Sprogg leapt from the saddle of the bike, over the side of the bridge and was gone. So quick were his actions that no one in the cars even saw him. Nobody even realised that Kevin had been carrying a passenger at all. Sprogg's quick action for once had saved the day.

Arriving at the village in a muddy and dishevelled state, Sprogg soon became his usual annoying self. He began to run cheeky to the bikers parked in the Market Square. Den had stopped by for a pint, and as he was going into town later that night he was wearing a suit. Sprogg was directing his sarcastic comments at Den, who began to get rattled. Sprogg grabbed a bicycle leaning against a wall and cycled round and round Den. "I saw your old man the other day and he said your bloody budgerigar talks more than you do". Den made a grab at him and Sprogg fell off the bike. Den tripped and tore the knee out of his trousers. He was furious. Sprogg ran and Den chased after him. He caught Sprogg by the scruff of his neck and threw him over a wall. "You bastard", yelled Sprogg, and ran away, trying to make his escape. This time he had pushed Den too far. Den had drawn a line in the sand. No longer was he prepared to put up with Sprogg's constant sarcasm and abuse. When it persisted further he seized Sprogg by the throat, dragged him down the alley leading to *The Smugglers* toilet, and thrust Sprogg's head deep into the pan and flushed the toilet.

We set off for The Yew Tree later that night. It was dark now and had been raining. Pud's girlfriend Terri was riding on my pillion, as Pud was still waiting to pass his motorcycle riding test. Suddenly a bike flew past us. Terri suddenly shouted in my ear, "It's Mick". The country lane was wet and mucky. Mick was her cousin. He had stopped by my house, but we had already left, and so he had come after us. He entered the right-hand bend outside the pig farm. We had a grandstand view. The bike skidded away on the wet surface. Mick slid along the road ending up in a ditch of water and worse. We stopped, picked up the bike, kicked the rear brake lever straight to free off the brake. We continued to the pub, but everyone gave Mick a wide berth for the rest of the evening.

A month or more had passed. Pud had now passed his motor-cycle test and had taken Terri out for a spin on the bike. Mick was waiting at the traffic lights on his Honda when he saw Pud and Terri cross the lights on Pud's Suzuki. When the lights changed Mick did a quick left turn and set off in pursuit of the couple to try to catch them up. Neither were aware that Mick was chasing them as they rounded a right-hand sweeper outside of Wannock Gardens, a popular tourist attraction. Mick, going too fast, could not make the curve. He crashed into the support wall. He was thrown over the wall and onto the lawn behind it.

Mick stayed on late at work that night. He was building a kit car with a glass fibre body based on an old Ford chassis and had stayed on longer at the workshop to manufacture some door mounting brackets for his car. He had these door brackets in the front pockets of his Belstaff waxed cotton jacket. With the impact of the crash he had collided with the rear of the petrol tank before being thrown clear. He was taken to hospital. He had broken both his arms. He had been lucky to escape really serious injury, but had very severe bruising around his loins. The car door brackets in his pockets on impact against the fuel tank, had led to damage to his genitals and had given him a blood clot which meant that his penis stayed semi-erect. At this time there was a film showing on cinema screens called *Percy* about a man who had a penis trans-plant operation, and so from then on Mick became known for the duration as Percy Penis. He sure took a lot of stick over that one.

"Hey", enquired Pud one day, "I am curious. How do you wipe your arse with two broken arms? Does your mum have to wipe your backside for you?" Percy said nothing, he was getting sick and tired of all the jokes at his expense.

CHAPTER THIRTEEN

New members and explosives

HERMAN arrived at our house. He had a stranger riding on his motorcycle pillion seat. "Aw, you old buggers", he addressed us in his normal manner, "this is Andy". Andy explained that he worked in the same office as Herman who had told him of some of our exploits. Herman had then invited him along to meet us. Andy had started his riding career on an old single cylinder AJS, which apparently leaked oil like a sieve. He had now been offered a Triumph 650 Tiger 110, the model fitted with a 'bathtub' rear mudguard, which he said was in good shape and so he may purchase it. The 'bathtub' was so known because it looked like an upturned tin bath and was designed to keep a girl's skirt from becoming entangled in the rear wheel, and also to keep mud and water from the pillion rider's legs; but for my money it did nothing at all for the bike's looks. Personally, I feel sure that these models, so adorned, lost Triumph an awful lot of sales, and therefore helped in the eventual demise of the original company.

On one occasion, with Andy riding pillion to Herman, we set off for another country public house. The group was ahead with Herman and Andy bringing up the rear. Worm's Ducati was of lower power than the rest of the bikes, so he was trailing perhaps a quarter mile or so behind some of the pack. There were many tight bends on this road and Worm was struggling to keep even some of the main group in sight. He misjudged a particularly tight left-hand bend. Going too fast, he left the road. He crossed the grass verge and crashed into a wall about four feet high.

Worm was thrown from his machine, over the wall and into the garden of a large and spacious country house. Herman arriving at the scene, turned his head, and shouted to Andy, "Aww, Worm has crashed", and continued on past. "Stop then, you idiot", yelled Andy frantically. He dismounted from the bike, "Quick, go and get the others". He ran over to the fallen bike and looked over the wall trying to locate Worm. We had arrived at the pub when Herman turned up and informed us of the crash. We remounted our bikes and roared back to where we found Worm sitting on the wall by his wrecked machine with Andy. There was a middle-aged chap ranting at him, who turned out to be the gardener. "My god, sonny", the gardener gasped, short of breath, "I heard a loud crash and saw a body fly through the air and land in my flower beds. You are lucky to be alive". Fortunately, Worm had managed to escape serious injury with just a few minor cuts and bruises, but the Ducati was no more, being a total write-off.

Shortly after this event Andy purchased the Triumph T110. One of the first things he did was to turn the standard handlebars upright. This looked very odd and made it look like he was riding a steer by gripping it by the horns. One weekend he turned up at our pad with a passenger. This chap eventually became known as 'One Ball' as he only had one testicle. Before long, he too had bought a motorcycle—a 650 Tribsa (a Triumph engine in a BSA frame). Andy and One Ball now became regular riders with the group.

Kiddie's bike had broken down. There was a motorcycle shop about twelve miles from our house which was open on a Sunday. A quick telephone call confirmed that they had the much needed part. The shop was known as 'Grabbers' because the owner also had his own finance company and would try to entice buyers into buying a new motorcycle on finance with his own company at higher than average interest rates and for over four years.

An unsuspecting buyer could also add a new helmet, leathers and boots to the cost of the bike which seemed a good deal until one stopped to check the interest rate. Grabber would also take virtually anything in part-exchange.

I offered to give Kiddie a lift to Grabbers, to buy the necessary part, but he refused my offer. "Fuck off, you're mad. I will go on the back of Griz, he's safe". So we set off with Grizzly on his Suzuki with Kiddie on the pillion, and myself, and with the now bike-less Worm, along for the ride, on my bike. It had rained earlier in the day, but the roads were now mainly dry. There were still a few damp patches under trees and in the shadows of buildings. The ride there was fairly uneventful, but on the way back it got more competitive. By the time we neared home we were neck to neck. As we turned into the end of the final lane leading to our house Grizzly made his bid for the lead. I was with him all the way. As we got to the farmhouse where our grandparents lived, there was a woman in a Mini trying to park outside. She swung into the road forcing Grizzly wide. He clipped the gravel at the edge of the road and the back wheel skidded out to the left. Grizzly wrestled with the bike, holding it briefly as it slid along sideways speedway style. Then he lost it, Kiddie fell off and skidded down the road on his backside. Grizzly hung onto the bike longer before slinging it down the road twenty-five yards further on. I stopped and we picked up the bike. Most of the backside of Kiddie's trousers was missing. Grizzly had gravel in his knee through being stuck under the bike as it slid along the road.

We arrived home. Our mother was unsympathetic. She looked at their injuries, then produced a pair of tweezers and began to pick the gravel from Grizzly's knee. She then turned her attention to Kiddie. His buttocks were a mass of blood and gravel. She bent him over the dining table. At this point Andy and One Ball arrived and were somewhat shocked to see Kiddie bent over the table with our mother picking the gravel from his arse through the large hole in his trousers using a pair of tweezers. They were horrified. "Oh, honestly, what a mess", exclaimed mother, "I don't know why you have to go so mad", to which Kiddie instantly replied with some vigour, "But Bird, we were in the lead".

This was not the end of the matter however, as Kiddie's backside became infected, the wound becoming poisonous as did Grizzly's knee. Kiddie could not sit down for a week and Grizzly's knee played him up for more than a few months afterwards. "Hey, Kiddie", I ribbed him, "Thought you said Griz was safe".

Around this time Grizzly ran into an old school mate called Dave. He owned a BSA which had expired at the roadside and he had to push it home. Grizzly told him we would take a look at it, so one day Dave arrived at our house having pushed the bike all the way there. On removing the timing cover, I found the contact points had closed up. I filed them up and set the gap. A quick wire brush on the spark plug and a reset of the spark plug gap and the Beezer started first kick. Dave was well chuffed and soon became a regular and enthusiastic member of the group. He had a great sense of humour, along with a schoolboy passion for concocting potions that exploded. Some of his antics were hilarious, but messing with volatile chemicals can be extremely dangerous. Just before I left school the headmaster had stood and delivered a stiff lecture to the whole school assembly on such dangers after a fourth form pupil had blown himself up in his garden shed, losing a finger.

Before long, Dave brought his younger brother Jeff along. Jeff, by his own admission was never a biker but would on occasion ride pillion with one of us as well as often taking an active part in the general exploits and excursions of the group. For the purpose of this book I have chosen to refer to the notorious brothers by their initials of DJP and JP respectively. The two certainly added a whole new sense of fun and humour to our already wild antics.

Here is an amusing contribution sent to me in more recent years by JP the youngest of the brothers which gives some insight into the character and general antics of the two boys.

A handful of our group worked evening shifts as petrol pump attendants in a local garage on different occasions over the years for extra income. At that time the fuel company Esso was running its 'Put a tiger in your tank' sales promotion and handing out free tiger tails with gallons of petrol. The tiger was the Esso symbol; the idea being that the tail was to be tied around the neck of the vehicle's fuel cap. Another such promotional item was a box kite.

Early Experiments with Rocketry

"I wish to turn the clock back to events in the back garden of our house around early November more than a few years ago. During that summer we had acquired some Esso promotions from the village garage, these being some tiger tails and a box kite.

The box kite was for home construction and comprised of about a dozen jointing clips and some white plastic sheeting embellished with the Esso tiger logo, along with a long length of string. Assembly took just five minutes or so—but the finished item looked better than it performed. After a few aborted trials the kite was left lying around the garden in a partly deconstructed state.

During the October/November period that year the elder sibling had been trying to improve on the performance of some fireworks acquired from the local newsagents. Although the rockets purchased would soar into the air emitting a suitable trail of sparks, there was no satisfactory bang with these modestly priced items. So it was that it occurred to the villain of this piece, to tape some bangers upwards to the stick of the rockets, so that any emitted sparks from the rocket may ignite the bangers and might well result in a satisfactory loud and pleasant bang.

So a couple of prototype rockets were constructed, and the youthful brothers climbed the large tree at the bottom of their garden to tape a section of the blue piping from the former box kite to a suitable branch near the top of the tree in as near a vertical position as could be obtained. The piping was to be the launch pad for the rocket.

So it was that the first rocket was ignited and it became apparent that the additional payload on the rocket had implications for its trajectory as it took off in a northerly direction, having only just cleared the roof of our house and landed satisfactorily close to a neighbour across the road, Mrs Hobden, in her front garden, but fortunately, as it turned out, with no final bang.

Adjustments were made to the second prototype to get the bangers closer to the rocket to improve chances of ignition; also it was considered that as the previous rocket had headed north, some compensatory adjustment to the pointing of the launch tube should be made in a southerly direction, which should see the resultant second flight take place in the required direction. So the brothers climbed the tree for a second time, adjustments were made to the rocket and launch tube, and the rocket was ignited by the elder brother.

Instantly it was apparent that too much southerly had been introduced into its trajectory, and the rocket took off south at an altitude of about twenty feet and flew horizontal to the ground. About 100 yards away were the back gardens and the houses on the main road, and the rocket seemed to be heading straight for the window of the house opposite. The brothers anticipated broken glass, but fortune smiled on them as the window was open and the rocket passed safely through the window frame without incident. They thought they detected a muffled explosion, but the distance was such that it was difficult to tell. So the two brothers beat a hasty retreat, and in the absence of further rockets, experiments were abandoned for the day.

It was a total surprise to the elder brother on catching the school train the following Monday to hear the following story. A fellow schoolboy called Trevor, a local resident of the area was recounting to a group the strange happenings of the previous day. It transpired that his father had a bout of feverish flu and had taken to his sick bed, but with the windows open in an attempt to reduce his temperature. Out of nowhere a rocket had entered his bedroom whilst he was in bed and exploded, scorching the bedroom carpet.

The other listeners thought the story to be highly unlikely and dismissed it out of hand. The elder brother, however, just smiled knowingly, whilst musing on the possible effect of adding some additional ingredients to the rocket and attaching a string of rookies—an experiment finally brought to fruition the following November.

It's probably best that you keep this under your hat Tony, in case him and his insurers are still looking for my brother."

JP

Moving on, the group was out on a run when we came across a new BSA broken down at the roadside. The rider stood by his machine in his new motorcycle helmet and motorcycle clothing. It was obvious that he was a new rider, recently kitted out with new gear and bike. There is a code among bikers, particularly back then, that you always stopped to assist a broken down biker. Bikes were a lot less reliable then than now, particularly British models. All motorcycles carried a tool kit, and owners would further carry spare spark plugs, a points file, electrical tape, fuses, etc. The general thinking being that the next breakdown could well be you.

The rider stood amazed as the whole pack pulled up beside him to help. His new leather jacket was open and he had a maroon college scarf hanging from his neck. He was fairly tall and wore black framed spectacles. He was very well spoken—he was clearly a college boy. He introduced himself, "They call me Ox. I am afraid my machine is poorly and it finally expired here, but it is, in fact a new bike. I would be most grateful of any assistance you can offer me". I removed the points cover, and sure enough the points had closed up just as they had on Dave's (DJP) BSA. The fibre heel of the points had bedded in while running on the cam, allowing the points gap to close up. A quick adjustment with a screwdriver and the bike fired up again. The cover was refitted. "Amazing", said Ox, full of gratitude, "Truly amazing, Sir. I am in your debt".

From then on Ox rode with us. He lived with his mother in a small bungalow, but she looked quite elderly to have a son of his age. He didn't seem to have a father or man figure in the house, but nobody ever made mention of this. Despite his good education, Ox's ambition in life was to become a London tube train driver. He was also impressed by the outlaw biker image. He had a poster of an outlaw biker, supposedly biting the head off a live chicken, on his bedroom wall. One time he asked me to take his bike out for a spin with him on the back. Whizzing through the bends at speed, he got quite carried away and shouted for more. "Faster, Sir, faster". Later Kiddie asked if Ox had passed me a chicken to bite its head off? Someone even drew a cartoon of myself, helmetless and across the tank of Ox's BSA with the helmeted Ox sitting bolt upright on the back, chewing on the neck of a startled chicken, with another in his outstretched hand, and the caption, "Want some chicken Tone?"

Around this time another school acquaintance of Grizzly and DJP joined us. He was known by his school nickname of 'Freshers'. Opposite Freshers lived another biker known as 'Dutch'. Both of these riders rode Hondas of the same cubic capacity. Then there was Dutch's mate who had the unusual nickname of 'Bidle', a guy with a brand new 500 Suzuki twin. Bidle soon made a name for himself on the front page of the local paper with the headline "ninety-eight miles per hour police chase", which cost him a large fine, along with a driving ban.

Our numbers were swelling fast. On occasions our house was full of biker boys and girls, sometimes twenty or more in number. Our parents took it all very well on the whole. Our mother became known affectionately as 'Bird' by all our biker friends.

Our mum had grown up with her brothers' biker mates around her parents' home. Sometimes, however, it all got a bit much and the old man once complained bitterly that they had to "sit on the stairs, as we couldn't get a seat in our own bloody house". On another occasion they had to take the dog for a walk as the house was bulging at the seams. There was a similar situation at the Warb family homes, the other biker open houses just a short distance down the road, but perhaps not quite to the same extent.

Worm also ran into an old friend from his school days. His name was Brian. He also joined the group and rode with us, as he still does to this day. Brian is a quietly spoken fellow, with a dry sense of humour. He was sometimes quite capable of coming out with a real gem. Brian soon became known as 'Brian the Sheep', or simply just 'The Sheep', owing to the fact that he lived on the edge of the Pevensey Marshes. Malicious and unfounded rumours spread within the group that he prowled the marshes late at night in search of sexual gratification. On one particular riotous night at the Black Horse he was ribbed relentlessly regarding his supposed nocturnal exploits. We then got bored and moved onto another subject. Perhaps 20 minutes had passed, when Brian suddenly stated, out of the blue, "They don't struggle you know". "What the hell are you on about?" was the general reaction of the group. "The sheep, they don't struggle when you shag them", whereupon the whole place burst into an instant uproar.

DJP was around our house with his BSA. We were talking on the driveway, when suddenly Grizzly rushed out, looking at his watch and carrying his crash helmet. "I'm off to pick up Worm from work he shouted. He fastened his leather jacket and helmet and fired up his bike, all in a bit of a rush. He spun the bike around, turned into the road and rode off with the front wheel of the Suzuki pawing three feet in the air. "He's in a hurry", observed DJP. We heard the revving bike go into second gear, and just before he would have changed into third gear we heard an almighty scrape, followed by a loud clatter and then a highly revving engine. With a joint exclamation of "Oh, shit", we ran like hell to the scene of the crash. It transpired that Grizzly had taken off so quickly that he had left his side stand down. When he had tried to take the slight left-hand curve, the side stand had hit the ground preventing him from making the curve. He had hit the kerb on the right-hand side of the road just behind a parked car and the bike had somersaulted across three open-planned gardens of the new housing estate. We picked up the bike and started to gather the debris. Grizzly was battered and bruised, but mainly unhurt. Still suffering from his damaged knee from a month before, when he had crashed with Kiddie, Grizzly limped back to our house. Luckily no-one seemed to be in at the houses involved, so I kicked the bike back into life and rode it home. DJP soon arrived and told us that he had just completed a clean up operation and had the bike's number plate behind his back when an elderly resident returned home and asked what the hell had happened to his lawn? DJP pleaded ignorance on the matter, stating he was merely a passer-by and knew nothing. He then made good his escape. A fortunate outcome indeed, one which could have been far worse.

CHAPTER FOURTEEN

Cafés and hot lead

WE rolled up at the Highlight *en masse* and parked among the other bikes lined up outside. The door was open and the jukebox was thumping. The familiar clanging of the three pintables at the back of the café was clearly audible as we entered. Sid (the proprietor) was behind the counter and greeted us in his normal friendly Greek Cypriot accent. "Hey, u fa kuffie?" Sid liked a lot of banter and so the standard reply came back , "No, you fuck offie". In a glass display case on the right hand side of the counter was an array of delicious gateaux and deserts along with some rum babas. "Hey Sid, have you got any cake?" "Ya want sum of ma cake, my lovely cake?" "no stick it up your arse, it's bloody awful," "You insult ma cake, ma luvley cake".

This by now had become the standard greeting, almost a ritual. We ordered our meals along with teas and coffees. "Hey Toni", chirped up Sid, "Wen we go shootin on your grandad's farm wagen". It was Saturday evening so we arranged to go the next morning. "I pick u up," Sid said. Geoff was also coming along. Our grandfather had sold some of his land and used the revenue to buy a second farm near Heathfield. Our uncle Norman and his family had moved to this latest farm to manage it for our grandfather, leaving our other uncle Gerry to run our local farm. Little did I know at this time that this last minute casual arrangement was going to leave me with a lasting indelible reminder of both Sid and the Highlight that would stay with me to this day and for the rest of my life.

Early next morning Geoff arrived at my home on his Suzuki, his single barrel 12 bore shotgun tied firmly across his back with a length of bale twine and the pockets of his Belstaff jacket bulging cartridges. Things have changed so much over the past fifty years. There was no such thing then as a shotgun licence or certificate. You just walked into a shop and simply bought a gun. My first two shotguns were ordered from Empire Stores mail order catalogue and duly arrived in the mail. In most cases a shotgun would simply stand propped up in the corner of a bedroom, a box of cartridges sitting in the cupboard. My grandfather had a matching pair of double-barrelled twelve bore hammer guns in his hallway, over his front door, mounted on two six inch nails, one facing one way and one the other. Furthermore, post-war, many country folk often still relied on the odd "one for the pot" meal of rabbit or game to supplement their meagre income with a free meal and so would often resort to ferreting to fill those needs and to feed their families.

Not long after Geoff, Sid arrived, and we all set off for the Heathfield farm in his car. After wandering around the farmland for a couple of hours and not seeing much, the sun came up so we stopped in the shadow of some trees. Geoff and myself unloaded our guns while Sid lit a cigarette, We sat down on the grass and had a chat. Sid finished his cigarette and asked Geoff what the time was. On Geoff's reply he jumped up suddenly with a gasp of, "Oh God, I hav to open da cafe". Geoff and myself got up and picked up our guns. Sid grabbed his gun and it went off with a hell of a bang. It blew a large hole in the ground right in front of me. Earth and grass flew up and stung my face. I jumped back, "Bloody hell Sid, that was close. Geoff followed the line of the shot with his eyes and calmly said, "You have been shot mate". I looked down in horror—pellet holes were visible in my jeans and blood was beginning to soak through the material

113

on my lower left leg. It had all happened in a flash, and I had not felt a thing apart from the dirt in my face. Now with those few words of reality, shock set in. I became hot and bothered. I felt faint. Everything went white, similar to when snow is on the ground, and I began to topple. Geoff caught me, "You can't pass our here mate, we are three fields away from the road". With Sid on one side and Geoff on the other, they dragged me over to a cattle trough full of stagnant green water and dived my head into it to revive me. I regained some sense of reality and with their help we made it to the farmyard. "What's up with him?" my uncle asked as they dragged me past. "Oh, he's been shot", was the reply. They shoved me into the back of the car and we set off at breakneck speed for the casualty department at Eastbourne hospital.

Once there, after the usual inspection, x-ray and diagnosis, it transpired I had collected seventeen shotgun pellets in my left leg, but by extreme good fortune none had touched anything vital. I was being kept in overnight, they said, for observation. I was appalled that nothing was being done to remove the pellets and expressed my disgust to the hospital porter as he wheeled me to the ward. His reply startled me. "Don't be such a baby, I still have a piece of shrapnel in me here from the war bigger than a golf ball". He pointed to his lower back above his kidneys, then he left me. Geoff came in. "That was a bloody close call mate. If it had been a direct shot it would have taken your leg off at that range". He was shaking his head in disbelief. I later heard from Manure who had been at the Highlight when Sid returned home, red in the face and somewhat flustered. He burst into the café and blurted out to his wife Doris, "Oh God, I shot Toni".

Although we did not realise it at the time, this was to be almost the last swansong for the Highlight. Within a few months Sid and Doris had split up and by the mid 1970s the Highlight closed for good. To say the clientele was gutted would be a serious under-statement, Now when we were in town we would need a new late night dining venue. We finally settled on the local Wimpy Bar at the sea end of Terminus Road with occasional forays to the Jolly Roger in Seaside Road. Both had extra basement seating when busy. The drawback with the Wimpy Bar was that it was a little too close for comfort to Macaris the coffee bar, being formerly frequented by our arch-enemy the Mods, and now by the Skinheads. Generally we attended these places in large numbers which tended to guarantee our safety to some degree—but not always. One evening a number of our group left the Wimpy on their bikes. Andy's brother Steve, who was now also riding with us, with girlfriend Wendy, were dragged from Steve's Suzuki and given a severe beating and kicking in the middle of the road in yet another typical "last one away" attack.

A few months on, a crowd of us were in the Wimpy on a Sat-urday night when seven or eight Skinheads came in. They were loud and boisterous. In a short time they began to abuse the staff and it all kicked off. The chef came out of the kitchen with a knife, but this one was on us—we had a score to settle. We waded in to the Skinheads with our superior numbers. We gave them a serious pasting. Kiddie seized one by the throat and threw him over a table. Fighting raged and in the middle of the scrap someone leapt up on their seat and yelled, "Where's my bloody burger?" When we were done we kicked them out onto the street. The manager was eternally grateful. The next lunchtime we were drinking in the Black Horse when an older couple came in for a drink with their son. The son was the Skinhead that Kiddie had thrown over the table the night before. He was as sheepish as hell and said no-thing. He just glared at us. After a while they drank up and left.

Not long after that incident a number of us were going into town in the truck. We rounded the railway station and the following right-hander. Halfway along the straight on our left a drunk was staggering along the pavement with his back to us. Without hesitation DJP hung right out of the passenger's side window and yelled at the top of his voice, "You bloody piss head". Quick as a flash the drunk wheeled aronnd and took two sharp steps to the edge of the kerb and punched DJP in the face as we went past. There was a loud bang, probably as the drunk's fist also hit the side of the van. DJP fell back into the van stunned. He was quite groggy for a minute or two. We continued on our way; recovering some of his senses DJP hazily asked, "What the hell happened, did we hit a lampost?". To which we replied with some amusement, "No that drunk you called a piss head was a bit quicker on his pins than you thought, he punched you in the face as we passed by".

The Wimpy manager was very friendly towards us. "You must try our Wimpy Special Grill, we have a promotion on". I ordered a Special Grill. We had been on the beer that night and I was hungry. I demolished the meal. That night I had a dodgy stomach and was up most of the night. The next evening we were again at the Wimpy. The manager came up with a promotion form for the Special Grill. He handed it to me and asked, "How was it?" I told him it kept me up all night. I seized the form and wrote, "It gets you up early because it gives you the shits", along with my name and address. The manager protested as I folded the form and shoved it into the box. A couple of weeks on I was surprised to receive notification that I was the proud winner of a Wimpy radio in the shape of a burger. The manager could not believe it. I can only imagine that someone in the promotion office had a really good sense of humour. I still have that Wimpy radio to this day.

CHAPTER FIFTEEN

Trans-Atlantic Series and home brewed ales

S OMEONE in motorcycle racing circles came up with the bright idea of challenging a team of riders from the USA to come to the UK to race against a team of British racers on tracks across the UK. This became known as the Trans-Atlantic Trophy Races. These races were scheduled for Easter 1971. The series was probably arranged for this time to fit in with US racing calendar commitments.

The first of these races was on Good Friday at our local track of Brands Hatch and we attended as a group on our motorcycles. The other two races of the series were to be held at the more distant tracks of Mallory Park in Leicestershire on Easter Sunday, with the third race at Oulton Park in Cheshire on Easter Monday. Being that the weather could be somewhat cold or inclement at that time of year it was decided to hire a large van for the second two events to transport a group of us along with our camping gear. My van was currently undergoing modification, a 3.0 litre V6 being shoe-horned in. We did this trip on two occasions during the early 1970s, although I cannot remember now what years they actually were. On hiring the van Kiddie was voted our designated driver as he was a lorry driver by occupation and so had a good knowledge of routes in general. He was also a few years older than most of us which helped for insurance purposes. On picking up the van we borrowed some hay bales from my grandfather, which we placed down each side of the van with old blankets over them as seats.

For the first few years the American riders did not fare so well against the British, particularly as they were not used to racing in the rain on damp or wet tracks; although they later had more success. The series did, though, lead to some good and exciting racing through the years, often with different machinery such as Cal Rayborn with his Harley-Davidson being a rare sight in the UK. As the years clicked by the sight and sounds of the massed Triumph and BSA triples, with the John Player Nortons also thrown into the mix, was an incredible sight to both watch and to hear.

So, van loaded, we set off with Kiddie driving, myself, my two brothers Grizzly and Worm, Bog Wright, Freshers, the notorious brothers JP and DJP, Robbo, Maz, Geoff and Kiddie's young brother Herb along for the ride, as there was no one left at home to look after him during Kiddie's absence. There was some good racing at a somewhat chilly Mallory Park with the wind blowing off the lake in the middle of the circuit. After the meeting we set off and after a meal stopped on the side of an A road somewhere for the night. We pitched our large tent and Kiddie parked the van right next to it to keep the wind off. It was a cold night and as our tent did not have a sewn-in groundsheet the wind whipped under the bottom of the tent. After a pretty sleepless night I was slightly annoyed to hear the van start up and drive away. I looked around me and realised that I was on my own, the rest of the tent's occupants having fled to the warmer climes or the van during the night. A while passed and after curling up tight I finally succumbed to a deep sleep. After an hour or two I was awoken by the van returning and the sound of cheery voices. It transpired that the bastards had left me in my tent by the roadside and driven away to find a café to fill their bellies. As I was finally warm now in my sleeping bag I was in no particular hurry to get up so they let my tent down, then took it away completely, just leaving me in my sleeping bag on the side of the road. At this point I decided that discretion was the better part of valour and so emerged. We set off for Oulton, myself on a grumbling and empty stomach. We pitched up at Oulton Park and foraged for wood for a fire to try to keep warm. Although the racing was good it was spoilt to some extent by the cold and some of our number never actually left the comparatively warmer interior of the van. On the way home there was a strong stench of bonfire smoke on all our clothing.

On hearing of our impending trip Dick the Undertaker had invited us to drop in and visit him and his family at their pad in the smoke (London) on our way home. We located the undertakers shop on a main London street and parked the van just around the corner. Walking back to the shop a double decker bus pulled up at a bus stop outside, its passengers bemused to see a whole group of dishevelled looking ruffians in leather jackets going into an undertakers. Dick opened the door and welcomed us. Geoff, who was the last one in turned to face the bus and waved his hands, beckoning to the bus passengers, inviting them in. Somewhat unsurprisingly there were no takers.

Dick took us up to his apartment above the shop. Later he showed us around. Opening a door to a large room where a couple of trolleys stood for moving coffins around, he leapt on one with a shout of, "This is where we do the go-cart racing"; he proceeded to scoot it around the room. Later he took us down into the cellar where lines of plastic beer barrels containing his home brewed beer stood. "Here is a special one that I want you all to try" he enthused, filling our glasses. Being in the cellar the beer was ice cold. After we had finished he asked for our opinions. Then with a clap of his hands he announced with glee, "Congratulations lads, you have all drunk a pint of embalming fluid!" Later Kiddie admitted the he felt quite pissed after a few pints of Dick's home-made wallop—and he was our driver.

Spring gave way to summer, Dick took his family on holiday to Cornwall. He had bought a small camping trailer to tow behind his car. He arrived back with it full of flagons of scrumpy cider. He erected his tent on the front lawn of his house to air in the sun. The tent was blue and igloo shaped with no poles but inflatable panels to hold it erect instead. It also had a round door. Dick cracked open some scrumpy. "Come in lads", he invited, "and sample the magic nectar". He began passing out some plastic glasses. We had tried a few different cider samples when Dick's children arrived and peered at us through the open door. Then they began to sing and dance outside. "Children", called Dick, "what is playing on the round television?" The children began singing and danced past the door as if they were performing on stage. We clapped their efforts. After a few more tasters we emerged from the tent. The neighbour on the other side of Dick's house was known by the nickame Old Nosey. She was unmarried and lived there with her brother. Nosey was forever hiding behind her curtains watching what was going on in the street. Us bikers would always give her a wave, whereupon the curtains would close with a sudden twitch as she realised she had been rumbled. Dick used a different approach. He would walk around with a glass, with a small amount of liquid in the bottom, and regularly hold up the glass and toast her at the slightest movement of a curtain.

On a Sunday lunchtime we would meet at the Black Horse for a few drinks. We would then go to our individual homes and grab a quick lunch before the masses all turned up at our house for an afternoon blast on our motorcycles. Dick had bought a brand new bright orange Citroen 2CV with a deckchair-like multi-coloured canvas roof. When asked why he had bought such a car he replied that it was a cult car, a Marmite car, a car loved by some but despised by others, similar to a Volkswagen Beetle.

On this afternoon around twenty of us were grouped outside our house ready to set off. A car came up the road hooting constantly. We spun around to see Dick driving past in the Citroen, his wife Jill at his side laughing with their two children in the back. Dick was half standing with his head out of the roof, but he was wearing his wife's headscarf knotted under his chin and his daughter's white plastic sunglasses and he was blowing us all kisses. A terrific roar of applause went up. Dick's sense of humour knew no bounds.

CHAPTER SIXTEEN

The winter of discontent

IN the 1960s and 1970s motorcycling was the cheapest form of transport. A prospective rider could purchase a machine with an engine capacity up to 250cc and ride it on a provisional licence on L plates. The rider needed no form of training or qualification whatsoever, nor initially any helmet or protective gear to ride a bike possibly capable of up to 100mph. He could simply purchase or mount a motorcycle or scooter and ride. This undoubtedly led to many serious accidents and a number of fatalities. Of course the machine needed to be roadworthy, taxed, insured and MoT tested if over three years old. The rider had to renew his provisional licence every six months or take his riding test to obtain a full licence. Many never bothered and merely kept renewing their provisional licence and continued to ride on L plates. After all it was much cheaper transport than a car where you either paid for driving lessons or had to drive with a fully qualified driver until you had passed your driving test. Because of this policy motorcycle sales in Britain boomed. Every town and village had a number of two-wheeled riders whose initial reason for obtaining a powered two-wheeler was for transport, particularly for trips to and fro from work, either being Mod or Rocker, depending on which side of the coin you fell on.

I know of one local rider, a photographer known as Hoot, who purchased a new 250cc twin cylinder Honda from a local motorcycle shop. The motorcycle was duly delivered by the company after first having been fitted with a rear carrier and top box to carry the owner's photographic gear for his employment.

Hoot flicked through the bike manual to familiarise himself with the controls, as he had previously only driven a car. Cautiously he mounted the bike, fired it up, pulled in the clutch, selected first gear and moved off. He managed to select second gear and arrived at the end of his road. He sat there revving up the bike with the clutch in. He took his left hand off the clutch to brush his hair from his eyes. The bike took off wildly on the back wheel, crossing the main road. Hoot and the bike ended up in a wooden bus shelter on the far side of the road. Hoot's recollection of this event shows just how easy it was for a novice to come to serious harm. The compulsory helmet law in Britain finally came into effect on June 1st 1973.

Having discovered the joys of two-wheeled biking the motor-cyclists began to meet at local establishments such as cafés or pubs and rode together as groups, visiting youth clubs, discos and parties around the area. This soon led to meeting up with other like-minded individuals from other areas. These groups would then, perhaps, start riding together. This was the case with our group as individuals or other groups would often join us on such runs or gatherings, swelling our numbers dramatically. It was like one big club of like-minded people all riding together. Such was one big Sunday ride out, when we were joined by many of the Highlight bikers including Stan and Russ on a trip to Ditchling Beacon which was caught on film on my movie camera. Stan's real name was Graham, but he got the name of Stan from Stanley Matthews the footballer as Stan didn't like football at all and he was crap at it anyway. It was a wind up.

This was how we first met Gozy and Weasel, two bikers from the nearby town of Hailsham. The pair would often attend discos at our local youth club. Discos were then in their infancy. The local discos were more often than not promoted and carried out by a lad of similar age to us known as Frenchie, who also supplied music for the intervals between different bands playing the clubs as well as many other venues in the area. Frenchie's disco was called Psychosounds and he went on to make it just one part of his huge lifetime entertainment empire which he built up over many years and marketed for the rest of his life, during which time he met and rubbed shoulders with many rich and famous people. Frenchie was also a biker, first owning a BSA Starfire and later a 750cc Triumph Bonneville. For all of our parties, weddings and many other events over the years Frenchie and his Psychosounds disco became the number one choice.

Gozy and Weasel were two inseparable friends who were always together. Of similar age to ourselves Gozy was around 5ft 10in tall with dark hair. Weasel was of similar height but with long blonde curly hair. Both rode in the standard leather motorcycle jackets of the day along with motorcycle boots with white sea boot socks turned down over the top. Gozy had a passion for Norton Commando machines and owned several over the years, before moving on to other marques and models. Weasel had a range of different machines over a period of time which also included one Norton Commando 850. When the pair attended such events they would always hit the dance floor. They were good dancers, especially Weasel, whose legs seemed to be super flexible and sometimes let to him being referred to as "old rubber legs". The pair along with others from the area began to put in the occasional appearance or two at the Black Horse.

A work colleague asked me if I would use my van, otherwise known as "the truck", to move an item of furniture for him—which I did. As we passed the Black Horse, Arthur, the pub landlord was bent over getting something out of the boot of his car. He had black trousers on and his enormous backside was sticking up in the air. My work colleague hung out of the van window and shouted, "The black arse" as loud as he could.

Fortunately, because Arthur was such a large man he moved at the speed of a snail. As his large neck turned slowly round I floored the accellerator and cleared off quick before he could see who it was. From then on the Black Horse became referred to as the "Black Arse" amongst ourselves. Later this was altered again and simplified. The pub then became known as "the cheeks".

A few weeks later Madge and Arthur held a raffle at the pub. Maz won a prize and we all had a good laugh as Madge called out M Maz-oo-waki as she made several unsuccessful attempts in vain to pronounce his Polish surname.

Amongst the regulars at the pub were two old country folk who liked us and with whom we got on very well. They were Harry and Old Ben. Ben was a real old countryman who had lived in the village near the pub for most of his life. Ben, a big chap, who always wore a trilby hat, was extremely deaf and so used to shout loudly in normal conversation. This could sometimes prove to be rather embarrassing. There was another chap from the same village who was a heavy plant operator. He was quite a porky bombastic person who would come in covered in muck and stinking of diesel oil. It appeared that he hardly ever washed or changed his clothes. He was known by all as Diesel Dick. This particular night Ben spotted Diesel Dick in the other bar. Ben suddenly shouted out, "Look at old Diesel in there, dirty bastard", at which Diesel Dick suddenly spun around. "You can bet his old marriage tackle ain't so clean either". Ben then followed it up with a huge belly laugh The rest of us couldn't help but laugh along also. One night Diesel decided to pick a fight with some jockeys from a local racing stable, who by the very nature of their occupation were small in stature. He realised his mistake when one hit him over the head with a metal chair from the beer garden.

Dilly arrived at the pub but did not come in for a drink. Dilly, Robbo, Fred, Pete and a few of the others just liked to ride and so didn't do all the discos, parties, etc. that the rest of us did. He had heard that Worm had been given a 500cc single cylinder Matchless by a neighbour. Worm had obtained and fitted a boarded sidecar chassis to the bike in order that he could ride it as a learner on L plates. Dilly said that he wanted to buy the outfit to race around the fields on his father's farm. Worm did not want to sell. Firstly, the bike was in good condition, having been well looked after by its previous owner. Secondly, Worm wanted to ride it himself and he felt it was too good to ruin by racing around muddy fields.

Dilly was a joker and told a good story. He had the gathered group in stitches while recounting a particular story of one of just many police chases, where after pulling him over the cop had turned his attention to the bike's open megaphone exhaust. As a finale Dilly stated that the cop put his head into the large megaphone and had a good look around without taking his helmet off.

A few days later, Dilly, Robbo, Geoff and a few others turned up at our house and waved £30 under Worm's nose to jointly purchase the outfit. That was about three weeks pay at that time for Worm and after a degree of mental struggle they managed to prise it from his grasp and ride it away.

Not long after Dilly's luck ran out. He was out for a ride with Sam and Tim from the village. As they rode through the country roads and passed a local pub, they took a downhill left-hand bend. As they rounded it a medium sized council work truck was parked right on the exit. The workers were sitting in the cab eating their sandwiches and pouring out their flasks of tea or coffee. Dilly could not stop and was forced to sweep around the vehicle. A Morris Minor Traveller was coming the other way. Dilly and bike collided with the driver's side front wing and were thrown over the car. The mirror fitted to the wing snapped off and the stem tore into Dilly's flesh, opening up a large gash. Apart from his bad injuries Dilly lost a lot of blood on the road. Later Kiddie and Kevin on their way home from work came across the aftermath of the prang and wondered what the hell happened there. The carnage was so bad that both Sam and Tim, after witnessing the crash, both virtually gave up riding bikes overnight. They never rode seriously again from that date on.

Dilly was rushed to hospital. Survival was touch and go for a while. Eventually he pulled through. Some of the lads went in to see him, but visiting was restricted. He was hanging up in bed with various limbs in traction. A young nurse had come in earlier to give him a bed bath. As she was washing around his loins Dilly began to get aroused. The nurse scolded him... "er, Mr. Dumbrell". "What's up nurse, have you never seen a stiff cock before?" "Mr. Dumbrell... you can do it yourself", she exclaimed. "How the bloody hell can I?", quipped Dilly as he hung there like a suspended wounded animal. The nurse threw the cloth over his private parts and stormed out. After that they put bromide in his tea.

Dilly was released to go home, but he was still in a lot of pain and on crutches. Typical of the man, he was determined to get back into the saddle. He bought a 250cc Yamaha YDS3 and had it delivered. Being left foot gear change he figured he would take it easy and use just the front brake. As soon as was at all possible he donned his gear, mounted the bike and set off carefully—but approaching Alfriston the car in front of him had to do an emergency stop. Stopping suddenly, Dilly put his bad foot to the ground which was his injured leg. His foot collapsed and the bike fell over pinning Dilly's bad leg under it. The local doctor was driving the car behind. He got out and lifted the bike off Dilly, then verbally gave him both barrels. He was not at all pleased.

Now, with plenty of time on his hands, and forced to wear a specially made shoe and a calliper on his right bottom leg and foot for life, he spent many hours in his shed working out how he could convert all of his future bikes to have both the gear change and the rear brake on the left-hand side. He was prosecuted for his part in the accident. Endorsements and a large fine were handed down from the bench as it was decreed that he was at fault for the crash as he should have been able to stop. However, awkward questions were also asked of the council workers as to whether it was wise or sensible to park your truck on an exit to a blind bend in order to take a lunch break, but, Dilly had history with the courts. It didn't help that in a previous accident he had taken the wing off the Chairman of the Bench's Alfa Romeo. The case made the local paper under the headline of "Motor-cyclist on crutches fined", along with a photo of Dilly's badly smashed Kawasaki Samurai. From then on Dilly adapted all his future machines to suit his current disability.

After this crash Dilly's father made a desperate, but unsuccessful attempt, to prise his son away from motorcycles. Dilly still did not have a car licence, so his father bought him a new Bond Bug three-wheeler. It was driveable on a motorcycle licence. It was not long, though, before Dilly clashed with the local constabulary yet again, this time with the Bug. Dilly was apprehended by Mick the motor-cycle cop for rounding a bend in Seaford with the Bond Bug up on two wheels. On pulling the Bond over the cop noticed that Dilly, as the driver, was driving with a broken arm and Fred as passenger, who had a broken wrist, was changing gear for him.

From Dilly's crash on we had a string of bad luck as a group. Our lovely neighbour Dick the Undertaker's wife Jill was diagnosed with cancer after the birth of their third child. Sadly she died aged only twenty-nine, leaving Dick and her mother to look after the children. We all felt Jill's death badly. She was one of us. She was generally there at her husband's side, along with their young family, putting up with Dick's wild ways and his strange sense of humour—but like him, she was an honorary member of the group. She was to be very missed indeed.

Summer crept on but our luck did not improve. One evening we had a dreadful phone call. Our good friend Maz had been killed in a motorcycle accident. We were totally shocked. Maz was our first casualty. Until now our exploits had seemed like some sort of wild game, a hectic roller coaster ride of life and endless fun with motorcycles, speed, runs and parties. I guess we felt we were somehow invincible. These incidents happen to others and we probably felt we were immune to such things happening to us. Later we heard from Manure what had happened. During the day he was on his way to an Eastbourne motorcycle shop to trade in his bike for a new Yamaha which he had previously ordered. On route he came across Maz and Manure pulled out behind him. Nearing a double bend Maz assumed that Manure would be turning off to the right to go home, but in this case he was not. Maz slowed, half turned and gave him a friendly wave. Then he gave the bike a small amount of throttle. On entering the left-hander he flicked the bike over to the left. The back wheel broke away. The bike spun around and threw Maz off. He slid across the road and a car coming in the opposite direction ran over him checking his slide. His helmet flew off on impact. Maz was pronounced dead at the scene. The cops on arrival asked Manure if they had been pace making or racing each other, which they were not. The experiment with the 125s had clearly failed and was abandoned for good.

The coroner seemed to think from the evidence that the bike's centre stand may have decked, lifting the rear wheel slightly, making it lose traction—but Manure saw nothing of this, the rear wheel just broke away. They had not been riding erratically or speeding, but simply going about their business within a 30mph limit. A split second and a simple misjudgement had cost our friend Maz his young life.

At this time we all thought we were tough, strong young men, but gathered around the graveside there was not one of us that did not try to fight back a tear as they lowered our fallen friend's coffin and we saw the brass plate with his name and age eighteen on it.

As a parting gift from autumn into winter both cylinder heads on my 250J cracked from the spark plug threads across to a head stud. The manufacturers agreed to replace them both for free under warranty, but there was a waiting list. It would seem that this was a common fault on that model. This meant that I ended the year bikeless.

After many months when I eventually got the replacement cylinder heads fitted, I was shocked to find the cooling fins were angled diagonally instead of straight in line with the bike as the originals were. Original replacements were no longer available. I was seriously disappointed. To my mind it spoilt the whole look of the bike.

To top it all Madge and Arthur announced they were retiring, and so would be leaving the Black Horse in the new year.

It had not been a good year for all, so we went into the winter in a state of depression. A winter which became generally known as the winter of discontent.

CHAPTER SEVENTEEN

A whole new beginning

OUR mood of doom and gloom was not helped by the cold, wet and miserable weather. Occasionally a few of us would still gather at the Black Horse. I drove up there in the truck as I was still waiting for my bike to be fixed under warranty. When I arrived there was hardly anything in the car park. I stood and briefly looked at the almost deserted pub. I entered the bar, Madge was serving, she looked up, "Hello stranger". I ordered a pint. A loud voice boomed out behind me. "Thirsty then?" It was Old Ben; he gave me a firm slap across the back. Harry looked on, "I don't half miss your mob", he said with a smile, "I feel ten years younger with them around." Old Ben joined in again, "It's been so quiet in here, I thought my hearing aid had packed up". He burst into a loud hoot of laughter and slapped me across the back again. Harry continued, "Your mate Kiddie is still in every night, certainly put his beer away, don't he?" Ben leant over, "He has bugger all else to do," he shouted. Madge served me the pint, "Tony's here, Arthur", she called out. Arthur looked around the corner and just grunted in acknowledgement. Arthur could be abrupt, but the couple were good to us. Back in the summer some tourists had come back early on a Sunday evening and complained, "We were in here at lunchtime and there were a lot of motorcyclists. When we got home our car petrol cap was missing, and we think they stole it." Arthur was fuming, "Don't be so bloody stupid. What the hell would our bike boys want with a car fuel cap? The best thing you can do is bugger off and not come back." Good old Arthur, we could always rely on him.

The door opened and Kiddie sauntered in having walked down from his farm cottage. "All right mush," he called out on spotting me. I noticed that in place of his well worn biking jacket he was wearing his work donkey jacket. We sat in front of the roaring log fire, had a few beers, discussed old times then had a game of darts. Come closing time we shook hands. We were all fed up at the moment. It was going to be a long drawn out winter.

Easter was coming up again in a few weeks time and still no sign of my cylinder heads. There had been a run on them under warranties apparently, so clearly it was a common fault. At this point it did not look like I would be making the first race meeting of the season this time around, but by pure chance that was about to change. Not only that, but this chance meeting was going to have a far reaching, but pleasant, effect on our gang for the future. As one chapter closes, another opens, as the saying goes.

I went along to the local newsagent's shop. As I left the shop I almost bumped into a young lad from our village who I recognised slightly. He nodded to me in passing. This youth was four or five years younger than myself. I knew this lad had recently become of motorcycle riding age, as I had seen him out riding. I enquired how the bike was going. He replied that the bike was going well but unfortunately he had been banned from driving for six months for speeding. I expressed my regrets and left with my bike magazine tucked firmly under my arm.

The next week or so passed quietly, then one evening there was a knock on the door. On opening the door I was surprised to see the same youth, who introduced himself as Dave, stood there uneasily with his hands in his pockets. "Hi, I heard your bike is off the road and I wondered if you would be interested in riding my bike to Brands Hatch with me on the back?". I was taken by complete surprise, but quickly recovered. I gratefully accepted his offer. Dave seemed pleased. "I'll have the bike ready and fired up at 9 a.m. at my place." He gave me a wave as he left.

I made my way to Dave's house for the given time. There were five or six motorcycles outside along with their young riders. "I hope you don't mind my mates coming along," Dave called, coming out of the house. "Not at all." I glanced around. I only recognised a couple of them, both local lads. The rest were strangers. One of the locals had a reputation as being a little on the shady side, a bit of a rogue. He had a nickname—he was known as Bar Steward, a take off of the word bastard. Coming from a family that was devoutly religious he was the black sheep of the family, a real rebel. At the age of only thirteen he had been riding a moped on the road when he crashed into some railings and was taken to hospital. The police tried to convict him on several counts, but the road was railway property, so was out of police jurisdiction—as a result he managed to escape prosecution.

A few minutes passed by. Gozy arrived on his 850 Norton Commando to pick up a petite young blonde girl who lived a couple of doors away. They came over and joined us. The line up was myself and Dave on his 250 YDS7, a 250 Honda, a couple of 250 Suzukis, the Bar Steward on his Yamaha 200 and Gozy with the young girl riding pillion on his Norton. We set off with myself and Dave leading, the rest behind, with the Commando bringing up the rear. I took the Yamaha up to the legal mph speed limit. I wanted to get the feel of the bike. After a few corners I found the brakes to be good and the handling to be superior to my own bike, even if it was not as quick. We cruised along the straight, the sun was shining and it was warm. A fantastic day to be out gobbling up miles on a motorcycle. Glancing in the mirrors I could see the others seemed, for now, to be quite happy to cruise along in convoy.

We came across some bikes in the distance. Yearning for some action I increased the pace. Dave seemed to read my mind and yelled, "go and get them" over my shoulder. That was all I needed. I dropped the Yamaha a gear and wound it up. Blue smoke belched from the exhausts of the two-stroke motorcycle. I changed back up a gear and hit the red line on the tacho. The engine screamed, I shifted up another gear. Glancing back over my shoulder I glimpsed the others giving chase through a haze of two-stroke smoke. I leant forward, Dave crouched across my back. A left-hand bend was coming up in the distance. I checked the speedo... 90mph... not bad two up. The bikes in front had seen us coming, they were going to make a race of it. They went into the left-hander fast, too fast, and had to brake throwing them off line. I caught them on the bend. The footrest and the centre stand on the Yamaha decked. We swept past them on the exit. Another glance in the mirrors and to my surprise Bar Steward was still with us, laying flat across his petrol tank just fifty yards behind. The others were still tearing up the other riders as we accelerated away. The run was now officially on. Into some long sweeping curves that we took flat out. Out of the corner of my eye a couple of farmers in a field spun around as we flashed past. We swept past a group of three big British bikes who gave chase. Briefly, after being held up by a car, one got alongside us, but we swept ahead again, our lighter, better handling bikes being faster through the corners. We flew down a hill, the Yamaha revving into the red. Nearing Tunbridge Wells we backed off our throttles, slowing the pace so the rest could catch up. We kept the speed down to the 30mph speed limit. Not wishing to attract the law, we did the same through Tonbridge. It seemed like walking pace after our high speed run. Seeing a police radar trap in the distance which had stopped two cars, I mused that it was about time they hid that somewhere else. We checked our own speed. A mile on we left the 30mph speed limit and wound it on again.

We came upon "death bend", a notorious tight left-hand bend, so named because of the large number of casualties that had come to grief there, owing to the poor road surface, the odd manhole cover and the fact that it was a deceptive bend. There was the usual crowd of ghouls sitting on the bank watching and waiting for someone to crash and to assist the unfortunate should it happen.

We swept in, Bar Steward hard on our tail. The stand decked, we left a trail of sparks. The watching crowd gave us a cheer. I opened up accelerating away. I looked back over my shoulder to see one of the Suzukis go down, his stand had dug in, the bike had spun around throwing him off. He slid down the road. A car coming the other way screeched to a halt. The shocked car driver jumped out. The lads on the bank had sprung into action. They already had the bike picked up. The rider was OK. It could have been far worse. He could have ended up under one of Henry Ford's mechanical creations.

We took the second short cut from Ightham to the circuit. The roads were narrower here and contained an extremely tight left-hand hairpin where many bikers have crashed over the years. If one failed to make the bend dire consequences awaited the unwary as bike and rider shot straight across the bend in front of other traffic and down a steep wooded bank beyond. If taking the bend successfully you then climbed up a steep hill before cranking hard right into a right-hander. Gaining speed you made a long dash down to the next junction, made a right turn, which took you down to the main A20. A left turn onto the main road, a fast blast past Johnsons motorcycle café and you finally arrived at Brands Hatch. Gozy came blasting past along the A20 on his Norton with its extra power. He had kept the speed down en route so as not to scare his inexperienced passenger too much.

An excellent day's racing was had at the circuit. Sidecar racing is often the last event on the programme, as in this case. I quite enjoy watching the sidecars perform. It is completely different to watching solo motorcycles race. Many do not like sidecars, so the circuit starts to empty, prematurely, before racing has finished. This time we stayed until all the racing was over and the traffic cleared a little. We then set off for home at more of a fast cruising pace. Around twelve miles from home, opposite Grabbers motorcycle shop was a Little Chef café. We had decided to stop there. On arrival we noticed a number of motorcycles in the car park. We went in and ordered our meals. Looking around I knew a few of the riders, some frequented The Highlight café in Eastbourne. There was a fair amount of banter going on amongst the different groups. We finished our food, stood up and picked up our crash helmets to leave.

We followed a group out of the café to the car park at the back where our bikes were standing. As we were putting on our helmets I caught one's attention. "How about a tear up?" I asked. The group turned and looked at each other. I knew that one of them had recently had his Honda CB500/4 "breathed on" by that famous Japanese tuner Pops Yoshimura. The bike had a sports camshaft fitted. I was interested to see how well it would perform. I was addressing my remarks to him. "Come on Chris, how about a blast?" Chris smiled and informed me that as he was still running in the motor he could only use limited throttle, so could not accommodate us that day. "What about the rest of you?" asked Bar Steward from behind me. I had not ridden with this individual before, but already on the run up to the circuit and then back to the café, he had proved to be extremely rapid. Both Yamahas had shown to be evenly matched as Dave and myself were on a 250cc machine, whereas Bar Steward, although riding solo, was mounted on a mere 200cc model. A general shaking of heads took place. "We are with him", said one pointing to Chris. Bar Steward growled... "What are you... women?"

At this point my attention was drawn to a figure beyond the group in the back corner of the car park. He had been eaves-dropping in on our conversation and was becoming increasingly excited. His face began to twitch, a roll-up cigarette fell from his lips and he began to shuffle his feet. I studied him for a moment. He was of medium build with dark lank hair. Over his well worn leather jacket was a dirty sleeveless denim covered in studs and chains. His grubby jeans had holes in both knees and were tucked into a pair of scuffed motorcycle boots, a pair of grimy seaboot socks were tucked over the top of the boots. In his hand was a battered crash helmet which had obviously been resprayed at some point with an aerosol can only to get chipped and scratched again. Next to him stood an immaculate Suzuki T500 motor-cycle, not new but looking like it had just been wheeled out of a showroom. There was something about his hunched stance that reminded me of a gorilla. Somehow the bike did not fit the image. He would have looked more at home on a battered ancient Harley-Davidson or a beaten up British bike that leaked oil like a sieve.

He was being joined now by a fairly short chap, also wearing a faded blue cut off denim, but there was an outstanding differ-ence, for while this chap's denims were also torn and shredded they were spotlessly clean. He had nothing on under his sleeve-less jacket, which was completely unfastened, showing off his chest and enormous muscular physique. He was a tough looking character. What he lacked in height he made up for in muscle. He was putting on a leather motorcycle jacket over the denim when his mate said something to him that made him look in our direction.

Suddenly the animal man stood upright and yelled across to us. "You want a tear up, I'll give you a fucking tear up". His face began to twitch uncontrollably. He spat on the ground, leapt on his bike and kicked it frantically into life. I grinned at Bar Steward. We mounted our bikes and Dave climbed up behind me. "Go on, show him what my bike really goes like", he shouted in my ear. We fired up our engines and the rest followed suit. I notched into gear and slowly let out the clutch. Already my mind was racing ahead. This animal was riding a much larger capacity machine than my borrowed steed. I was confident in being able to see him off around the corners where Dave's smaller, lighter bike would out-handle and outbrake his, but the animal's bigger engine would give him more speed and the advantage along the straights. In my favour was his obvious inexperience. We both had pillion passengers, but the extra weight would affect our Yamaha most. Somehow by fair means or foul I had to gain a large advantage. Slowly we rolled out of the car park and across the garage forecourt that adjoined it. As we got to the road I saw a gap in the traffic. Catching the animal unawares, I suddenly snatched the throttle open fully and we were gone. We tore down the road for half a mile before making a right turn onto a very bendy road. As we made the turn there was only Bar Steward behind me. Here we had the advantage. I threw the Yamaha from footrest to footrest through the corners to try to maximise our lead. I overtook cars whenever it was safe to do so. The foot pegs and stand scraped several times. We rushed down a slope, through a village, uphill and out to the other side. From here on the road was wider, the bends more open and we lost our advantage to some extent. Bar Steward was still with us, flat across his fuel tank, but still on our tail. After several miles we came to a roundabout and flew across it. Now the animal had the advantage. Long straight road, we tucked down as low as we could. I held her flat out. This is where I needed the extra sixth gear on my Suzuki which made it a faster bike. The animal was not in sight. After a mile or so he appeared in the mirrors behind us but still far back in the distance. As we neared Dave's home he caught us up and followed us there. We pulled up and switched off our engines. Our exhausts were so hot they were ticking. A few seconds of silence and Dave said, "My poor bike". The animal took off his helmet and gloves. He had an adrenaline rush. The nervous twitch on his face when he got excited went into overdrive. He tried to roll a cigarette but his hands were shaking. He started stammering, "Cor... cor... f... f... fucking 'ell." He got the tobacco into a roll of paper and went to lick the glue, but as he was twitching so much the tobacco all fell out again. "Oh f... f... fucking bollocks", he gasped, giving up. He threw the roll-up remains on the ground. Once he had calmed down and was back to normal we all had a chat. They said they lived in "the Bay" on the coast a few miles away. He seemed to know Dave and Bar Steward. He asked where we normally hung out and I told him about the Black Horse, after which he and his mate, who said his name was Nick, mounted their Suzuki and rode away. "Who the hell is that animal?" I asked as they left. Bar Steward grinned, "Oh, we call him Fucking Bollocks, because he usually manages to get at least one if not both words into each sentence."

CHAPTER EIGHTEEN

Names and wild escapades

WITH the weather improving we started returning to the Black Horse in ever-increasing numbers. The black mood of depression cast over us all by Maz's untimely and early death lifted a little with summer just over the horizon. The new cylinder heads finally arrived for my bike and were fitted under warranty by Park Motorcycles where I had bought the bike brand new. I have been dealing with Barry, the owner, for over fifty years, and I have always had good service from the company. The head problem had been a manufacturing fault and nothing to do with the dealer. It was just fortunate the problem had occurred during the winter months—however, I was no longer happy with the bike because the new style modified heads spoilt the bike's looks.

Glad to have the bike back, I joined a few of the others on a ride over to the Pioneer Run, a London to Brighton ride for old pre-WWI vintage motorcycles. We stopped in a café on Pyecombe Hill for a bit of breakfast. Hearing a tapping noise we saw Herman with his lunch box open on the table, tapping and shelling a hard-boiled egg into the ashtray, then pouring a flask of his own tea. We told him, "Herman, you don't do that in a café, they won't like it". To which he replied, "Aww... then I'll tell them to fuck off". We finished our food and rode amidst some of the old bikes down to Brighton. After looking around the old motorcycles for a while we set course for home. Kiddie pulled over to relieve himself in a field gateway. As he stood there, his manhood in his hand and his back to the road, a battered old white Luton backed Transit van stopped behind him. Kiddie glanced around uneasily. A loud voice called out, "Jesus loves you man". Startled, Kiddie replied, "Oh, does he, I'm glad some bugger does". The caller held up a sunflower head and said, "Hey man, ain't that pretty". Kiddie replied, "I suppose it's all right if you like that sort of thing". The caller said, "Hey man, if you looked like that I would say you were mighty pretty". Having recovered his poise Kiddie gave a shout, "Just piss off you bloody weirdos". The back of the van was full of hippies in flower power clothes with long hair and beads around their necks. Kiddie stuck his fingers up at them. As the hippies drove away they gave us a peace sign. The next night on the TV local news, those same hippies were featured dancing around a tree singing and playing guitars at Plumpton Green. Turned out they were part of the Children of God, a fanatical religious sect.

Feeling refreshed Kiddie quickened the pace and a run developed. I got out front, but Kiddie was right on my tail. I rushed into a bend, but on approach I noticed it was a little damp under the trees. I eased up slightly and feathered the throttle, holding it as open as I dared. My two-stroke engine chattered, yan... an... an... an. Kiddie swept past but as he did so, he lost it big time; the bike skidded away from him on its side. Kiddie fell on his back and was sliding down the road right in front of me with his legs wide apart and my front wheel between his legs. A look of sheer terror spread across his face. I braked as hard as I dared to avoid him, without joining him on the tarmac. A second or two later, I succeeded in missing him and he spun around and off to one side, a big grin of relief appearing on his face, so I waved to him while he was still sliding along the road. We all stopped and picked up his bike. "I thought you were going to run over my nuts then, you bugger", said Kiddie thankfully.

Another close call happened during the week on a ride through the country lanes around Litlington, when Robbo dived under

Worm on a right-hander, then fell off. In a desperate attempt to avoid him and with nowhere to go, Worm rode up a steep bank, wall of death style, across a flight of steps and down the other side, but somehow managed to stay on the bike and miss Robbo.

Johnny had decided to emigrate, so he sold his Montesa to Geoff, who soon sold it on to Robbo, who took the bike racing and won the 1974 Southern 67 Championship. This was to be the start of a very long, successful and illustrious racing career which included many Manx Grand Prix and Isle of Man TTs—along with many other prestigious races worldwide. Not bad for a man whose parents wouldn't even let him have a motorbike; so he had bought an old Ariel single cylinder sidecar outfit and parked it in the next road with his bike gear hidden in the sidecar. Living in a nice area, his mother used to complain about a scruffy old sidecar outfit in the next road which lowered the tone of the whole estate. One day, riding through Eastbourne, he came across a woman on a zebra crossing and had to stop for her. It was his mother and she recognised him. His cover had been blown.

The following Sunday we were going out for a run again. I got a call from Monty from Hailsham. Was there a spare seat, as he wanted to ride with us, but his bike was off the road? I said I would take him, so we rode around to his house to pick him up. I had to ride really hard to try to stay with the others and everything was decking on most bends. When we got back to Monty's house his shoes were worn away so much that he couldn't walk in them. They had been scraping on the road surface during the hard cornering. He took them off, lifted the lid off the rubbish bin and dropped them straight in. He told me they were new shoes when we left and he had put them on for the first time that day.

It was Spring 1976, when out for a ride, I stopped by Grabbers bike shop. There was a lovely light metallic blue new Suzuki T500 two-stroke twin on display in the showroom. I was completely overwhelmed by the bike and just had to have it. The GT500 model had just come out with a different fuel tank and a disc brake up front, but I preferred the earlier shaped model. I sold my old bike to Tim, a young lad who lived near me, who had just come of riding age and who had heard the bike was up for sale. The first thing he did was to get the front brake upgraded, with the shoes relined by Joe Dunphy, a well known motorcycle brake expert. I ran the new bike in and started to open it up. The quicker I went, the more disappointed I was with it. When we had been out on a run in earlier times with Stan, who had a similar model, I remember thinking that Stan on the bigger, faster Suzuki should be ahead of the 250 and 350 models, but it was not to be. Now having bought such a model myself I soon found out why. It was not that Stan was a slower or any less of a rider, to the contrary he was as good as any of the rest of us. The answer lay with the bike. The 250 and 350 models were lighter and of a shorter wheelbase, but the extra bonus was that sixth gear, something more like an overdrive to help get the maximum speed from these smaller bikes, also giving more of a correct gear ratio for every corner. In reality the 250 was 247cc whereas the so-called 350 was actually only 315cc, but that extra 68cc difference from an overbored 250cc engine made a hell of a difference in power, particularly hurtling out of corners where the front wheel would lift skyward without effort. The T350 was a superb country road "scratching" bike in its day, as was the 250. The 350 model was rightly named as the Rebel, a highly suitable name for this machine. My brother Grizzly owned such a bike.

Flat out on the T500 showed that it was only a mere 5mph faster than my old 250 on the straight, even with more than a few thousand miles on the clock. That extra long wheelbase of the bike meant that it was unable to corner as fast on tighter bends and the front brake was rubbish. T500 owners would openly joke in the bars about buying a pair of Ferodo soled boots to drag along the ground or putting a foot in the front wheel to try to stop quicker. What made it even worse was that Sprogg, on buying an identical bike later on, had a few miles per hour over mine if we were side by side wringing their necks, even though mine was set up perfectly. All these facts together gave an insight as to why Bollocks and Nick had so much trouble catching up with myself and Dave on his Yamaha on the way home from Brands Hatch at Easter.

Madge and Arthur were leaving; they packed up, said their goodbyes and left the pub for good. We were sorry to see them go. They had been good landlords. In their place came the new landlord, Doug with wife Eve.

Bollocks and Nick started to show up at the Black Horse. Nick brought two friends with him, Bean who owned a Suzuki Hustler Mk 1 and Richard. After a while Nick bought an orange 250. Kawasaki triple, on which he would arrive at the pub. Now with a spare pillion seat Bollocks brought along a young chap with long fair shoulder length hair. He was called Douglas, although this was not his real name. Douglas was younger, only fifteen years old, but had already been in trouble with the cops. He had bought a Triumph Tiger Cub and had ridden it illegally and under-age on public roads. He had lost control of the bike, went up a kerb and crashed through a wooden fence, breaking both ankles and ended up in a water filled dyke next to the road. Nick on jumping into the dyke to rescue the floundering Douglas, had landed on a broken bottle. He had cut the sole of his foot open on the bottle. Douglas was a great guy, always laughing and joking. He loved life and women. He lived life to the full, which made it so much more tragic that he was destined to lose his life so prematurely. Bollocks did not keep his T500 for long, soon chopping it in for a mustard coloured early 1970s Triumph Bonneville 650 which suited his animal man image a whole lot better than the Suzuki.

Bar Steward brought along an old school friend who was now serving an apprenticeship with him as a car mechanic in a local garage. His nickname was Box. He got the name because his parents owned an old square classic car in which they delivered him to school, which was nicknamed "the box". Box was known to do some crazy things on occasions. Another motorcycling friend of theirs who joined us was known by all as JB, simply because these were his initials. JB, like many of us at that time, had long dark shoulder length hair. He owned a Yamaha. Another local lad, nicknamed Fortesque, as he spoke with a posh accent, added further to our numbers. He owned a 500 Vincent Comet.

Gozy and Weasel, turning up at the pub, brought with them a couple of new faces from their own town, Ogri, so-named after a cartoon character and his side-kick, the spotty-faced Malcolm, also named from the same cartoon strip drawn by Paul Sample in *Bike* magazine. There was Buck, who rode a Kawasaki Samurai and later on got a Norton 750 Atlas then a 750 Honda. Finally, there was the previously mentioned Monty, who after a few different bikes eventually ended up with a water-cooled Suzuki GT750 triple.

The Black Horse was gaining in popularity as more and more bikers cottoned on to it being a good meeting place. A group started turning up from Eastbourne. They were Mayo, Mick and Allen, with Allen's sister Lori and another girl called Gill. Mick was not actually from Eastbourne, but just rode with them. He came from Pevensey Bay, as did Bollocks, Nick and Douglas. When Bollocks saw him at the pub he decided he should have a nickname and started to rattle through his own repertoire of disgusting suggestions—"Flem, Puke, Gob, Slime, Pus..." A show of hands cast the vote. Slime it was to be.

A chap known as Sondel Steve turned up from another area of Eastbourne with a group of friends. Steve had this name because he had built a probably as near to racing bike on the road as you could get, being road legal. It was a 350 Yamaha two-stroke twin with the engine race prepared by Sondel Engineering. The bike was in full racing Yamaha colours, as was Steve's helmet and racing leathers to match. The bike went like the clappers and was featured in an article in *Bike* magazine, along with the owner. Steve himself was no slouch. The riders he brought with him were Daffy, Colin, Harry the Dog and Mac.

Tim, who I had sold my old Suzuki to, came along with his older brother Andy. These were the Gibbons brothers. Andy had a raced-up and lowered Ford Anglia. One night, Andy was coming home, when he hit a piece of steel pipe laying in the road. It flew up, jammed in his anti-roll bar and jammed the car's steering. The car left the road, hit a tree, and with no seat belt or seat belt law Andy was thrown through the shattered windscreen. He collected a face-full of shards of broken glass on the way through, which came to surface from under his skin periodically. He was able to remove chunks of glass at different times for the rest of his life. Andy decided to buy a motorcycle, another Suzuki T500. A record came out about a dance called 'The Funky Gibbon'—so Tim got the nickname of Funky. Sadly, neither of the two brothers would outlive their parents.

One night the other Andy told us that Herman was in trouble at work. As he trundled his trolley of office paper files from one department to the other, he would crash through the fire doors without opening them first. When the office women complained he would lose his rag and swear at them. He had been pulled into his manager's office countless times, so was on his final warning.

Herman worked in an annex of the Dental Board, perhaps half a mile from the main building, and above a large car dealership on the main road into town. Whenever we passed by in daytime we would yell abuse, "Herman, Herman Munster", and other obscenities. He was named after the character from the American Munsters TV programme. His head would suddenly shoot up in the middle of the office; he would dash to the window and press his face against the glass looking up and down the road for us. A few weeks later we heard from Andy that a jet plane had screamed low over the town roofs and the office. Herman had leapt to his feet and shouted, "Fucking hell, Concorde", and so was dismissed. He then obtained a job at a local plumbers' merchants, which only lasted a couple of months. When we asked what had happened, he said he had lost his temper because they had locked him in the bog house. We had seen Herman lose his temper a few times. One time when we pushed him into a lift, hit the button, vacated the lift quickly, sending him up to the top floor. Another time Worm had seen him carve someone up at a level crossing. The driver hung on his horn; Herman stuck his fingers up and told the driver to fuck off. The car driver stopped his car, leapt out and started punching Herman around the head. Herman did his usual when he had bitten off more than he could chew, and started yelling at the top of his voice, "Fuck off, you fucking bastard, just fuck off". His next employment was as a petrol pump attendant at a local garage, but he was sacked when he refused to go out in the rain to refuel a car.

Herman had traded his Honda for a new Kawasaki Samurai two-stroke twin. We thought we would have a bit of fun with him, so we sent him back to the dealers to buy a jockstrap for his crash helmet. Later, we conspired that wherever he went, someone would listen to his engine and tell him that his tappet roller bearings had gone. We had tipped everyone off previously of the wheeze. We told him that he must get it done under warranty, but the dealer would try to wriggle out of it, so he must be firm and insist. He returned to the dealership and had a blazing row with the mechanic, who told him there was no such thing. Later on we were horrified to see the stainless steel mudguards on his new-ish bike scratched all over. He said he had cleaned them with a Brillo pad pot scourer. He was certainly a strange character, but harmless enough. Not long after he sold his bike and bought a car and so stopped riding with us. Sadly, many years later, he was to tragically lose his life crossing a railway track on an unmanned crossing.

Andy brought another couple of chaps along. One was known as Length, not just for his 6ft 6ins height, but also for the size of his manhood, of which he was very proud. The two men's girl-friends were long-time friends. Length had once been a Mod, but had finally seen the light. Andy had won him over, when out as a foursome, he had plied Length with endless tales of tear-ups, the roar and power of the big British bikes and the whole bike scene in general. Now converted, Length was hot for a piece of the action himself. He went out and bought himself a 650 Tribsa. The other character was soon named by Worm as Jaws, because of his teeth. Jaws rode a Honda 750 four—and he rode it to the full.

There were a lot of changes going on within the gang at this time. The BSA of DJP had prematurely expired. One Ball knew a chap that was selling a BSA 500 twin for £30, but when we went along, he denied that he was selling it. One Ball was furious, so he took the money himself and later came back with the bike. The problem was that DJP had not passed his bike test, but knew where there was an ageing child/adult sidecar. My uncle had given me an old book on fitting, setting up and riding a sidecar out-fit; so we fitted it and rode it to Park Motorcycles for its MoT test.

DJP arrived at our house to collect the outfit. L pates were duly fitted, and I gave the new owner instructions on its use from the book. Sidecar outfits are an unknown quantity to many, an evil-handling beast ready to bite the unwary. Riding an outfit is completely different to riding a solo motorcycle. Without realising it you corner a solo largely by leaning the bike rather than by steering it. With an outfit you cannot lean the bike as it is fixed rigidly to the sidecar. The book said use the handlebars to physically steer as you would the tiller on a boat. If the sidecar is on your left and you open the bike's throttle, the bike steers to the left as it drags the weight of the sidecar. When you shut the throttle, the opposite happens, and the sidecar over-runs the bike, steering you into oncoming traffic, a rather disconcerting experience. If you have an independent sidecar brake fitted, you can use that brake to check the sidecar over-run and swing making it a safer proposition. This outfit did not have such a brake, so I instructed DJP—on the left you go in slow and accelerate around the sidecar on the exit. On a right you can come in faster and wrench it around, even drift the outfit once confident. Too much speed on the left will cut off the sidecar and lift the chair wheel into the air.

Andy had arrived and elected to ride in the sidecar on the outfits inaugural run. We unclipped the hinged hood, laying it across the bike's seat, opened the sidecar door and ushered Andy in. We shut the door and clipped the hood down. Andy was laughing, joking and pressing his face against the window. With all the instructions whizzing around in his head DJP fired up the Beezer 500 and they set off down the road. Approaching the first left-hander DJP's mind became a muddle, it was all too much to take in. He entered the bend too fast, wrenched the handlebars round and lost control of the outfit. Outside the scrap yard were a number of ramblers striding up the hill. The outfit shot across the road heading directly for them. The ramblers scattered. The outfit went straight through the middle of them as they flew in all directions. It continued onwards, its rider unwilling to return by the same route to risk the wrath of the irate ramblers. Our intrepid heroes eventually arrived back at our house, a pair of nervous wrecks. Andy was as white as a sheet. In an instant they had seen their lives flash before them. The experiment over, the outfit was to be no more, being dismantled and both items sold off again separately,

Hurtling homewards on a run out, as I rounded a bend my visor flew off. Knowing the pack was not far behind I quickly pulled up fifty yards past the bend, parked the bike by the kerb and ran back to pick it up. Box came around the corner, braked hard and stopped in the middle of the road level with me. I yelled a frantic warning, "Don't stop there Box... you idiot". The words had hardly left my lips when Bollocks appeared. Just missing Box he pulled over hard against the kerb. Nick was next, at speed on his Kwacker, he couldn't stop. He flashed past, directly between Box and Bollocks, up the kerb and across the wide grass verge, his rear wheel locked solid, the bike snaking frantically, throwing up clumps of turf. Bollocks let out a huge gutteral laugh, "Fuck-ing grass cutter", he yelled after him. Unwittingly Nick had just earned his new nickname. He was to be Grasscut from then on.

Getting his bike test out of the way Grasscut bought a 1969 Triumph Thruxton Bonneville fitted with a Morgo big bore kit, a production race bike on the road. Built by a local motorcycle mechanic it was geared for 130mph. On the way to the pub one day, Grasscut threw the Bonneville down the road with Douglas on the pillion. They slid along the road. Grass jumped up and chased after the bike. Bollocks saw that Douglas was still laying in the road and ran to his aid. Tugging, he tried to get his helmet off. Struggle as he might, it would not budge—and all the time

Douglas was making strange gurgling noises. Grass came over and asked what the hell he was doing and informed him that model of crash helmet was fitted with an extra safety strap, so it had two fastening straps. "I thought you were a gonna", said Bollocks, "you were making gurgling noises". Douglas retorted, "I'm not surprised, you prat, you were throttling me and you nearly pulled my bloody head off". When they got to the pub, we noticed that as Douglas had been wearing a cut off denim jacket with studs on the back under his leather; the studs had worn small holes through the back of his leather jacket like a colander.

Now with a spare seat, the boys from the Bay brought another future biking candidate with them. His name was also Andy. "It's no good," Bollocks decided. "There are just too many Andys, he will have to have a nickname". He started to run through his choice repertoire, "Flem, Gob, Puke... Pus... Ah yes, that's the one, suits him perfectly". So Pus it was.

Later on, running into us when we were out with Manure, Bollocks stated "Manure... why are you being so nice to the bastard? Why don't we just call him Pigshit?" So Pigshit he became. It was a name that haunted him and he began to dread, particularly in later life, when out shopping with the wife and it was shouted across Tescos.

A pub a few miles away called The Plough started having discos on a Friday night, so we rode over. A couple of trendy chicks in tight jeans and knee-length boots were strutting their stuff to 'Long Cool Woman in Black Dress' by The Hollies on the dance floor. Grass hit the floor, dancing behind them in his leather motorcycle boots keeping perfect time and formation with their every move. Bar Steward got pissed. He went to the bar to get another drink, but it was busy. He leant over and helped himself to a rum from the end optic. The barman turned, and spotting him he quipped, "Ere, you just nicked that". "I know,"

151

replied Bar Steward, "cheers". He raised the glass to the barman and downed it. A few more measures and he was thoroughly wrecked. He stripped off to his underpants, leapt onto a chair and started dancing to the music. Brian the Sheep had just bought a ploughman's lunch. He unwrapped a small packet of butter just as Bar Steward dropped his underpants shouting, "Look at my lunch pack", he continued on the chair. "Look at old Bar Steward, the prat," chuckled the Sheep. He threw the knob of butter, which hit Bar Steward on the back, between his shoulder blades. The butter, initially, stuck to his back, but his body heat melted it. The butter slid slowly down his back as he danced, wedging between his buttocks. He didn't even notice and continued dancing. On the way home on the bikes after a few beers, Kiddie thought it might be a good idea to take Sprogg and his girlfriend, Sally, on a right-hand bend, but he hit the gravel on the edge of the road and went down the road on his backside. It certainly was a night to remember.

One Ball threw a party. His parents were away, so he had the house to himself. His family owned a nearby leisure park with its own clubhouse and swimming pool. They sometimes had discos or functions at the clubhouse. They also owned a farm. They lived in the large farmhouse which had been extensively modernised and extended with its own sauna. The party was in full swing. Dick the Undertaker spotted a big ornamental clock with a barometer and a round thermometer all incorporated set in gilded marble. He asked what was wrong with the clock. One Ball explained it was an old family heirloom, but the clock did not work. Dick replied that old clocks were a passion of his. Much to One Ball's concern, Dick started working on the clock. Party in full swing, there was a large table full of food with a tablecloth that hung right to the floor. Myself and girlfriend Jayne were under the table. Kiddie was dating a tall, athletic girl named

Pauline who excelled at sports. After a few drinks and midway through the party, she suddenly launched herself at Kiddie, shouting his name. Kiddie fell backwards with her on top of him onto the food table. The table collapsed, coming down and hitting me on the head. One Ball was furious, it was an expensive antique table. The lights all came on and the party pretty much finished at that point. Dick came over to say he had fixed the clock temporarily and it was working. He would see his clock-maker friend who would make a new part for it. We went to leave but Grizzly was missing; we couldn't find him anywhere. It was a cold night and foggy, so we drove up and down the road shouting his name. We heard a muffled reply. We found him laying in a ditch down the road, in a drunken state. Got him home. Our father was concerned that his middle son was fast becoming an alcoholic, especially after tripping over him previously in a drunken state in an open porch with a layer of frost over him at five o'clock in the morning.

We had to do a bike recovery. This was quite normal practice, bikes not being as reliable as they are today, or sometimes the odd accident. There was not usually a shortage of willing helpers. We picked the bike up. On the homeward leg we stopped at a former transport café, now another Little Chef restaurant. After our meal Bar Steward disappeared into the toilets. A few minutes passed. "Where's Bar Steward?" enquired Grass. "In the bog," I said. "Fuck him," said Bollocks, "let's go without him". So for the crack, we left the restaurant, piled into the truck, drove out of the car park and the fifty yards or so down to the junction with the main road where we were making a right-hand turn. We had to wait for a gap in the traffic. A gap came. As we started to move and turn right Bar Steward rushed out of the café, across the road; jumping up he threw himself at the side of the van, catching hold of the roof rack. We took a left-hand curve. His body and feet came up horizontal to the roof rack with the centrifugal force. On the straight, he managed to work his way forward enough to try to open the sliding door. He hung onto the rack with one hand, grabbed the door handle and wrenched the door back. As he went to swing into the door, Sprogg's hand came out and grabbed his testicles. There was Bar Steward hanging onto the roof rack with one hand, jerking and jumping around like he was suffering a major electric shock, whilst fighting Sprogg off with the other hand as we drove along. Eventually Sprogg relented and let him in. We continued our journey without further incident.

One evening passing through town Grass saw a bunch of Skinheads out of the back window. They were our hated rivals. He opened one of the back van doors and yelled, "Bloody Skinheads". Unfortunately Bar Steward was laying against the other back door in a drunken state, which flew open and he fell out. In the absence of any rear seating, I had acquired a number of plastic milk crates, which placed upside down with old cushions on top, served as seating. As Bar Steward toppled out backwards his legs came up under DJP's thighs as he sat on his milk crate. In his drunken state DJP glanced down; what the hell was Bar Steward doing? He regained his senses in a flash, grabbed the unfortunate Bar Steward's legs, physically hauling him back in— but not before Bar Steward's hands had dragged along the tarmac and been skinned where he put his hands down to save himself. He was in agony. He tucked his hands under his armpits and sat there in agony, grimacing. "Sorry about that," said Grass, apologetically. "It seemed like a good idea at the time".

CHAPTER NINETEEN

High speed chases

I GOT laid off at the Birds Eye frozen food factory where I worked along with a number of other staff, so I took employment at a nearby rope factory instead. I had been there a few months, when I went to the bike shed where my motorcycle was parked and found an attractive little blonde waiting by my bike. There were two attractive girls that worked in the rope factory offices, a dark haired one and this blonde. "Hi, I'm Deirdre, will you take me out on your bike?" Not one to turn down such an opportunity, I agreed. We arranged to meet at the bus stop near to her home, about ten miles away, on Sunday morning and to take a spare crash helmet along with me.

Sunday morning came and I met her as arranged. She was waiting at the bus stop wearing the shortest of mini skirts and a trendy little black leather jacket. Far from the best riding gear, I thought, but then I was not about to quibble. She said she just wanted to go for a spin on the bike so we went in search of the others. I was keen to show her how well the bike would go, so I set the pace with all the rest all following along behind. Under normal circumstances it was usually a race, everyone in competition for the lead. Today, however, although I set a fast pace, no one pushed to take the lead from me. I congratulated myself on my performance as no one got past us. Later on in the evening I dropped Deirdre home and then went back to the pub. Kiddie informed me that they had all been quite content to sit behind and take in the view of Deirdre with her miniskirt up around her neck. My ego took a tumble at this point.

A couple of weeks later, I was rushing to work in the morning when I hit some spilt diesel oil on a bend and went sprawling. I was just limping over to recover my bike when a big wholesale bakery van came along and stopped. The driver got out and asked me if I was OK. I told him that I was, but the bike had suffered somewhat and I had the usual gravel rash on my left knee cap. He drove away and I continued on to work. Later in the afternoon, Kath, one of the women that worked part-time at the factory, came in to start her shift. She told me that it was her husband that had helped me in the road that morning.

Over the years there were many different girls that hung around with certain members of the group, us being such young hot-blooded males. Some girls dated two or three different bikers over a period of time before ending up marrying, settling down and having a family, with one or another member of our crowd. Many of these girls loved the excitement, the thrills of speed, general partying and a constant life on the edge as we did. One such girl was Julie, who became affectionately known as Pike, after a character from a TV series called Dad's Army; who perhaps was not the brightest tool in the shed. When Dick the Undertaker was around she would make herself scarce and hide because he would smother her with kisses. She was good fun and liked a good laugh, so one time we caught hold of her, tied her onto a long tree branch and carried her hanging like a dead deer. We dumped her on the front lawn next door, where Dick the Undertaker spotted her and dashed out of his house. "Julie darling, what have they done to you?" he asked smothering her with the usual kisses before untying her. She was a good sport and went along with most of our escapades for the sheer hell of it. First she dated Grizzly and later myself; eventually she dated and married Dim-widdy who was a great guy, a keen and safe motorcyclist—one of the best. Unfortunately as it turned out he would not live long enough to collect his state pension.

Another such girl was Louise, who dated Andy Gibbons. She was known as Louse, a happy-go-lucky girl who liked a good laugh. On our way into town one night with Gibbo leading, he also hit some diesel on a big roundabout. The pair were sent sprawling, sliding along on their backsides behind the T500, which was emitting a vast quantity of sparks from its underside. Myself, being next in line, I heard a large amount of screaming. I realised it was Louse. She continued to scream all the way to the kerb where she eventually came to rest. Gibbo jumped up and retrieved the bike, placing it on its centre stand. Louse got up and punched him in the face. I asked her why she did it, and somewhat agitated, she replied loudly, "Well, he bloody frightened me". Later, when we arrived at the Wimpy, she said that skidding along behind the bike she thought the sparks were going to ignite spilt petrol.

Another biking girl was Gill, who first turned up at the Black Horse with Slime and his Eastbourne crew. Gill bought a 125cc motorcycle to take her test on, but a woman in a car brought her off of the bike. The woman tried to get Gill's helmet off as she lay winded in the road, but like the Douglas episode it would not budge. Some other cars stopped to assist, but by then Gill had got her breath back. She stood up and took her crash helmet off. "Oh," they said, "It's a girl, are you all right young lady?" Gill reassured them she was fine. Girls that rode motorcycles were very much in the minority at this time; most preferred just to ride pillion. Worm took a shine to Gill and asked Slime which of the girls he was dating. Slime replied with a vast exaggeration that he was dating all of them, so Worm took a chance and asked Gill out. Much later they eventually got married. A few years down the line, Gill bought and rode a Kawasaki 400cc triple.

Having said that, a rumour went around that there was a new chick in town who was riding around on an RD200 Yamaha. A tall, leggy, attractive blonde had started work in a florists shop on the High Street. Being a florist she soon got the nickname of Daffodil. As soon as she passed her bike test she bought a red Suzuki GT500. She had the right build to ride a bigger bike as she looked like she had some Nordic ancestry, perhaps Norwegian or Swedish, but she was soon bombing around at speed on her bright red steed, her long blonde hair flowing out the back of her white crash helmet with a dark visor fitted. She certainly did not hang around, and when out riding with the gang, had no trouble being up there amongst the rest. Bean had recently sold his Suzuki Hustler to his elder brother Alan, who had just started riding. Bean and Grasscut had just bought themselves a pair of gleaming new matching black Honda 500 fours. Alan got the name of Dimwiddy after a character he kept joking about that we saw in a film at the late night cinema. Dimwiddy started dating Daff, so she began to ride with us. Sometimes she would take Wendy on the back of her bike. Wendy was dating Andy's brother Steve. One quiet night at the pub, it was decided that Steve should have a nickname. No one could think of a name for him. On his way to the bar, Worm suddenly turned and in desperation said, "I don't know, maybe we should just call him Mawanga or something". With some agreement Mawanga it was. "That'll do"—When Bollocks heard about Steve's new nickname he said, "Sort of fucking silly nickname they would give the prat". It was my turn next. Worm came up with Aitch, a throwback from my early days as a butcher. Aitch is a cut of beef joint and is pronounced simply as the letter H.

Another long term girl member was Sue, who later married Spud. They had a three bedroom apartment together over some shops opposite the top of the High Street. The flat was nicknamed The Hotel, as many bikers stayed there on occasions, but they had some great wild parties there. Sue's hobby was dressmaking and making soft cuddly toys, so they threw more than a few fancy dress parties as Sue enjoyed making her's and Spud's costumes. I remember one such wild party, when Worm arrived as Elvis, Gill as Catwoman and Sprogg in an outfit of his own design. He had on black tights, black shorts with a teeshirt emblazoned with Fart the Fantom across his chest, along with a long blue cape, mask and a pair of large hobnailed boots. About ten p.m. the booze supply was running low, so we decided to walk down to the off-licence for more alcohol before it closed. We got to the Post Office and there were three young teenage girls in the old fashioned red telephone box outside. They were probably talking to some boys as they were giggling a lot. Sprogg climbed onto the wall at the back of the phone box on its blind side. He got on the roof of the phone kiosk and started dancing. The girls inside were screaming like mad. Eventually, they made a dash for it. Sprogg jumped eight feet or so from the top of the kiosk and chased them down the High Street, holding his cape outstretched behind him, with them running flat out and screaming like crazy. That was such a wild party.

Another girl who rode bikes with us was Linda who dated Bar Steward. She owned and rode a 250 CZ, not the best of machines. Sprogg's girlfriend Sally bought a Honda ST70 monkey bike for transport. One night after a football match Sprogg was wheelying Sally's bike on grass. Bar Steward was drifting Linda's CZ when he flipped it, so Linda gave him a roasting.

Back at the Black Horse two more new riders turned up. One was known as Have a Fag Carl, because he was always offering his Players No. 6 cigarettes around, saying "Have a fag mate". He lived just around the corner from the Highlight Café and rode a blue Honda. The other was another one of the Bay boys known as Walrus. On a Sunday lunchtime it was customary to tear up the main road as fast as possible leaving it to the last second before anchoring up hard, changing down a few gears and throwing the bike around the left turn as fast as possible, as you knew there would be a crowd of onlookers watching. On this particular Sunday, Bollocks, with Pus riding pillion, was about to do just that when something made him hesitate. Out of the corner of his eye he thought he glimpsed a flash of a dayglow jacket to one side of the assembled crowd outside the pub. He pulled in the clutch, changed back up and rode on past the junction and up the road. Further up he turned around riding slowly back, making a right turn, he toodled up to the pub. Parking up he noticed there was a motorcycle speed cop there, who had pulled three bikes off to one side. He was ranting and raving at them. Bollocks sidled up to Walrus and discreetly asked what had happened. Walrus replied, "Look at it this way, the cop came in last".

It was a regular occurrence for us to get chased by the cops; fortunately they had only two cars in the area at that time that could even stay with a reasonably fast bike. The standard issue motorcycle for speed cops then was the 650 Triumph Saint (a detuned, down-geared version of the Trophy) and the Norton Commando. Both of these bikes were hampered by a lack of radio communication whilst on the move, as they were fitted with a radio telephone mounted into a cutaway on the fuel tank. As previously mentioned the speed cop had to actually be stationary to use the radio telephone receiver, also a police Saint was no match for any decent bike over 250cc. The two fast police cars in East Sussex were a 2.5 litre Triumph PI and a Lotus Cortina Mark 2. The rest of the police fleet was made up of Morris 1000 cars and vans, Ford Anglias, Austin Cambridges, Morris Marinas and the odd Minivan—all fine for town work but no comparison to a fast motorcycle. It was a heavenly time for us. If out on a run and we got chased, you simply split up and turned off, then turn off again and again, as many times as possible, everyone going different ways. Each time you came to a junction and turned off, you cut your chances of getting caught dramatically, as police cars would radio ahead and set up a road block. It was fatal to continue along the same road. Later we would all meet up at our previous agreed destination, all arriving via different routes. If on your way home the same would occur, after splitting up we made our own way home. After a while this riled the cops immensely. They were determined to get us any way possible. On one occasion, after splitting up, we arrived at home and turned into our drive to find the motorcycle speed cop waiting for us in our own driveway, leaning on our fence, having already removed his crash helmet. He was beside himself with glee. "What kept you?" he asked with a grin, and collapsed into a fit of laughter. On another occasion there was a cop car hidden in a gateway. I went past at ninety mph. I looked back to see the car pulling out, so I dropped my speed to the legal seventy mph and held it there. The cops pulled me over and told me they had clocked me at over ninety mph. At that time they had no speed detection devices fitted in police cars. They had to rely solely on the speedometer, which was supposedly calibrated regularly over a measured mile at a constant speed, using two solid white lines painted across the road exactly a mile apart. Two officers in the car had to clock you for three-tenths of a mile at a constant speed. I told the cops I was doing only seventy mph and to catch me up they probably had to do over ninety mph from a standing start, but they lied and nicked me anyway. I pleaded not guilty, went to court to fight my case, but the judge found for the cops. Lesson learned, never ever trust a copper.

Soon Bollocks got caught in similar circumstances. He, too, put his unfounded trust in the British legal system. The judge found for the cops and issued his verdict, the statutory endorsement and a fine of £20. Bollocks was outraged, instinctively he replied, "You bastard". The judge asked, "Did you say something Mr. ...?" "Errr, no your honour". An usher stepped in, "He called you a bastard, M'laud". "Oh, did he, fined another £10 for contempt of court".

Our cousin had come of motorcycle riding age. Hearing our tales of police chases came in useful when out testing his bike, flat out, on a long straight stretch of road known as the Broyle, he was chased by the police. Remembering what we had told him he turned off, off again and again, losing the cops, he got clean away. He had the nickname of Mauler, as when we were kids we used to wrestle, and his pet saying was, "Get your maulers off me".

On a run with Bar Steward, One Ball and Andy, myself and Bar Steward were both riding solo with One Ball on his 650 Tribsa with Andy riding pillion. We weren't hanging around, so I was keeping an eye out for the law. One minute we were on our own, next time I glanced around, back in the distance was a police Triumph 2.5 litre PI with its blues and twos going, hurtling up the centre of the road in pursuit, just cresting the top of a rise. Myself and Bar Steward had just passed a left turn, so we had no choice but to carry on. I looked again and there was no one there. One Ball, Andy and the cops had all disappeared. There was a layby further down with two bikes parked in it, so I throttled back and pulled into the layby. Bar Steward asked why we had stopped? "Didn't you see?", I asked him. "The cops were after us, and now they have gone, they must have turned off and chased the others". Bar Steward hadn't seen them. We suddenly realised that one of the other bikes in the layby was our friend Fortesque. He had recently bought a new BMW motorcycle and a full set of racing leathers. He was currently riding with the BMW set.

We told him what had been going on. Some minutes later the cop car arrived in the layby. "Excuse me", asked the cop, "have you seen three motorcycles speed past here?" Myself and Bar Steward tried hard to suppress a grin. "No", we said, shaking our heads innocently. The cops started walking back to their car when one said something to the other one. They turned and came back, "Ere, you are one", pointing at me, "and you are another", pointing at Bar Steward. He then pointed at Fortesque, "And you... are the third one". Fortesque broke into sheer panic, "I am not with them, keep me out of this", he grovelled. I thought he was going to have a coronary. Eventually the cops went on their way. We continued on, expecting to find the others at the agreed destination, but they were not there. When I got home our mother asked what we had been up to. Two traffic cops had arrived at her door, caps in hand, and solemnly asked if her sons were out on their bikes. Both of my brothers being out, my poor mother feared the worse. "Don't worry", they said, "They're all right, but we can't identify the two people on one motorcycle". "Oh, my god, that was...", giving the cops their names and addresses. "Thank you", the cops congratulated her, "because we couldn't catch the so and sos". Our poor mother, at this point realised she had been duped into spilling the beans. Andy and One Ball had been sitting at home chuckling about the day's events, when suddenly there was a loud, slow knock on the door. It was the long arm of the law.

When the matter came to court, it transpired that alerted by Andy, One Ball had made a hurried turn left and then wound it on again; the cops were in hot pursuit. As the bike rounded a corner, they encountered a horse and its rider along the straight. They slowed, chugged past, then wound it on again. The police car came hurtling down the lane, blue lights flashing, two tone horns blaring meeting the horse on the bend. The horse reared up, threw its rider, and took off. Because of the chaos, One Ball and Andy got clean away. They tried to prosecute One Ball for the horse incident, as well as reckless riding. One Ball took the stand, defending himself. He was able to prove that his family owned a farm and horses, so he would not have acted in the manner so described. The horsewoman gave her evidence, angry and out for revenge. One police officer gave his evidence, stood down and sat on in court. His colleague took the stand. Basically, "On this day we were in pursuit of three motorcycles at speed, blah, blah, blah. On the last motorcycle the pillion passenger suddenly turned and appeared to wave goodbye, the motorcycle then turned hard left and took off again at high speed". At this point, myself and Bar Steward burst out laughing, knowing that in fact Andy had spotted the cops and was hitting One Ball in the back, shouting, "It's the law, it's the law". The sitting cop glared at us. The judge ordered, "Silence in court". Having escaped prosecution over the horse fiasco, One Ball was convicted and fined on the dangerous driving charge. Our mother had learned the same lesson—she would never trust the police again.

CHAPTER TWENTY

Throttle crazy

KIDDIE gave a sudden shout. "You little bastard..." Herb made a dash for the back door of the house. Kiddie, servicing his bike, had put down his spanners, taken the cap off the oil tank and gone to the shed to get some oil. He returned, "Now where the hell did I put that spanner?" Looking around it could not be found. Searching, he spotted the top of it—his brother Herb had dropped the spanner into the bike's oil tank while he was away and was now making a run for it. Kiddie was up and after him. Their dad was in the kitchen.' Herb flew past, into the hall and up the stairs. "What the hell is going on?" he enquired. "That little sod has dropped a spanner into my oil tank". "Leave the boy alone, he's only young." "He won't get much older if I get hold of him." Disgruntled, Kiddie went back out to finish the bike's service. With a creak the upstairs wooden sash window of the cottage opened. Herb called down, "You think you are quick on that bike, but you are a tosser, Kiddie. Soon I will be old enough to get a bike and I will blow you into the weeds". "I will kick your bloody arse boy, when I get hold of you," yelled Kiddie in   defiance as he fished for the spanner with a bent piece of wire. The brothers had a love/hate relationship, as on the other hand during school holidays Kiddie took Herb to work with him on the back of his bike, as there was no one else at home. Herb would ride with him in his truck as Kiddie drove around making delivery drops around the area.

We all knew that Kiddie finished work at 5.30pm, so if any of the lads were around the Lewes area at that time, we would wait outside his yard for a dust up on the way home. I know that Robbo and Stan did this a few times. On this occasion when I waited for Kiddie the phrase "dust up" was about to get a different meaning. I was waiting when Kiddie came out. We set off, myself first away with Kiddie following. We left Lewes, heading south. Heading downhill towards the railway on a slight right-hand curve there was a box lorry further ahead of us. On the left was the entrance to a country lane with a staggered junction. I noticed a tractor and trailer waiting to pull out. The tractor was fitted with a front loader and bucket, which was in the fully raised up position. As we sped downhill towards it, the lorry briefly blocked our view of the tractor, but above the top of the lorry I saw the bucket of the loader start to move, so I eased up. Kiddie sped past me about ninety mph, just in time to see the truck clear the tractor and trailer, which pulled out across the main road ahead of us. Kiddie suddenly sat up braking like crazy, but with the tractor and trailer across the road he had no choice but to crank left. He went flying down the narrow country lane towards Glynde from where the tractor had just emerged, still doing about eighty mph and kicking up clouds of dust and grit. I chuckled as I continued along the main road behind the lorry waving to him, until he eventually managed to stop, turn around, come back out and give chase again.

Kiddie, Fred and some of the others were out for a ride around the Ashdown Forest area. As they neared Uckfield on the way homeward, those close to the back noticed a red Vauxhall Ventora keeping pace with them. The car followed them through the town. The pack turned left at the traffic lights, taking the Framfield road, opened up, increasing speed with Kiddie and Fred out in front. Those at the rear held back though, unsure of the red car. Fred and Kiddie had swapped machines to check out the performance of each other's bike. As they hurtled out of a bend, a few hundred yards down the straight the police had set up a road block and stopped them all. The red 3.3 litre Ventora pulled up behind. The two occupants got out donning their peaked caps. It was the latest police scourge, an unmarked police cop car known as a Q car. The latest tool in the armoury of the cops to chase down speeding motorcyclists and car drivers. They had radioed ahead. Kiddie and Fred used the confusion to swap bikes back. A cop gave each a ticket to produce their documents. Checking it out, Kiddie said, "That's not right, this is my bike here". The cops ranted at them, accusing, you did this or you did that... "No, not me, this is my bike". In the end the cops gave up and let them all off with a caution and a severe rollicking.

The next clash with the unmarked Ventora came with Robbo, Stan, Trevor and a few others from the Highlight. Trevor was running in his 250cc Kawasaki triple and so could only use limited throttle. They don't know where they picked up the dreaded Ventora, but it seems another case of the police having to do eighty-five mph to catch up with the distant motorcycles. The driver was a particularly officious and hated speed cop who usually rode a Norton Commando and he had a particularly ruddy faced complexion.

With TT, the other bike cop in our immediate area, we figured that he had a job to do, so he had to perhaps book offenders if he caught them in the act. He wasn't exactly a bad person—but this guy was. He would have certainly been equally at home with Hitler's Gestapo or SS. He was a nasty piece of work. He was known by all as a complete arsehole. On this occasion he stated he had followed the motorcyclists for four miles at eighty-five mph driving round corners with one hand, whilst using his other hand to jot down their registration numbers on a pad balanced on his knee. Obviously, his evidence was completely false, but those apprehended went to court and pleaded not guilty. When

Smed heard of the incident, he wrote a letter to the Court in his capacity as an RAC/ACU Instructor/Examiner, stating that Trevor was running in his bike at low speed. Furthermore it was impossible to drive a large and heavy car, such as a 3.3 litre Vauxhall Ventora—to hurtle around the bends on that road steering with one hand whilst writing down registration numbers with the other. Also, in this very case, what he was doing was actually committing the offence of dangerous or reckless driving himself. In those days the police had to serve a Notice of Intended Prosecution within fourteen days of the alleged offence. If they were unable to serve this legal notice within the given time space, then the participant could not be prosecuted. Robbo and Trevor were served with a prosecution notice, but Trevor alerted Stan and the others. They all made themselves unobtainable. Out of the seven motorcyclists booked, only these two were able to be prosecuted. Despite good legal representation they were convicted. It was a complete sham. Outside the court, the cop, somewhat full of himself, said, "Nice try". He obviously was going to hold this against Smed, as sometime later whilst he was booking another motorcyclist at Polegate, Smed rode past on his Z1 Kawasaki, upon which he said to the motorcyclist he was booking, "There goes Lord Smedley, "I'll have him..."

Fred is a small bloke with a lot to say for himself. A real livewire, and he hasn't altered with age. Being honest, I would have to admit that the fastest and the best riders back then were the originals, Dilly, Den, Fred and Kiddie. They had been around longer than the rest of us. All these riders were about the same age and probably five years older than us up-and-coming riders, Next, I would probably put Geoff and Robbo, along with the rest of us, in no particular order. If Geoff was not in the first three places, it was usually because he had fallen off trying. Years later Geoff had a spot of hip trouble. On getting checked out by a doctor, x-rays were taken. Somewhat confused, the doctor asked, "So when did you break your pelvis in three places?" Geoff replied that he didn't know that he had. There had been occasions when he had bounced down the road, and thought, Christ that hurt, and he had been off work for a few days. The doctor replied that he had been a lucky man.

None of us were known to hang around as we had good teachers. Fred excelled at joking and practical jokes, but things didn't always go his way. During the 125cc experiment we were all out riding hard on country roads. Try as he might, Fred could not stay with our bigger bikes. We came to a fork in the road, but the leader was not sure which road to take. It should have been a left turn, but unsure, three bikes stacked up next to each other. Fred came hurtling round the corner, and finding the left exit blocked he shot off down the lane on the right and disappeared, so we all cleared off homeward. Nearing our house we all slowed down, that is all except Fred who kept flat out to make up ground. As Fred overtook Worm, there was a man with a bulldog starting to cross the road. He seized his dog by the collar and made a frantic dash for the opposite kerb. He was the local policeman who lived just around the corner in a police house. One time Fred was out with the Highlight boys. He was slipstreaming Smed down the straight as Smed had a bigger bike. Smed suddenly felt a few seconds of vibrations as his bike seemed to lurch forward. Smed looked round. Fred was about ten yards back, sitting up looking all around as if he was innocently taking in the countryside on a Sunday ride. When they arrived at their destination, Smed checked his big Kawasaki over. There was a black rubber mark on his rear mudguard. Fred had got so close, that as Smed eased up slightly, Fred's front tyre had rubbed his rear mudguard.

Fred decided to go racing, he had planned to do this earlier, but circumstances had prevented it. Now he bought a Honda

CB500/4 and prepared it for racing. Dixon Racing and Hastings Motorcycles sponsored him. He actually did really well, but we would not admit it, and kept ribbing him, he was a hopeless slow-coach. I even had a tee-shirt printed with a Honda 500/4 on the front and a slogan on the back stating that Fred was "full of shit". I lost no time parading my new shirt. I would stalk the racing paddocks of the tracks where Fred was racing. If he didn't actually see it himself—others informed him on his return. I became a thorn in his flesh. In 1976 he won the BEMSEE 500 Production Championship. We were on the bottom bend at Brands Hatch when he came around on the control car. As he passed by we all yelled abuse at the top of our voices and stuck our fingers up at him. He heard and saw us. He had to laugh.

One of the girls held a "tastefully outrageous" party at the Hotel Norfolk in Eastbourne. Fred turned up as a punk rocker wearing a black bin bag, complete with large safety pins. Halfway through the evening I ripped his bin liner to pieces, leaving him wearing only his boxer shorts. Later he came up behind me and tore my teeshirt off my back. It was last seen blowing in the wind, tied to a lamp post on Eastbourne seafront. Fred had finally got his revenge.

Several other members of our group went motorcycle racing, including Andy, Length and even Sprogg. One Ball bought a 750 Ducati, on which he sponsored Andy. Daffy, being a printer, printed off a number of "Count Uno Bollicko", one bollock racing team stickers which found their way into pubs, clubhouses and cafés around the land. A spin-off with Fred's racing was that we got to buy used practice tyres at £5 apiece. These tyres had the scuffed sidewalls, but the centres looked almost new. After a while we found other bikers would be checking on our bikes, saying "Bloody hell, look how far these nutters have been cranked over". I also bought a pair of Girling rear shocks and a Boyer ignition system from Fred. His racing career was both varied and exceptional. We saw him romp home in sixth place in the 1000cc Formula 1 race at Silverstone, a good result against strong professional opposition. We also watched him race in two Isle of Man TTs. I had a new fan teeshirt printed and wore it in the bar of his hotel on the Isle of Man. "Fred... for wanker of the year". He was not impressed.

On the racing scene, myself Grizzly, Worm, Pud, Spud and Bar Steward, all took to the stock car tracks as a six man banger racing team, for three years. When the team finally stopped racing, Pud and Bar Steward continued to race on alone for a number of years. They fared pretty well at it.

CHAPTER TWENTY-ONE

Forest Frolics

DURING the summer of 1970, both halves of the Warb family decided to go to the New Forest on a camping holiday together and they invited us all to go along with them. Companies at that time only gave their employees two weeks' annual holiday, plus the compulsory few days at Christmas, Easter and a few other Bank Holidays reluctantly granted by law.

During our childhood and teenage years, only the rich could afford to fly. Package holidays abroad were things of the future. Many a family still holidayed their vacation away at Mrs Brown's seafront guest house at Margate or some similar such dwelling house in some other resort, often booking next year's break at the same abode on leaving.

Camping was a very popular form of holiday for many families trying to make ends meet, and during the 1950s it was normal to see more than a few old well-worn plodding motorcycles fitted with enormous sidecars full of kids, along with the wife riding pillion, chugging along fully laden down with camping gear. Sometimes a small home-made trailer was being towed behind to help spread the load of all the equipment. One or two caravan companies marketed a small model of caravan, which was advertised as being towable by a motorcycle combination, but few could afford them.

By the late 1960s many such worn out motorcycle combinations had expired for good and their owners moved on to purchasing their first secondhand car. These old bangers were equally loaded down with normal essential camping equipment,

172

some often dispersed onto a roof rack for the annual family holiday. Holiday camps were formally opened at seaside resorts by Fred Pontin and Billy Butlin. They became a popular and credible alternative for families to take in and enjoy the seaside air. Many families though, still stuck with the familiar camping, or even a caravanning holiday if they were a little more affluent.

So it was that the two Warb families set off for the New Forest, with a number of bikers also in tow, including Spud, Pud, Mad Mongol, Dutch, Bidle, Herman, Grizzly and myself. Both of the Warb fathers were tradesmen and both owned vans, so the camping gear was duly loaded aboard the vans and the families sat in the back atop of the gear. We in turn followed on our motorcycles with another car also in the convoy.

After about a hundred miles, we arrived at the former WWII airbase of Stoney Cross. Originally this had been an RAF base but later in the war had been taken over by the American Ninth Air Force, who flew B26 Martin Marauder medium bombers and P38 Lockheed Lightning fighters out of the base. The old camp water tower was still in existence, as were some of the foundations of the original huts and services of the site now known as Longbeach. The campsite was currently being run by the Forestry Commission.

On entering the site we found it rammed to almost full capacity with tents and caravans. We eventually found enough space for all our tents and vehicles and set about making camp. After cooking a decent meal, it became apparent that the Warbs knew the area well and we all set out to a nearby pub in the forest called The Sir Walter Tyrell. The pub was well liked by campers and caravanners alike for its popular bands, discos and fine ales. It was and still is, a popular New Forest pub.

Spud had bragged earlier that he could drink fourteen rum and cokes, and was again on course to down the same amount that night. A great evening was had by all and we all had too much to drink. There was a stuffed head of a stag on the wall, a fine specimen. Someone took a picture of me cuddling it. We made our way back to camp. Spud was the worse for wear. During the night the sound of violent vomiting was heard. We got up in the morning to find Spud had crawled out of his tent. He was laying face down in the grass, next to a pool of vomit. He was hungover all day. The rum in these parts must clearly be stronger than most.

We had a good time down at the New Forest. As a group we played all sorts of sports. We erected a rope swing which led to some crazy antics, as well as touring some of the other local hostelries. This trip set the trend for a start of a love affair with the New Forest. During the mid-seventies we would return with ever-growing numbers over and over again to the Forest, and in particular Stoney Cross. On occasions, we still do this today.

On the way home whilst on a straight road, Herman suddenly turned off and followed another car. We stopped and he eventually came back and said that he had followed the other blue Austin, to which we pointed out that the one in our convoy was in fact green!

On our annual trips to the New Forest, someone would drive the truck loaded with camping gear, food and usually a spare motorcycle with a dozen or more motorcycles in convoy. On one trip Grasscut pulled alongside me on his Thruxton Bonneville at the traffic lights. I had the sliding door hooked back, so I leaned out and switched his bike's ignition off as the lights changed and drove away. A few miles on he came roaring past. The van died—he had leaned in and turned the ignition off trying to take the keys with him. Fortunately, this was before the days of ignition steering locks. Arriving at the Forest site we found it to be almost completely full. We toured around looking for somewhere big enough for the group, but there was nowhere. Eventually we spotted a clearing amongst the trees but it was off the road and at the bottom of a grass bank. After a quick survey and discussion we felt that there was enough of us to help to manhandle the truck back up the slope if necessary. The bikes of course would be no problem. I drove the truck down the bank and reversed it back under the trees. We unloaded all the gear and decided to do a trial run. We found that if three or four people stood on the rear bumper and held onto the strong roof rack for extra grip, we could make a run up the bank and out onto the concrete road. If we needed more grip the hanger-ons on the back simply jumped up and down. So the camp was set up to give the truck the best run out of the trees at the slope. Tents and bikes positioned accordingly. Generally when out and about we were on our motorcycles, the truck was left at the site. On one afternoon however, we all piled into the truck and went into Southampton on a pub crawl and then to the ice rink next to Southampton football ground. After a good evening's ice skating, on our way back to the truck, we were verbally abused by a group of Skinheads. Driving by in the truck, we caught them up by surprise, pelting them with empty beer cans. Setting off back to the campsite whilst travelling along the A31, a police car coming the opposite way on the dual carriageway, slowed down on spotting the truck despite the darkness, and then sped up again. Clearly someone had called the cops, but in this case they had to race down to the next junction to turn around to pursue us along the westward side of the carriageway. I floored the truck, got to Stoney Cross making a right-hand turn across the carriageway onto the road towards the camp site. The cops probably spotted us making that turn whilst still way back in the distance. Turning into the site, we nipped along to our pitch, down the bank and into the trees. We evacuated the truck and disappeared into our tents, laying low for ten to fifteen minutes at least. The police drove slowly down through the site looking around. Later they came back past again, but still failed to spot us in the dark. Half an hour later we felt the coast must be clear. They had finally cleared off.

The next year we were back. This time Worm drove the truck. Once again the site was pretty full. Luckily we found a suitable pitch big enough to accommodate us all, at the very bottom of the site around a large oak tree. Everyone else gave us a wide berth, so we ended up with a good hundred yards of clear space around us. A couple of young girls on horses came riding through the Forest past our camp, so we treated them to the usual cat calls and whistles. They must have liked it because they were back the next day and stopped for a chat. We ribbed them about their horses calling them "dog meat that should be in a can". Bollocks was in his tent. "Bet they couldn't even jump over that little tent over there." One of the girls took up the challenge, rode her horse to the gallop and jumped clean over Bollocks in his tent. He came steaming out of the tent. "What the bloody hell... you bastards", when he saw us all laughing. One girl was slim, dark haired and attractive; the other blonde, plain and a bit on the plump side. Two of the guys arranged to meet them that evening. The girls took them to an empty farmhouse at the stables and took them upstairs. In the bedroom was just a double bed with a mattress. They all had sex. Douglas said afterwards that he didn't really fancy the blonde he was with, so he had to check out the dark attractive one naked on the bed next to him to get aroused. It started to rain hard; the bedroom had a slatted window operated by a handle. The two guys pissed out of the window. Bob finished first and pulled the lever, shutting Douglas's cock in the slatted window.

In the morning the rain had stopped. Getting breakfast we found a couple of angry hornets in our Sugar Puffs cereal box.

We spent most of the day playing football. That night we decided to ride on our bikes the mile or so through the forest trails, to The Sir Walter Tyrell pub. When the pub merriment was in full swing, Bar Steward put a knot in each corner of his handkerchief and said he was an Englishman on holiday, reminiscent of the male beach sunbathers of the day. He draped it over his hat and then put the hat back on his head. A little while later, Bollocks, who was sitting behind him, turned his lighter up full and set fire to it. It was well alight when some geezer rushed in from the other bar and said, "Excuse me, did you know your hat's on fire?" If quick enough, we should have replied, "If you whistle it we'll pick it up from there". Bar Steward jumped up, threw the hat down and stamped the fire out on the wooden floor. Later he put a cigarette in the mouth of the stag's head on the wall. When the pub closed we rode back through the Forest all well oiled. We gunned our bikes out of the trees in a large group to find that our no man's land had been compromised. There were many newcomers' tents and caravans all around us. Alerted by throbbing engines and blazing headlights, shocked faces appeared in tent doorways and hanging out of caravans. When we got up in the morning they had all gone. We had our clear hundred yard exclusion zone all to ourselves again.

The next evening a couple of the lads kept throwing up and went down with food poisoning. An ambulance duly arrived and took them to Southampton General Hospital. A few of us followed the ambulance to bring them back to camp. Treatment took a while, so the rest of us fell asleep stretched out on the seating in the waiting room. We were awakened by an angry matron. "This is a hospital, not a doss house." It was almost daylight when they released our sick friends. We returned to camp with little sleep that night.

That morning there were sudden hoots of laughter. A young lad, nicknamed Mouth, had come with us on this trip. He had got this name after sarcastic ranting with Grizzly. Sue, his girl-friend, was fed up with waiting for him, so sarcastically announced loudly, "Come on Mouth… we are going home". She got a round of applause. Like Herman previously, Mouth was the latest butt of everyone's jokes. Mawanga had played a prank on him, so to get his own back Mouth had dropped a Rendalls contraceptive pessary into Mawanga's tea and stirred it in. Mawanga had drunk the tea.

On the last night of the trip we all had too much to drink and things got out of hand. Mouth, being the youngest, had got fed up with being constantly pranked. We got hold of the emergency fire beaters from their rack and started play fighting. I think someone may have got hit harder than intended, and we started arguing amongst ourselves. It was a case of the beer talking. Someone, maybe Worm, I think, stated that something I had done had sparked the incident. I cannot even remember what it was all about now and probably no one else can. I got angry and behaved like a total prat. I told them all to get fucked, got on my bike and set off home. Luckily, I had a full tank of fuel but in my anger I screwed the bike hard, going flat out where I could. It had got dark and as I neared home on a dark unlit country road, I suddenly saw white ghostly shapes floating around in the air four feet from the ground. I thought I was seeing things. Not knowing what it was I sat up and braked like mad. Before I could stop I was amongst them. It was a whole herd of black and white Friesian cattle in the road. My actions stampeded them. Taking fright, they turned and charged back the way they had come, almost trampling the two police officers that had rounded them up and were trying to return them to their field. They were furious. They shouted and hollered at me, asking me what the hell I thought I was doing. Now they would have to start all over again. I kept my visor down for fear of the smell of alcohol on my breath. They set off running after the cows. I had been lucky not to hit any of them. On my way again, my bike started faltering, so I switched to the reserve position. It picked up again, but ran out of fuel completely a mile from home. I was fearful that the angry officers might come along, so I ran as fast as I could pushing the bike. I arrived back home completely exhausted. Three bikes broke down on that trip and had to be transported back in the truck at the holiday's end, including Pus's Honda CB72.

From media sources, on 15th April 1979, a group of up to thirty Hell's Angels armed with guns, axes and knives ambushed a party of so-called Greasers from Windsor, who were dressing as, and calling themselves, Hell's Angels. The Greasers were ambushed in a car park at Brockenhurst in the New Forest. Richard Sharman, the leader of the rogue Windsor bikers was lucky to survive after being shot three times in the head. Richard Jessop received a fractured skull, and another Windsor biker took a blast from a sawn-off shotgun. Twenty-four Hell's Angels were convicted for the attack and were imprisoned or given other sentences in 1980. As a result of this Forest clash the Windsor Chapter officially became Hell's Angels in 1985.

Panic gripped the New Forest. From this incident on, most of the Forest pubs banned bikers. On our way down that year we happened to stop at a pub. The landlord opened the upstairs window and yelled for us to clear off or he would set his dogs on us. I pulled the starting handle from its mount under the truck driver's seat and told him to send the dogs out as we were ready. He shouted that he would call the police. It was no use arguing with such people. All around the area now there is signage outside many public houses, "No Bikers". Luckily, our favourite hangout, The Sir Walter Tyrell, did not, nor even The Green Dragon, a lovely Forest pub at Brook. The Bell Inn, opposite, had no signage to state that bikers were banned, so we went in and ordered a round of drinks. The barman served us. After a while the land-lord appeared and reprimanded the barman for serving us. Then he told us to finish our drinks and leave. Pus left the last half inch of beer in the glass with bits of hops floating in it. He went right up to the landlord's face. He banged the glass down on the bar and said menacingly, "You can keep the fucking seaweed" and left. Forty years later a group of us camping in the Forest in our motor homes, went into what is now The Bell Hotel. We told the young landlady that forty years ago we were thrown out of the pub. She asked why, and we told her of the Angels shoot out. As a parting shot (no pun intended) Bar Steward turned back and said, "It was probably you that did it". She laughed.

Worm at age 14 testing our BSA 'bitsa' Bantam field bike.

Snout (left) and his Triumph Bonneville outside the Highlight.

Photo: Julia Gorringe

Dilly with his 'Opal Mint' Kawasaki 250ccc triple, so called because the colours were the same as on the mint pack.   *Photo: Mick Robinson*

Dilly with his Bond Bug.   *Photo: Mick Robinson*

Robbo's championship winning 250cc Montesa in 1974.

Photo: Mick Robinson

Fiery Fred on his way to winning the BEMSEE Championship title with his Honda CB500 Four. *Photo: Fred Huggett*

The gang at "the cheeks" summer of 1977.   *Photo: Dick the Undertaker*

Kiddie at "the cheeks" with his Suzuki GT750.

Grizzly's crashed Yamaha RD400.

Dilly and Pete on the ex-Worm outfit.   *Photo: Mick Robinson*

The hotted-up "truck" fitted with a diesel front and a Ford 3 litre V6 engine.

God, we could party back then ... Bar Steward's party at Eastcote.

The author on his motorcycle shortly after recovering from a broken arm.

Worm on his Suzuki T200 Invader during long hot summer of 1976.

The author's Suzuki GS1000.

Sprogg on his Suzuki T500.

Photo: Clifford Hylands

CHAPTER TWENTY-TWO

Suicide Jockeys

I TURNED twenty-one years of age whilst working at the rope factory. The women that worked there were kind and I had quite a few birthday cards, some with silver keys on them. Back then you were not an adult until you reached twenty-one, then supposedly, you were old enough to be trusted with the key to the door of the family home. Soon after this Kath told me that a neighbour of hers worked on a milk delivery round and there was a vacancy for another milkman. The dairy worked a four weeks on and one off system with good pay and extra commission on goods sold. I liked Kath. She was a good sort and a younger thinker than her years. I had met her husband too when I dropped my bike on the way to work. Her neighbour arranged for me to meet the manager of the dairy. I went for the interview and got the job. During my working life I was destined to do eighteen years in total on milk delivery rounds. For a young, fit guy this was an excellent job, as I could run around a delivery round in four to five hours from start to finish and be back home again. Later on the company wanted to increase the size of the round, but instead of increasing our pay they altered our working shift pattern to fourteen days of work and seven days off with double pay if you had to work your week off. This was a brilliant system which enabled me to strap a tent and sleeping bag onto my bike and clear off on trips, both throughout Britain and abroad at will. After a while a young lad came and found me on my milk round. He introduced himself as Kath and her husband Ray's son. He asked if I needed any help on my round on

Saturdays when I had to collect the money, so I employed him and when we finished the round I would drop him off home on my motorcycle. Doubtless to say, as soon as he was old enough, he too got a bike and started riding with us, although he was much younger. He was to eventually get the previously mentioned nickname of Mouth. On many occasions in those early years of milk delivery it was not uncommon to have a handful of drunks hanging off the milk float, helping me to deliver milk early on a Sunday morning

A similar situation had happened with Bar Steward. A young lad who lived in the next street was attracted to motorcycles. He would come around to help Bar Steward with the bikes. Bar Steward would then take him out on the back of the bike. He got the nickname of Weed because he was so skinny. He too started riding with us as soon as he was old enough to ride a bike. After Herman left, Weed, being the youngest, became the butt of everyone's jokes. When Mouth joined he took up that dubious honour, not always one that he rejoiced in. One night Bar Steward had been out until late with a girl. When he got home his parents had locked him out. In desperation he went round to Weed's house and climbed up, tapping on the bedroom window. He could see Weed fast asleep but could not wake him. The small top window was open, so he climbed through it, but with nothing to grab hold of, he fell on Weed, who woke up screaming.

As mentioned earlier, in our quest for entertainment with our second generation biker gang we travelled far and wide to bands, discos and to wild parties. There was always some action somewhere, generally in pubs, youth clubs or village halls. We would meet at "the cheeks" and then ride over en masse. Sometimes the venues may be flagging a little when we arrived—but our arrival certainly livened things up a bit. Our merry band would instantly crowd the bar and hit the dance floor; that was if the massed arrival of up to twenty noisy motorcycles with guys and girls, had not already woken the place up. Worm worked with a young couple who with their friends invited us to all of their parties, as we did with them. Our parties at the Dicker Village Hall became legendary. With a bar supplied and Frenchie blasting out the music with his disco, they were always packed. One night Have a Fag Carl left the hall after such a late night bash. When he got to the junction by the Little Chef, where Bar Steward had hung onto the van roof rack, he failed to stop, went straight across the main road and into a hedge on the opposite side of the road. He stepped from the bike and it was left wedged firmly upright in the hedge.

Someone saw an advert for a disco at a place called the Wallis Centre in East Grinstead, so we headed over there. The venue was about twenty-five miles from home. The Wallis was a new one for us. It was a well run youth centre, run by a youth leader called Steph, who was well liked and seemed to command a strong sense of loyalty and respect from his patrons. It was perhaps, one of the best run youth clubs in the county. On our first visit I noticed a memorial plaque and a photograph on the wall of a young chap on a Suzuki GT380. I asked Steph if the guy had died on his bike. He replied that he did not, he took a swim in a gravel pit and drowned. A sad end to a young lad with his whole life in front of him. There seemed to be a strong camaraderie between all those that attended the Wallis and during the period which we frequented the place it was strongly biker orientated. I don't remember seeing a single Mod or Skinhead in the venue at any time. A real bonus for sure.

On our third or fourth trip, after leaving the Wallis and heading homeward, we arrived at East Hoathly. Those of us in front suddenly realised that those near the rear had vanished. We realised that they had probably stopped for fuel at the village garage where there was a twenty-four hour automatic pump which took £1 notes in the machine. You then got around three gallons of fuel for £1 at that time. We stopped in a field gateway to answer the call of nature, and before long we heard motorbikes in the distance. We ran back to our bikes and fired them up. Mawanga was riding pillion to me that day. With Worm and Length already ahead I gunned the Suzuki away after them. The rest of the pack were howling down on us, so I wound it up... flickering headlights behind us, we cranked into a left-hand corner, but the bike would not go around... a screech of tortured metal... the back wheel stepped out... the harder I cornered the more traction I lost... I tried desperately to control the skipping bike but couldn't... the engine must have seized I thought; so I snatched in the clutch to free it... then I lost it completely... and as if in slow motion the bike skidded away sideways. A headlight shone bright in the treetops... I flew gracefully through the air... Mawanga passed me skidding along the road surface face down, going straight as a die like a human torpedo... thump... a terrific bang as I smacked into the side of the front wing of a car on a garage forecourt... I slid across the bonnet, curling over, then fell off the other wing onto the ground, coming to rest by the opposite front wheel of the car... sound of the revving of many bikes being frantically stamped down through gearboxes... others ahead turning around and racing back... shouts and worried voices... the garage owner and his wife came rushing out of the house and joined in the melée... a torch flashed on and waved around... silence... then sirens in the distance... "what the fuck had happened?"... I started cursing and swearing at the top of my voice... I had gone into shock... where was Mawanga?... was he injured— or, was he dead?

Mawanga's legs and feet were found protruding from under the front of another car. He was out cold. It had all happened in a flash. After some time Mawanga's feet started thrashing around like crazy. He had been knocked unconscious by the sump of the car. The impact had split his crash helmet. Now unaware of where he was, he was fighting to try to stand up. The others calmed him; grabbing his legs they gently pulled him out from under the car. I am sure the cops must have been there soon, but I didn't see them. The ambulance had arrived and took us away. Worm made his way home. Our mother called down from upstairs asking where I was. Worm said I would be home soon. Our mum pressed him for more information, but he simply said that an ambulance would bring me home, but I was OK.

I had been lucky. I had only broken my left arm. Mawanga was detained in hospital with concussion. I arrived home in the early hours. The crash had been caused by being in a hurry and leaving my side stand down. As Grasscut and Funky had caught us up from behind they had noticed the side stand was down and were frantically flashing their headlights to try to warn us. Funky said later that the sparks flying from my side stand, as it dug into the road surface were up to his waist. This was a serious design fault on Suzuki's made throughout the 1970s, as the stand came too far forward and past the point of no return. If someone was foolish enough to leave the side stand down and it hit the ground on cornering, there was no way the stand could flip up and your fate was sealed. The exact same thing had happened to Grizzly months previously.

Later that morning Worm had summoned a few willing helpers and we all set off with him driving the truck to retrieve my bike. The garage was open for business so we all went into the office. I gave the garage owner my name, address and insurance details. I apologised to him and his wife for my abusive language the night before, but they understood that I had been in a state of shock. They had locked my bike away for the night and now released it. On checking it over, there was surprisingly little damage. For some strange reason the left-hand side of the handlebar had been bent straight downward, but in doing so, the clutch lever had become tightly wedged between the handlebar and the indicator. The bike had entered a ditch at the end of the garage forecourt and sat there a few yards into the ditch, bolt upright, still running and in gear, lights ablaze. The clutch was engaged, held in position by the damaged bar. The bike was found just three feet from a telegraph pole. Someone had switched off the ignition. We got the bike home and unloaded it. With my left arm to be in a plaster for six weeks, I sat down to try to figure out how to convert the bike to ride one-handed.

Worm had changed the high bars on his Invader for a set of straights and the old bars were in the shed. I found that by fitting the narrower Invader bars I could tip them back and tighten them in a position that fitted my plastered broken arm perfectly. This was fine on straight road, but to corner I would have to lift this hand from the bar as my left arm was set in a fixed position. I then looked at the controls. I simply moved the clutch lever to the right-hand side of the handlebars in a straight down position under the throttle grip. Job done. I did a test ride—perfect. I found that my black leather jacket sleeve fitted over the plaster. With no hope of getting a leather glove on, I found an old black woollen one which stretched over the plaster. Within an hour I had mastered it and could ride as good as normal, even to the point of racing each other, as myself and Bar Steward were to find out. Dick the Undertaker came around and asked where I was. Our mother replied that I was out on my bike with the others. Dick replied, "My God, if that had happened to me I would be in bed for a week looking for sympathy". A week in bed was what Mawanga got before they would release him from hospital. I felt pretty guilty about that.

Within the week the East Hoathly village cop came to our house and served a pink slip of paper on me. It was a Notice of Intended Prosecution. I protested. We were not speeding, having just pulled away. He told me that his Inspector had deemed that leaving your side stand down was paramount to Driving Without Due Care and Attention and as such I should be prosecuted. Several weeks later however, the same cop returned. They had withdrawn the Notice of Intended Prosecution. Apparently a Lewes motorcycle cop had also left his side stand down. He was not so lucky however, and was thrown through the windscreen of a car travelling in the opposite direction, breaking his neck and killing him instantly. The police felt that if a highly trained police motorcyclist could make the same mistake they could hardly convict me.

Bar Steward had bought himself a maroon Suzuki T500. We had been to see a band and were returning home in the early hours of the morning. We were racing each other and approaching a village on the fast main road. There was a police house in the village and the officer on duty must have heard us coming from afar. As we swept around a right-hand corner the policeman ran out in the road to stop us. With my arm in plaster there was no way I was going to stop, so I went around one side of him and Bar Steward the other. With full throttle we cleared off. I had to put my left arm behind me to get down across the petrol tank. I was always a bit sceptical about two-strokes seizing up, so when riding one, it's second nature to keep a couple of fingers over the clutch lever, but then what do they say about "if needs must"? This was always at the back of my mind after top motorcycle racer Bill Ivy met his death that way. He took his left hand off the bar to fasten his helmet. The two-stroke seized at that point, threw him off and killed him. A great world class rider he was too.

A couple of weeks later on a Saturday our mother took a phone call. It was from the police. There had been an accident at Friston they said, and those involved had requested that I pick their motorcycles up. Worm came with me and we set off wondering what or who we were going to find there. As we neared Friston the police had closed the road, but they let us through. As we approached I could not believe the scene of utter devastation. It was like a bomb had gone off, a war zone with a trail of destruction two hundred yards or more long. There were two smashed cars and three bikes spread out in various states of destruction. I suddenly realised that here I was with these cops all around having driven there with a broken arm. In the truck was an old suede coat with a fur collar that I wore sometimes on my milk round. It was a hot summer's day, but I had no choice but to wear it, to cover the plaster on my broken arm.

We found Bean's Honda in three pieces. The front forks were banana shaped, badly bent, torn clean from the fork yokes with such a force that the top of the fork legs had turned blue from the friction heat. They were still attached to what was left of the front mudguard and wheel, both totally smashed, the wheel having completely collapsed, as was the rear wheel. All lights, indicators, clocks, smashed, as were the rear mudguard, exhausts, side panels and engine cases. The fuel tank had been torn off and thrown down the road. The front of the seat ripped up into the air, as if by some giant hand, scattering the tool kit and instruction manual all along the road. The only thing left visible and untouched was the carburettors—everything else was totally smashed. I wandered through this mechanical wasteland in disbelief. Bar Steward's bike was propped up, mildly damaged, but had a cracked engine case and was leaking oil. I picked up Sprogg's crash helmet. It had blood inside. You could not see through the visor as it was so scored. Sprogg had clearly been thrown along the road on his face, but most worrying was a near perfect Dunlop TT100 tyre print across the helmet. Sprogg's bike was further up and laying on its side with the forks bent back and the fuel tank dented in. The lead car on the other side of the road had been hit head-on and was clearly a write-off. The car behind it had been hit on the side and the door was caved in. The only vehicle left there unscathed was Grasscut's black Honda CB500/4 sitting on its side stand. We loaded the bikes and left the scene. Worm riding Grasscut's bike—the rest in the truck.

Later, we found out what had happened. Coming home from Seaford by the longer route, Bean had come from the back of the pack to overtake everyone at perhaps ninety mph. He left it too late, tried to take Sprogg. who was the front runner. By then he was into the curve, laid the bike hard over on its left side, but was going too fast. Everything decked, Bean ran out of ground clearance, drifted across the white line and smacked head on into the front car coming the other way. He was thrown clean over the car and onto the grass beyond. His bike disintegrated. The fork and wheel assembly, torn from the bike took Sprogg down. Sprogg's bike ploughed into the second car. Other debris took Bar Steward down. Bar Steward's bike then ran over Sprogg's head. The occupants of the lead car had been on their way to get the Newhaven ferry to go on holiday.

Grasscut was extremely fortunate to be the only one to pass through all the wreckage unscathed. Bean spent some time in hospital with a smashed leg, but by some miracle only received other relatively minor injuries. Sprogg had put his teeth through his bottom lip and broke his wrist; whilst Bar Steward had minor leg damage, which required crutches for a week or two. Given the devastation, matters could have been far worse. Later, Bean received an eighteen month driving ban and a hefty fine for his actions. Whilst writing this book, I asked

Grasscut to write an eye-witness account of what happened. This is his story:

BEAN AND A BLACK HONDA MISSILE

TONY has kindly asked me if I could elaborate on Bean's "monumental mishap". Well, where to start? At the beginning, I suppose, maybe a little before is best to help you understand how we got there that day, amidst the total carnage created by a suicide jockey red-lining it on a black Honda missile.

I first met Kev, who soon became known as Bean when we both attended the same secondary school together. We soon became great mates and after a few years we both bought old motorcycles which we rode along an old disused railway track on evenings and weekends. Perhaps it was about now that we should have noticed Bean's determination to defy the laws of physics and gravity. He certainly had a talent for coming off. Some might say his riding style was bravery and no fear.

As the years passed we were finally able to legally ride bikes on the road. We went through the usual two-strokes, a Suzuki Hustler, a Kawasaki KH250 and later I had a Thruxton Bonneville. By the age of eighteen we'd got some dosh together and an opportunity popped up. Honda had brought out a stonking 500/4, so we graduated to nice quiet civilised wolf in sheep's clothing four-stroke machines that revved to over 9,000rpm that would not attract the cops too much. We both decided to get our first bikes from Hydes of Horsham as they had two we could have. We picked the bikes up, chuffed as Punch or what, happy as pigs in excrement, you wouldn't have found two happier mates, road warriors, kings of the road we were, an unbelievable feeling. You had to run new bikes in, which involved low revs for 500-1,000 miles to get your first dealer service done then you could gradually wind them up slowly as the miles crept up.

As with every different bike you need to find the limits of its adhesion. Bean in his boundless enthusiasm found his after bottoming out his centre stand and exhaust pipes outside of *Pevensey Castle*. He slid gracefully across the road, promptly ending up on his arse sitting beside his pride and joy outside the castle entrance. He picked her up and rode home without any further determination to reduce his long term residence on this planet. He decided to claim on his insurance and spun them a yarn about something jumping out in front of him. The upshot was; could he get some quotes and send them off? They would then deal with them and let him know what to do. Bean phoned Kennards, a motorcycle shop in Seaford, where coincidentally Sprogg was working, to see if they could do a damage report. Eric the boss said it was ok they could, so we arranged to go over the following Saturday.

Saturday came, and I rode over to Bean's place. Bar Steward joined us on his T500. He was just passing Bean's house as we were about to leave, so he joined us for the ride. We all set off for Kennards of Seaford. We arrived and Eric did the assessment. As we were about to leave, it was around knock-ing-off time for Sprogg who was always up for a ride, so he finished work and joined us for the ride home. We decided Sprogg could lead as he was the quickest, Bar Steward next, then me with Bean bringing up the rear. Not that we were riding hard, more of a cruising, running-in amble really. We were going back the longer way round. After you climb out of Exceat valley there is a slight left, sweeping right, sweeping left then right—not much at all, really, more or less straight for close to a mile. It must have been about here that Bean had his temporary dislocation of brain function and a total commonsense meltdown. He wound it up along that straight. He planned to take us all on the straight, then throw it into the corners. If he had started his run another twenty seconds or so earlier he would probably have made it.

Sprogg, Bar Steward and myself were just approaching the beginning of the right, left, right combination at the end of that straight about 400 yards from Friston Pond, when all of the sudden, just as we took the first right-hander, this black and chrome Honda ballistic missile with Bean tucked in, went past me like a bat out of hell with his arse on fire. He flew past Bar Steward and was just about alongside Sprogg, who was now just entering the tight left-hander, when the unthinkable happened. Even though Sprogg had

191

kept a tight line going into the left-hander, not thinking that anyone would be coming by. Even so, this only left Bean about three feet to get through before white-lining into the danger zone and imminent disaster… oncoming traffic. He laid her down as hard as he could for the left-hander, trying for the gap between Sprogg and possible oblivion… he ran out of road, the side stand dug in… sparks… screaming engine revs… tyre smoke, the bike spun, screeching car tyres. A massive impact… **whumph**… *both Bean and the bike went straight into the oncoming traffic. Bean was thrown off, he bounced and hit the rear of the first car, slid between that and the second car and then straight into a large fence post on the other side of the road. His bike seemed to explode and go everywhere, the impact so hard that later we found it ripped the front forks out of both yokes and them turned the tops of them blue with the impact heat stresses of pulling them out. As this happened the front wheel, I think, bouncing off the car took Sprogg out bringing him off. He had a TT100 tyre mark across his skid-lid, his bike slid into another car; by now there were two cars, two bikes, one bloke in the road and another wrapped around a post. Bar Steward had nowhere to go, coming off his bike after debris from Bean's Honda hit him and took him out, or possibly Sprogg's bike took him out, it was hard to tell, it was mayhem. It's true what they say about everything happening in slow-motion. I saw all this happen in total disbelief. Twenty seconds ago we were four mates riding home, now we are in a war zone and one of us could be dead.*

I was next, there really wasn't anything I could do; there were now three bikes, bits of bikes, two blokes and two cars, plus Bean all over the road. I did what all bikers might do in this situation, shut my eyes, braced myself for impact and prepared to kiss my arse goodbye. The next few seconds were a bit of a blur, it all seemed to go quiet, nothing happened. A little voice in my head said **open your eyes you daft bastard**, *I opened my eyes… good news, wasn't dead… bad news, I was heading for a wall. I swerved, just missed a car and slewed to a halt beside a line of traffic. Looking back it was total carnage laying in the road, broken bikes, broken blokes, broken cars, the sickly smell of hot oil smoke, petrol, antifreeze steam, acrid burnt rubber smoke,* people screaming. Luckily no one in the cars was hurt. One woman had wound down her window and was screaming, "I saw it all, I saw it all... you maniacs". Bar Steward limped over to her, he looked like he'd just done ten rounds with Mike Tyson; he stuck his head in her car window and told her to "Shut the fuck up, our mate could be dying over there"... She shut up. I ran back to find Bean lying beside the big fence post, hardly moving. He was just making a horrible sort of gurgling/growling noise. I looked down at his legs and one didn't look right. If he had busted an artery he was in trouble, big trouble, let alone any other internal injuries he may have. All this happened before the advent of mobile phones; I had to find a phone box ASAP and pray that it worked. The nearest phone I knew of was at the bottom of the hill in East Dean village. Got down there, luckily this was back in the days before they invented random vandalism by retards. Result, it was working. I had never made a 999 call before, so when she said, "Police, fire, ambulance or coastguard?" I said, "just send the lot... now". I got back to the carnage, people were wandering about out of their cars, someone had found Bean a blanket, checked on Sprogg and Bar Steward, by now both vertical, both walking wounded, but thankfully they said they would be OK. The cops arrived pretty quick, but it seemed to take forever for the ambulance to arrive. When it did arrive Bean was in a very bad way and totally out of it. The ambulance guys gave us that sort of "it's not good" look. I felt helpless, scared shitless, went with Bean, it really felt that we could lose him, but if it was his time to go, it was right to have mates with him. His parents would have wanted that.

Thankfully, Bean must have had a guardian angel there that day, he survived, but he spent months in hospital getting R&R... "repaired and rebuilt". While he was in hospital we would go and visit him often, one time after I was unlucky enough to have spiked my foot on the weir while we were swimming in the river. It needed some stitches and stuff at the hospital. When finished they gave me a wheelchair, so I thought, Yeehah, you know what, I'll go and visit Bean, and lo and behold, they had given him a wheelchair as well. So, once again we got a bit creative and did what every self-respecting pair of *bikers would do. Be rude not to, wouldn't do it? We had a race around the hospital corridors... this time we didn't get a bollocking or detention.*

> **In the space of a couple of minutes that day all our lives changed forever.**
> **It's about then that you realise how special, yet fragile, life is on a bike, on the edge; in a blink it could be gone forever.**
> **Don't take it for granted you will always make it home to your loved ones. We were lucky.**
> **Bean's bike never made it to its first service.**
> **Mates are mates, through thick and thin, no matter what.**
> **Bean is the brother I should have had.**
>
> Nick "Grasscut" Goble.

CHAPTER TWENTY-THREE

"I kicked the Bonneville over and the bitch kicked me back"

PETE had bought a new Ducati 24 Hour model, a lovely look-ing café racer style bike, resplendent in red and white. We all sat in the square at Alfriston and admired it. We decided to go for a Sunday afternoon run, but as Pete was running the bike in and could only go relatively slowly we told him to lead and we would follow. We were in no hurry. Pete set off, myself next, the rest behind. Alfriston is an old historic smugglers' village with narrow main streets. Pete had only gone about fifty yards when a tourist coach came around the corner. The road was narrow with walls on both sides, so the coach took the corner wide, leaving Pete hardly any room between the coach and the wall. Pete aimed for the small gap and braked hard. The coach driver swung to the left as far as he could. The Ducati front wheel locked up under hard braking, throwing Pete off. He bounced along the side of the coach and for one awful moment I thought he was going under its rear wheels, but instead he just scuffed along its entire length as the coach was still moving. We stopped and picked up Pete's bike which had minor damage. It was no one's fault, just the perils of manoeuvring such a large vehicle in a confined space. Pete had been very lucky indeed.

Grizzly, out riding alone one night on his bike, got sandwiched while overtaking between two cars, and broke his right foot, ending up with him on crutches. Some time later the same hap-pened to Bollocks, strangely enough on the same road and in the same location. A group of us were ahead. I was riding at the back of that group. I looked back to see Bollocks behind us overtaking between two cars travelling in opposing directions. The car heading towards him suddenly drifted over, narrowing the gap. Bollocks had just become the meat in the sandwich. The car hit him and I saw the front chrome wheel trim go spinning twenty feet into the air. The car didn't stop, but increased speed and cleared off. I slowed; Bollocks caught me up—he was laying across his petrol tank in severe pain when he stopped. It was a hospital trip for sure. Same as Grizzly, he had broken his right foot.

In true biker form, Bollocks was not going to let a small matter of a broken foot curtail his enjoyment or affect his life. As soon as he was released from the local hospital casualty department on crutches, with a warning not to put any weight on the injured foot, he set about adapting his bike accordingly. The model of Triumph 650 Bonneville that he owned was still fitted with a right foot gear change, so Bollocks moved it around on the splines so that the gear lever now stood bolt upright. Somehow he managed to start the bike and he found that with one or two painful attempts he could manage to select gears by simply kicking the upright gear lever either forward or backwards with his injured plastered foot. Within a few days he turned up again at "the cheeks", riding with his foot in plaster and sitting on his crutches, along with a sock over his toes on the injured foot. When out on a run it hadn't slowed him down. He would come storming past flying into a right-hand corner with everything on the deck and a large puff of white plaster dust flying back from his foot, his crutches wedged firmly up his backside. Sometimes he had to make several attempts to get the bike into gear, as his changing method was perhaps a little on the Heath Robinson side.

Apart from his normal day job, Bollocks still worked odd evening shifts at the local garage as a petrol pump attendant. You can imagine JP's surprise, when arriving to start his shift at the garage, Bollocks came roaring in with his foot in plaster nearly to his knee and his crutches wedged firmly between his buttocks. It was a long hot summer that year. Bollocks was a mechanic in his day job. He was not exactly known for his personal hygiene. This was made even worse when he gave up his job as a car mechanic and became a fitter/engineer looking after machinery in sewerage plants. One evening JP was utterly astounded to see Bollocks, after complaining that his "leg chucked up a bit", disappear into the garage workshop, produce a tin of Gunk engine cleaner and a paint brush and proceed to "gunk" his injured leg down. Satisfied with the result, Bollocks hobbled over to the garage hosepipe. Turning it on, he stuck the hose into the top of the plaster, washing the Gunk out of the bottom by his toes, with a satisfied "the fucker will dry out by the time I go home". The plaster did not fare too well however from its degreasing episode and constant contacts with the road surface, so after a few days Bollocks mummified the plaster, binding it up with a roll of electrical tape. Eventually he was forced to go back to the casualty department for repairs, where they chastised him with a stern, "We told you not to walk on it", to which he replied, "I didn't bloody well walk on it, I kicked the Bonneville over and the bitch kicked me back!" He continued to hare around as normal until the plaster was removed and beyond.

One day I got a phone call. The Bonneville had expired by the roadside and could I pick it up; so the normal recovery team sprung into action. I had finished the Transit's modification with the three litre V6 engine now fitted, and this was one of its first outings. A Jaguar pulled up next to us at the traffic lights and tried to burn us off, but the Transit blew it into the shrubbery— a satisfactory result. The only problem was, it drank the fuel. We recovered Bollocks and his Bonnie.

Afterwards, we set off into town to the Wimpy. There was a

large group of Skinheads there as we drove in. Puss shouted through the ventilator on the side near the back of the van, "Fucking Skinheads". We were in slow moving traffic. I said, "You idiot, the traffic lights are red". Seeing their chance, the Skinheads came charging up the road after us. The traffic lights changed to green. The traffic started to slowly move. I sat right on the last car's tail, but the Skinheads were almost on us. The traffic started to increase speed. Most of the Skinheads gave up, but one was running flat out just a couple of feet behind us with his chin stuck out. Everyone in the back was jeering and sticking their fingers up at him. "Brake", yelled Bollocks, "Brake". I stood hard on the foot brake. With a loud bang the Skinhead ran straight into the van's back doors. As he hit the deck we drove away to a loud cheer.

An exhaust clamp came loose at the manifold, which made the truck engine backfire on the over-run. It was so much fun that we left it. You could spot a likely target ahead and change down a gear and with no throttle, count to three to produce an enormous backfire right behind an unsuspecting target. Old ladies nearly jumped through shop windows, a cyclist hit the kerb and fell off his bike and girls screamed. Locally we heard someone in the pub say, "Don't tangle with that lot, they carry shooters in there". What fun. Sadly it came to an end when after a fast run to One Ball's park clubhouse, the DJ announced that there was a van on fire in the car park. The constant backfiring had split the seam along the top of the silencer wide open and allowed hot gases to play on the van floor. The floor had got so hot that the old bit of carpet on the floor had started smouldering. Bear, a big guy who hung around with us, borrowed the truck while we were away at the TT Races, tightened and fixed the exhaust. The backfires were no more.

Bollocks was soon tearing around again and after every tear

up he would suffer the same adrenaline rush with the uncontrol-
lable face twitching, the shuffling of the feet, the tobacco falling
out of the cigarette roll-up and the usual, "Cor... f... f...
fuckin...'ell. Then, in true fashion he would wipe his nose along
his sleeve. He was a true "animal" if ever there was one.

A group of us piled into the revamped truck and set off for
Santa Pod Raceway to watch the drag racing. A great weekend.
After leaving the drag strip on the way home, the engine began
to backfire and stopped. Checking it out I found that somehow
the ignition timing had slipped. I turned the distributor around
to reset it and we continued on our way. Halfway down the M1
motorway the motor expired again. I had just lifted the bonnet
when Frenchie came along in his disco Ford Transit and pulled
in front of us. Frenchie's Transit was well sorted. It was a long
wheelbase, twin rear wheel job. Like myself he had fitted a three
litre Ford V6 engine with the diesel front grille to allow for the
extra length of the bigger engine. Further, he had fitted a Reliant
Scimitar gearbox with overdrive and when he read that a minibus
differential was the highest ratio you could get, he hired one, and
suddenly overnight Frenchie's Transit got faster and the hire company's minibus got slower. Inside the van behind the normal three
seats, he had a row of reclining seats from an aircraft, complete
with headrests. Behind that was a load stop partition to stop the
disco gear sliding forward under heavy braking. When his van
had broken down and he asked me to transport his gear for him,
I found that he and his sidekick had girls in every town. I guess
you could call them groupies.

Frenchie hitched up my truck with a tow rope. We had a lot of
guys and girls aboard, but he said he would at least tow us off the
motorway, which he did. He towed us to Hemel Hempstead. We
found a quiet street and parked the truck, then we all squeezed
into Frenchie's van for the ride home. I went back a week later

with a local builder who towed me back with his truck and would only take petrol money for the task. What a really decent guy. I found that a fibre timing cog with a steel middle had come unbonded, allowing the timing to slip.

One lunchtime I had been at Pigshit's house working on his bike with him, when a petite, pretty young girl strolled past. She was wearing a little black miniskirt with black knee-length boots and a red leather jacket with a few badges on the sleeves. Her long brown hair hung down to the centre of her back. I mentioned to Pigshit that she was "a bit of alright". He said that she lived at the top of his road and her name was Christine. A few months later we all went to a speedway ball at Eastbourne's Winter Garden. She was there with her parents. Grass went over and told her that I fancied her and we dated for a year or so. She was a really nice girl, but was very quiet and didn't have much to say. She was like a timid little mouse, so it was a real shock one day while in the Wimpy Bar that she suddenly picked up a mustard dispenser and shot a large amount of mustard into Bollocks's coffee while he was distracted. We sat there grimacing, trying not to laugh as Bollocks took two noisy slurps of his coffee. He saw us looking and said, "What are you all looking at... fuck off". He stuck his fingers up at us. Taking a further long slurp... he suddenly stiffened, he smacked his fist down hard on the table, nearly choking he gasped, "Funky, you bastard". He had a line of mustard along his lip. Everyone fell around laughing. Funky protested his innocence, "It wasn't me. Why do I always get the blame?"

After a while I decided she was not the girl for me, so we finished. A week later I crashed the bike, breaking my arm and putting Mawanga in hospital with concussion for a week. Otherwise, Christine would have been riding pillion that night. Soon she was dating Funky. They were together for perhaps six months.

200

One night Bollocks dropped in at Funky's house. Bollocks asked, "Where's the bird then?" Funky replied that they had just had an argument, so he had finished with her. I could never understand how he could have managed to argue with her as she was so mild mannered and hardly spoke. Bollocks went on his way. After an hour or so Funky got to thinking that perhaps he had been a bit harsh on her, so he got on his bike and went round to her house to apologise. When he got there he found Bollocks's Bonneville still steaming outside. Bollocks dated her from then on. After a while she became pregnant, and later, when they were getting married, Bollocks asked Length to be best man. Length agreed. When it came to the wedding, Length said, "I didn't know you owned a suit Bollocks", to which Bollocks replied, "I don't, I got this one from the old lady's club book, and it's going back on Monday".

CHAPTER TWENTY-FOUR

The trip that never was

I HAD become fed up with the performance of my T500 Suzuki. I still liked the look of the bike but it didn't perform as well as I wanted. Fortesque had a used black Honda CB500/4 with a loud exhaust pipe, the same model as Grasscut and Bean had just bought; also Fred had just won the BEMSEE 500 Championship on the same model. I bought the bike from Fortesque. When I got the bike, I initially struggled to get ninety mph on the clock. Fortesque was not a fast rider. The bike was very clogged up and would not rev, but by holding it flat out through the gears everywhere I went, I eventually saw 115 mph flat across the tank. It was a much better bike than the T500. It was faster, it handled and cornered much better and the brakes were good, as it had a disc brake up front. Also it had both electric and kick starting. By modern standards the front disc would be considered woefully inadequate, but back then it was a revolution. Bar Steward later bought a Honda 500/4, as did Mouth, once he had passed his bike test.

One evening saw several of us polishing our bikes in the driveway of our home when Mouth came hurtling up the road; turning into our drive, he weaved through the assembled bikes and disappeared around the back of our house. He had hardly dumped his bike and gear and dashed back to join us, when we heard the familiar throbbing of a police Norton Commando. The cop rode straight into our drive. He was particularly obnoxious. Traffic police in cars wore peaked caps with a white top. Traffic cops were worst than most. They seemed to pick them for their arrogance. If a traffic cop wore his cap tipped forward with the peak over his eyes like a guardsman, it was usually a sign that he had a complex, as his parents were not married. However, I had never seen a bike cop before with his crash helmet tipped forward so that the peak was over his eyes. He dismounted and looking around, he said sternly, "Whose are all these bikes here and whose is that Jaguar? We don't like Jags because they are villain's cars". Our mother was in the house and overheard him. After her last encounter with the police she was in no mood to let that slide. She came out, "How dare you, that is our Jag and we are not villains", she came back at him. The cop seemed a bit bewildered. He had charged in here looking for a certain bike that he had been in pursuit of and he could not see it amongst his prime suspects. After a few minutes he gave up and cleared off. "That was a close one", said Mouth with a grin.

It was decided we needed to do a road trip. I shut my eyes and stuck a pin in a map. Opening them, the pin was stuck in Great Yarmouth. "Sounds good enough," we agreed. We packed the usual tents, sleeping bags and camping gear onto our bikes and set off for a four day long Bank Holiday weekend run. Recently I had fitted the Boyer electronic ignition to my bike, which I had bought off Fred. I had no experience of such items. The unit looked like a black ring doughnut that took the place of the points assembly and backplate. As I was unsure of the system I packed the original set up in a plastic bag in my luggage. Good job I did as it turned out. There was myself, Grizzly, Kiddie, Geoff, Mouth, Spud, Sue and Grasscut, but Grasscut had brought along Basil, who was his workmate. Initially, we didn't get very far, as Geoff picked up a rear wheel puncture just outside of Otford, near Sevenoaks. We pulled into a layby. Luckily, with all bikes together and no recovery truck along I had packed a foot pump. The puncture was not too big, so Geoff pumped up the tyre, saying that he would set off home, stopping regularly to re-inflate the tyre with the foot pump and would meet us back in the layby again the next morning. We decided to pitch our tents on the grass verge next to the layby and cook some grub. Later, we decided to go and find a local pub in Otford. It soon became clear that there were some in Otford that perhaps weren't too chuffed to have a group of bikers visit their establishment. One posh twat was downright rude. Basil called across the bar to me, "Did you hear what him over there, with the dead rat under his nose said to me? (the guy had a moustache), he just said, 'Now listen here, Sonny Jim'." We went in search of another pub, but ran into a large group of young Skinheads. There were ten or twelve of them, nothing we couldn't handle, them being generally younger than us. One of them came up to Mouth with his chest stuck out. I shouted a warning, "Watch it Mouth, he's got a brick behind his back". Mouth took the brick off him, but as he did so, the Skinhead swung around. He had another large brick in his other hand and caught Mouth a glancing blow across the side of the head. Mouth's reaction was swift. He battered the Skinhead into submission. He really hammered him. The rest held back; they wanted none of what their mate had just received. They carried their injured mate away bleeding, battered and bruised with him shouting abuse at us. We found another pub, then later went back to our camp.

In the morning we got up and cooked breakfast, then sat around and waited for Geoff's return, but by lunchtime he had still not shown. We were wasting time. This was pre-mobile phone days, so Geoff had no way of contacting us. I rode into Otford and found a phone box. I rang Geoff's parent's home. Geoff answered the phone and he had decided not to come back. I rode back to find the others had struck camp while I was away and were ready to leave. I strapped my gear on my bike and we set off again. Further along the route my Honda did three large backfires and died at the roadside. I removed a spark plug and checked for a spark—there was none! I had been right not to trust the modern electronic set up. I had to convert the bike back to the points system at the side of the road. While I was doing that I noticed in the road there was a dead rabbit, a bit of road kill. The rabbit had been squashed by passing traffic so many times that it was now just a strip of fur that had dried out in the sun. I saw Grizzly sneak over, pick up the deceased rabbit, lift the lid of Kiddie's top box and slip it inside, shutting the lid again. It has to be said at this point that none of us generally rode with carriers or top boxes. We preferred our bikes sleek and naked, as light and agile as possible. The top boxes would remain bolted to the carriers, then the whole lot was fitted as one, only when needed for trips such as this.

We set off again, but I had to laugh riding behind Kiddie, as a small tuft of fur was visible flapping about in the wind from the edge of his top box. I could see Kiddie keep looking in his mirror trying to figure out what the hell it was. When we stopped for fuel he opened the top box and threw it out. Grizzly was on it in seconds, spiriting it away to another location and another victim. I picked up my crash helmet, pulled out my gloves and the dead rabbit fell out. Mouth was paying for his fuel, so I popped off his bike's plastic side panel, slipping the rabbit underneath and putting it back on. Just in time as he came out. Fur was visible, but he did not spot it. Mounting the bike he fired it up, and away we went again. Somewhere near Colchester disaster struck. There was a bang from Kiddie's bike, the rear wheel locked up and there was a large pool of oil on the road. Closer inspection showed that the locking washer on the large nut on the front sprocket had failed. The sprocket retaining nut had become unscrewed and had disappeared. The sprocket had come completely off the shaft and jammed under it. This locked the rear wheel solid and pushed the bottom clean out of the gearbox. Shit, this was terminal.

Just as we were wondering what to do next, a Dunstall 750 Suzuki in Texaco colours came along and stopped. It was a guy with a stunning petite blonde on the back. He introduced himself, "Hi, I'm Roscoe, what's the problem here?" We explained the situation. "Well, I only live about half a mile along this road, just on the left as it starts to go uphill, you are quite welcome to push your bike to my place. There's plenty of room and you can leave it there until you can collect it." We thanked him and he set off home. Basil dismounted from the back of Grasscut's bike and helped Kiddie push the stricken Suzuki to Roscoe's place. We all met up there to decide our next move. We decided that Great Yarmouth was out and perhaps we should stay local. Roscoe told us of a campsite with a clubhouse a few miles away. He would take us there. We dispersed Kiddie's gear between us. Kiddie got on the back of Grizzly's bike and we set off after Roscoe. Arriving at the site we booked in and pitched our tents. Roscoe told us there was a fete in Colchester that weekend. If we wanted to go he would come back in the morning and take us there. We agreed and settled down for the evening. Roscoe and his gorgeous girlfriend bade us goodbye.

Sitting having a meal, I casually asked Mouth what he thought of his 500/4. He replied that it was a good bike. Grizzly jumped in, "umm, goes all right, does it?" "Yes, why?" Mouth was getting suspicious, "I bet the bloody rabbit's in there somewhere!" He jumped up, unlocked and lifted the seat. Finding nothing there he stood back. He started pulling off the side panel but on the wrong side of the bike. We all burst out laughing. Replacing that panel he came around our side and spotted it. "Bastards", he exclaimed, and threw the rabbit out. Before he had even refitted the side panel the rabbit had moved on again. He put on his jacket and... "For fucks sake", as he put his arm in the sleeve, the rabbit fell out. More laughter. After a night in the bar we settled down for the night. Mouth got into the sleeping bag, he jumped up, "I'm sick of this, that bloody dead rabbit is in my sleeping bag." Grizzly cut him a look; he took a long, slow drag on his cigarette and with a puff of smoke he said firmly, "Mouth, you're pissed, you're in Basil's sleeping bag". The rabbit continued to do the rounds for the rest of the weekend. It was a source of constant entertainment.

Up and about the next morning, Roscoe and his bird arrived. He took us into Colchester. I tried to remember landmarks to find our own way in and then back to the site. We stationed ourselves in the beer tent. The weather was warm and sunny and there was plenty to do at the fete; a couple of Roscoe's mates were there also. I saw a poster for a group called Medicine Head, whose hit "One and One is One" was in the charts. They were playing that night at the Top Rank in Colchester. I thought I would like to see them and Mouth said he would like to come with me; the rest wanted to stay on site to use the bar and clubhouse. Roscoe led us   back to the camp site. He gave us his phone number and we thanked him for all he had done. We would call him, we said, to arrange collection of Kiddie's bike. We would be away home in the morning.

After a wash and brush up, Mouth and myself headed back to Colchester on our bikes. We found the Top Rank, parked the bikes up and watched the gig. When we came out it was dark. We had supped a few beers and were unsure of our way back to the site, so we were taking it easy. We pulled up at some red traffic lights. There was no one ahead of us. I was suddenly struck in the back by a heavy blow, which made me lurch forward. A fairly big guy with short hair ran on past me and started laying blows on Mouth from behind. He bent forward under the blows. I quickly flipped the side stand down, and glancing around there was another one almost on me. As he lashed out I socked him hard. Mouth had somehow recovered his shock at this unprovoked attack and had like me, whipped his bike onto its side stand and was exchanging blows with his attacker. There were a few cars behind us now, who started hooting their horns as the traffic lights changed to green. The third car back was a light coloured Triumph 2.5 litre PI with its doors open. There had been a third person running from the car to join in, but with everyone hooting he thought better of it and ran back to the car. Including the driver that made four of them. I hit my attacker as hard as I could and knocked him over. Mouth had already dispatched his, so we leapt on our bikes and gunned them away, We were doing sixty to seventy mph through an unfamiliar town and we didn't know where the hell we were going. Behind us we could hear car tyres screeching around corners. They were gaining on us because we did not know the roads or the route we needed. Suddenly, I recognised a fair sized roundabout ahead from the afternoon when we had been riding with Roscoe. I raced my bike towards it, Mouth on my tail. We needed the third exit. We leant our bikes over hard round to the right. With a huge squeal of tyres the Triumph PI came drifting around the roundabout the wrong way, trying to head us off. From this direction it was the first exit. We cranked our bikes hard left and gunned the throttles hard as we took the exit. The Triumph driver threw the car hard right to try to take the exit but was going too fast and spun completely around in a cloud of tyre smoke, the car ended up going backwards into the kerb. We had been saved by the fact that roundabout exits are designed for the users to exit from the left. By hurtling around the roundabout the wrong way, to try to cut us off, the junction for the car was a very tight turn and he spun the car trying to make it. It had been a close run thing though, as he nearly had us. Mouth and myself tore back to the site as fast as we could, being flat out once we hit the carriageway. To this day we don't know what this incident was about. Nor could we be sure if our attackers were Skinheads or Army squaddies, as Colchester is a garrison town; we just noticed that they had very short hair. We got back to the camp site and told the others of our experience. They had had a good evening, but suddenly the couple in the next tent started having a noisy love-making session on an inflatable Lilo mattress. The rubber mattress was rasping and the girl was wailing, so the rotten devils popped a tent peg or two. The next weekend we returned with the truck to retrieve Kiddie's broken bike. Roscoe had given us directions on the phone to his local pub, so we met him and his friends there; we all shook hands and then bought them a pint. Over the years I have often wondered what happened to Roscoe. He was one of the best.

CHAPTER TWENTY-FIVE

Tales from Mona's Isle

A CROSS the Irish Sea and jut nineteen miles from the coast of Scotland lies a lovely little known island with its own parliament. The island has all that the mainland has to offer and more besides. It has the world's largest water wheel, it has castles, its own electric mountain railway, steam trains and horse-drawn trams. It is the home of the tail-less Manx cat and has so much more... but to the biker it is Mecca. It is the home of the annual Manx Grand Prix and the famous and legendary Isle of Man TT Races... once visited it will have you returning time and time again, as there is nothing quite like it anywhere else in the world.

It was in late May, 1977 that a number of us set off for the "Island' as it was commonly known, intent on watching practice week as well as the famous IoM TT races. After a wet ride we arrived on the dockside at Liverpool and were somewhat surprised to find that they were still checking how much fuel you still had in your fuel tanks. My uncles, from previous experience, had warned us to arrive at the Liverpool terminal with as little fuel as possible. If there was more than a couple of pints if fuel in your tank they would pump out the excess and hand you a sticker which read "Tank Pumped Out". This left you just enough to get you to the nearest Manx garage. After a fairly rough four hour crossing we arrived at the quay at Douglas, IoM. It was low tide when we arrived so they were craning bikes off, four at a time, with a lifting frame; it all looked decidedly dodgy.

We had booked a guest house on Douglas seafront. On arrival we were greeted by an older grey haired lady of about retiring age and her daughter. She introduced herself as Mrs Crowlin (the proprietor). Those of us who had taken girlfriends along were fortunate enough to have a double room, but the single chaps were billeted six to a room in bunk beds, or occasionally had to even share the same double bed. This of course would lead to the obvious high spirited chaos. Our behaviour could not have been too bad however, as the ever suffering Mrs Crowlin and her daughter were to welcome us back in ever-increasing numbers during the 1978 and 1979 TTs when the great, many times motorcycle world champion Mike Hailwood would make his return to racing and the Isle of Man after an eleven year retirement. I suppose you could say that 1977 was perhaps a more low-key affair, as it was our first trip and we were smaller in number. However, for the benefit of this book I have chosen to write all our TT 1970s experiences into one chapter. By 1979 the number of us booked into Mrs Crowlin's establishment had grown to twenty-seven souls, including a number from other towns around our locality.

On arrival at the B&B we found it to be an old, but fairly clean, run-down property, of similar stature to John Cleese's (of TVs Fawlty Towers) hotel. It was an ideal cheap and cheerful base for a band of young hooligans like ourselves. Having got established we soon got used to the system where a bell would ring five minutes before meals. Mrs Crowlin seemed to do most of the catering, whilst her daughter managed the chambermaid and cleaning side of the business. Mr Crowlin seemed to have another job and had little to do with the business other than to reside at the same guest house—but, at the sound of any riotous behaviour he would suddenly appear. They employed several young teenage schoolgirls to wait on tables at meal times. A first trip to the IoM TT, or any other street racing for that matter, for the first time is a real shocker. Newbies are physically shocked at the incredible speeds reached by the bikes as they flashed past close by as you sit on a wall or grass bank just feet from the action. Situated roughly in the centre of Douglas promenade, we were in the thick of the daily race-goer high jinks and action. There were motorcycles parked everywhere on the main streets, side streets, on pavements and the promenade itself. All day and night there were the sounds of revving motorcycles racing around. The IoM was packed to capacity with bikers and with advertised bike events all over the Island. The Island police in their white helmets and carrying white truncheons the size of a baseball bats were strict and fair, but they stood no nonsense.

We hit the pubs and Brian the Sheep had a few too many. In the night he was sick in the wash basin in his room which blocked the basin's u-bend. Length and Andy had to share a double bed. On returning to their room Andy changed into pyjamas and got into bed. Length stood at the end of the bed in his underpants with a large erection. "Lift up those sheets, Andy, here I come." "Get away from me, get away," Andy yelped. When recounting the story next day Length recalled, "Screamed like a girl he did, just like a girl" The next morning the breakfast warning bell went and all six in the room were still asleep. Gozy leapt out of bed and beat them all to the wash basin. He filled the wash basin and started to have a quick wash. Washing his face he got soap in his eyes. "Don't mind if I share the same water do you Gozy?" urged Length. "No, no, that's fine", replied Gozy trying to wash the soap from his eyes; he glanced over to see length washing his testicles and penis in the same basin just a few inches from his face. Gozy was appalled, "You dirty bastard". "But Goz, personal hygiene is important", came back Length with a chuckle.

Down to breakfast we went to wind up the young waitress. We would hide a breakfast under the table. "Excuse me, I haven't had my breakfast yet". They would bring another one. We would pass it to the next table. They would deliver breakfast to the next table. "Thank you, sorry but I've already got mine". Poor girls did not know if they were coming or going. The B&B was built in an L-shape and was three storeys high. One part of the L was built a half storey lower than the other which meant that you could see into the windows of some of the other block. When we arrived to book in there had been a young couple checking in at the same time. She was a very attractive little blonde. One evening one of the lads looked out. "Bloody hell, they're having it off". They all rushed over and climbed onto the double bed, hanging out of the window. Someone farted loudly and with a great roar of laughter the bed collapsed under the weight. The couple making love looked up to see six faces cheering them on. From then on they never attended meals. He told Mrs Crowlin that she was ill. He came down each day to get their food and take it up to their room. Mrs Crowlin, concerned for her health asked how she was, but we knew better. Each time we saw him we couldn't help but smile—nor could he help but smile back, but she couldn't bear to face us all. Length got the metal rubbish bin, turned it upside down and put it under the bed to prop up the damaged leg. A few days later an irate Mrs Crowlin accosted him on the stairs. She had to get a plumber to unblock the basin u-bend she said, and now the bed had been broken. "It's just vandalism, just wanton vandalism," she raged. Length tried to explain it was an accident, but she was having none of it. He got angry, "Its not vandalism", he snapped and in desperation he hit the banister with the flat of his hand. The whole section of banister fell out in his hand. "Whoops, sorry", apologised Length, as he quickly bashed the ageing, shoddy banister rail back into place on its mounting grooves. The next morning Mrs Crowlin went into the community lounge to open the curtains. There she encountered Box. He had not made it to bed that night and was fast asleep on the sofa wrapped in a long "Bike TT Supporters Pub" banner that he had "borrowed" from a nearby pub. As Mrs Crowlin pulled back the curtains he woke up with a start. Rubbing his eyes and stretching, he blurted out, "Oh, what I need is another pint of Newcastle Brown". To which Mrs Crowlin snapped back, "Huh, strikes me as you could do with one less", and stalked out of the room. While Mrs Crowlin fumed her daughter just smiled realising that these incidents were just youngsters' high jinks with no malice or vandalism intended.

We had a ride down to Castletown, where we toured the castle. Box put himself in the standing stocks and Length grabbed him from behind and simulated sex for foreign tourists with their movie cameras. After a few lunchtime beers we rode down to the Calf of Man. Laying by our bikes in the sun a few of us nodded off only to be awakened by a buzz of excitement running through the crowd. Opening my eyes I saw people pointing in the direction of the cliffs. Squinting, oh yes, hang on, there was a figure, a streaker, running stark naked in slow motion along the clifftops. But, wait, there was something familiar about that tall lanky figure. He ran to the highest point where he stood thrusting himself for a few seconds and then he was gone; but, man that streaker sure looked like Length.

That night Daffy, Sprogg and Box, along with their girlfriends went into an Indian restaurant. Box was drunk and in trying to eat his curry and rice succeeded in getting much of it all over the table. The waiter came by and grabbing Box firmly by the shoulder he said loudly in his ear, "You eat like a peeg". Box was having none of that, so as the waiter scurried past again, a plate of food in each hand, Box grabbed him, spun him round and belched in his face. While this was going on Sprogg picked up the water jug and tipped water into the waiter's pocket. The next night when we passed by the Indian there were a couple of large bouncers on the door to keep any riff-raff out. Later Sprogg arrived back at our hotel with a roar on his Honda four with girlfriend Sally on the back. She was so pissed that she was sitting facing backward on the bike laying over the top box with her arms wrapped around it.

In the morning Box's girlfriend decided to wash out some pairs of her knickers in the sink. She rinsed them out and shut them in the window across the sill to dry. Box, coming into the room, thought it was hot so threw open the sash window. The knickers blew away into the yard below. At evening meal they announced that if someone had lost their knickers they could come and claim them. She was too embarrassed to go so made Box collect them. He got a standing ovation.

A few doors down from our guest house near to an entertainment venue, the Villa Marina, was the Punch and Judy burger restaurant. Downstairs was a takeaway burger bar and upstairs was the sit down restaurant. It was good cheap grub so we used it a fair bit on more than a few occasions. Upstairs on the counter where you ordered your food was a large bowl of sugar lumps probably about eighteen inches in diameter where you helped yourself to sugar for your tea or coffee. We were eating in the restaurant when Box came in. He had that look of devilment in his eyes. He went up to the counter and grabbed two big handfuls of sugar lumps which he then threw at us. We were ready for him so we all ducked. He completely missed us but hit a party of Germans behind us on the next table. The Germans jumped up, gathered up the sugar lumps and returned fire as did we. Box grabbed the bowl and threw more handfuls of sugar lumps at us. A terrific sugar lump fight broke out across the whole restaurant. A middle aged woman leapt to her feet in the middle of the throng yelling "Call the police". As she did so a sugar lump skimmed across her forehead and parted her hair. Time to leave, we beat a hasty retreat while the fight was still raging. The next day Box tried the same thing again but his first handful of sugar lumps hit a family with a young son. The father leapt to his feet and grabbed Box by the throat. Pushing him up against the wall he told him exactly what was going to happen to him should he try anything like that again. "Serves you right Box, you bastard", said Brian the Sheep, "You asked for that".

1978 was the year that the famous "Mike the Bike" Hailwood made his triumphant return to racing and the Isle of Man TT circuit after the infamous eleven-year lay off. I had seen Mike race when I first started motorcycling so I was convinced that he could come back and win. Those that had never seen Mike in action thought he was probably a has-been, would come nowhere and should have perhaps stayed retired as motorcycle racing development had moved on so much in eleven years. This led to much wrangling and argument in the pubs that year on the run up to the TT. Spud was my biggest adversary. He was an out and out Barry Sheene fan. Sheene had only raced once on the island and had fallen off, crashing out at Quarter Bridge. He made himself unpopular with TT fans as he and the former world champion Phil Read had called for the TT to be banned on safety grounds. Furthermore they had been instrumental in the TT losing its world championship status. Read, despite speaking out against the TT, had been quite content to return to the island in 1977 when the prize money was right. He too was unpopular with TT fans and the Manx people and he was booed on his return. I told Spud that Hailwood was going to win and he bet me he would not. Spud and wife Sue left it too late that year to get a booking with Mrs Crowlin. Manx Radio had announced that there was not a spare bed on the island because of Hailwood's return and had appealed to the ordinary Manx people to throw open their doors and provide B&B facilities to desperate motorcyclists. Spud and Sue managed to get one of the those bookings and so travelled to and fro daily to Mrs Crowlin's establishment.

One pub landlord on the TT circuit, I think it may have been the Crosby Hotel, was so convinced Mike would win, that he papered over the pub sign with posters stating "Well done Mike" before the racing even started. Mike romped home to a comfortable win on the Sports Motorcycle Ducati, an incredible feat and the fans went wild. The rest is TT history. Sadly that great hero Michael Stanley Bailey Hailwood MBE, many times world motorcycle champion, awarded the George Medal for walking into the flames and pulling fellow Formula 1 car racer Craig Regazzoni from his burning car, was to die alongside his young daughter in an ordinary, but fatal road accident whilst out buying fish and chips with his children.

We had a chap called Reg holidaying with us. He was a train driver with a Suzuki GS1000E fitted with a large red after market fairing. One Ball had also brought a friend along who he let ride his Triumph 750 Jubilee Bonneville with him on the back. The chap's nickname was Frozzie but unfortunately the poor fellow suffered from a severe case of piles (haemorrhoids). To ease his pain he had inflated a scooter inner tube and tied it across the front of the bike's saddle so his uncomfortable area was suspended over the centre of the tube. On arriving at Mrs Crowling's that year the bike was parked outside on the pavement and regularly drew a crowd all trying to figure out the purpose of the inner tube. After a few days we decided to inflate it further. Recounting his painful ordeal some years later, Frozzie stated, "I came out and those bastards had inflated it to the size of a bloody tractor tyre". There was an unholy argument going on between One Ball and Frozzie as the bike kept blowing halogen bulbs at £8 a time, a lot of money back them. Halogen bulbs were relatively new to motorcycling, but on this trip eight bulbs blew.

One Ball was furious and accused Frozzie of revving the bike too hard, but in reality I feel the real cause was that you must not touch the glass of the halogen bulb with your fingers or it will quickly blow. A few days later a rear suspension unit on the Triumph broke, so a search for such a unit on the IoM ensued.

Buck had not been able to make the booking that he had already paid for, so had sent his younger brother along in his place. He was riding pillion passenger to Gozy. He became known to us as Baby Buck and owing to the fact that he was much younger could not handle his drink as well as us, so spent much of his time pissed.

Now installed at Ma Crowlin's in '78 I found that along with my girlfriend that year we had a front facing room on the third floor above the communal lounge which was directly over the hotel main entrance. That night we were in the room when I saw Andy pull up on his bike with girlfriend Carol, who he had brought along that year. I filled up the metal waste bin with water. They came up the path and started to climb the four steps leading to the front door. As Andy's foot hit the third step, allowing for a deflection shot, I tipped the whole bucket upside down. Just as they got to the front door there was a loud scream from the darkness. It had been a direct hit. I quickly shut the window and made myself scarce. Unfortunately they had been carrying their skid lids upside down which got soaked inside. The helmets remained wet for the rest of the holiday. I had not bargained on that one.

During the day we did a few laps of the TT course on our bikes. That night we hit a few pubs in Douglas town. Mouth's girl Sue had bought herself a cowboy hat. As we strolled through the town one of a group of people coming the other way stole her hat, one guy putting it on his own head. Mouth told him to give it back. The guy said, "Make me". An altercation ensued between us and them. Mouth was certainly up for "making him". Just as it was all about to kick off we saw two IoM cops approaching on their normal beat from behind the guy. Mouth decided to bait him. He succeeded and as the guy lashed out the cops grabbed him from behind. The cops returned Sue's hat and took the other guy to one side with the warning of "a night in the cells and off the island on the first boat in the morning or on your way".

In the morning in one of the dormitories of six people some of the lads pondered. Reg was in bed but he had packed minimal luggage. "Hey", said Goz quietly and gesturing, "Where's Reg's boots and clothes?" When Reg awoke and got out of his bunk bed he was fully clothed. He was even wearing his big hobnailed boots in bed.

Mad Sunday, for those that have never set foot on the Isle of Man, is the first Sunday of TT week. It is known as Mad Sunday because everyone goes wild and tears around the thirty-seven and three-quarter mile circuit at high speed. The Isle of Man police are pretty lenient on this day only enforcing speed limits in towns and villages along the route. Furthermore the mountain section that runs from Ramsey to Creg ny Baa was made one way only, but I gather that now this is the case for the whole of TT fortnight to stop some of the annual carnage. On Mad Sunday we were out for a run round the circuit when we stopped at the Glen Helen Hotel for a few beers. Sitting on the bank watching the action it was pretty disappointing for Mad Sunday, being more of a procession. "What a bunch of wankers", said Gozy out loud. "Someone should show them how it's done". We continued to lay on the bank watching and drinking beer. About ten minutes later a bike came flying through the corner with a big red fairing. Everything was on the deck including the bottom of the fairing which was being scuffed along the tarmac, and then it was gone. "Fucking hell", we all leapt to our feet. "Hey, that didn't half look like Reg", exclaimed Gozy. We all looked around. Reg had been sitting directly behind us on the bank. Now both Reg and his crash helmet had gone. When we got back to our bikes Reg returned wearing a big grin from ear to ear.

For some strange reason the IoM pubs were only open for one hour on a Sunday evening. "What a bloody silly idea", was the general consensus of the group. "Hey Aitch", said Length. "I know what I'm gonna do. I'm going in bang on opening time and buying six pints". All those in the hotel lounge agreed that's what we were going to do. We had hardly made our decision when Reg came along with a whole armful of bottles of spirits, "For the lemonade boys", he said with a grin as he disappeared. Most of those from his home town did not drink so this was Reg's pet name for them. That night we were first in the queue outside the nearest pub when it opened its doors. We each bought five or six pints and so started our drinking marathon. Reg and the "lemonade boys" had stayed at the hotel. On closing time we made our way back there. The "lemonade boys" were already bladdered. They were falling about all over the place, their speech slurred, most were unable to string a sentence together. Reg had successfully laced their drinks. We grabbed Weasel, stripped off all his clothes, opened the gate and pushed him out onto the pavement. He was staggering up and down the promenade stark naked trying to find his clothes. We started up a chant, "more, more, more". This was soon taken up by the hordes on the seafront. Heads were appearing out of the windows of other hotels all along the seafront and they joined in, "more, more, more". The chant grew louder and louder. Ogri and Baby Buck staggered out of the hotel into the front garden. The same happened to them. They were instantly seized, had their clothes stripped off and were pushed out into the street. Gozy was hanging out of the lounge window pissed as a fart yelling, "What are all those people looking at? Fuck off, just fuck off", and giggling like a girl. The chants grew louder. Alerted by the noise Mrs Crowlin appeared at the front door just as Ogri was staggering up the steps naked to gain access to the hotel. She tried to shut him out. "Get out, get out, you dirty beast!" Ogri was pushing the door from outside trying to get in and Mrs Crowlin was the other side trying to shut him out. Feeling sorry for him Spud joined in. He pushed the door open just enough for Ogri to wriggle through the gap and past Mrs Crowlin. With a quick, "Thank you, Ma'am", he staggered up the stairs, his manhood slapping from leg to leg. Mr. Crowlin appeared at this point wearing a pair of silk pyjamas and asked what the hell was going on. Weasel and Baby Buck had returned to the garden looking for their clothes. We had thrown them over the fence into the garden of the hotel next door. Weasel spotted his. He climbed on the three feet high wall and scaled the iron railings. Pissed as he was, he still had the presence of mind to gently lift his ball sack over the pointed railings as he went over the top. He and Buck managed to retrieve their clothes and eventually get them back on. The rest of us were in the garden laughing about the incident when the cops arrived. "OK, we know that you were involved by that stupid grin on your faces, so where's the nude party that's been going on on the lawn?" We denied any knowledge of such an event. "OK, any more of that sort of behaviour and you will all be off the Island on the first boat in the morning." Later that night in their six man dormitory Ogri leant out of his top bunk and was sick. Gozy, who was still pissed, slurred, "That will teach you, you bloody piss head" until he saw where the vomit was going directly downwards into Gozy's own motorcycle boots. I went into their room the next morning to find a disgruntled Gozy with his arms folded standing over Ogri who was clearly still suffering badly from a major hangover slowly scrubbing away at Gozy's bike boots over the sink.

The next night we were down in Douglas town in a restaurant

when Baby Buck came by. He was so pissed he was crawling along on all fours. We banged on the window and stuck our fingers up at him. He tried to crawl into the restaurant but it had a swing door which swung back shutting his neck in the door, so we had to rescue him.

Later, back at Ma Crowlin's attic dormitory, One Ball jumped out of bed. "I'm going to be sick". "Well, don't be sick in here, be sick out of the window", was the urgent reaction of the others. One Ball slid up the sash cord attic window. Being an attic room the hotel guttering ran across the outside of the window. As he leaned out, vomiting, One Ball clutched hold of the guttering for support. The guttering support brackets must have been rotten as all of a sudden the guttering gave way and all the cast iron guttering along the side of the hotel broke free. Falling three storeys it smashed to pieces with a terrific clatter in the alleyway below. Immediately all the dogs in the near neighbourhood started barking furiously. Whoops!

When you decide where you are going to watch the TT racing from each day it is always wise to spectate from a point that has another exit access road to it so that if you wish you can move elsewhere during or between racing. Failure to do so means you are stuck at that same spectator point until the roads re-open when racing has finished for the day. The roads are re-opened by a marshal's "Roads Open" car (a car with a large sign on the roof). As it speeds past each viewing point barriers are opened and the masses of bikes flood out onto the circuit, all going hell for leather, usually in the direction of Douglas. It is a dangerous time with so many massed bikes all tightly packed and travelling at high speed together and I have witnessed a couple of incidents where someone has gone down taking another four or five bikes down the road with them. TT racing on closed public roads of course can only be described as extremely spectacular.

TT week done for 1978 we all set off home. It was getting dark when we rolled off the ferry. We found a nearby garage with a queue, eventually got fuelled up and set off. Geoff was leading as we had found out on the way that at seventy to eighty miles per hour his Kawasaki S2 triple two-stroke was only able to make sixty-five miles on a tankful of fuel before going on reserve. After a few fuel stops the time was approaching three o'clock in the morning and the sky was beginning to lighten. I was fighting hard to stay awake until the next fuel stop where we would take a break for food and coffee. When you get a lot of varied motorcycles together all travelling at different revs but at a constant speed on a motorway, the combined noise resonates into a rhythmic pattern of sound, further lulling you to sleep, vrooma... vrooma... vrooma and you really struggle to keep your eyes open at that time in the morning. I had set my trip meter at the last fuel stop so I knew that Geoff would be stopping at the next services. Suddenly Geoff swerved violently into the empty right-hand lane. In my tiredness I had not been quick enough to avoid the obstacle. I hit a lorry inner tube that had been laying in the road at eighty miles per hour. The tube was no longer a circle, but was one whole length of rubber about six feet long. I looked behind to see if Gozy had hit it, only to see that my bike had thrown it into the air. It had caught Gozy squarely round the neck at eighty mph and was flapping out both sides like a giant scarf. It had caught Gozy completely by surprise, the sheer weight of the inner tube had pulled him backwards on the bike, opening the throttle and instantly increasing his speed. I opened up and accelerated into the next lane to get out of his way. Buck on the back leaned forward and was grappling with the inner tube. I was killing myself laughing as I watched the situation unfold as the pair wrestled with the long expanse of flapping rubber. Buck eventually managed to pull the tube from Gozy's neck, but as they kicked it away it wrapped around Gozy's leg, dragging his foot from the footrest. Gozy was bent right forward across the handle-bars with one leg right back and the inner tube flapping wildly behind them, whilst still wrapped around his leg. Eventually they managed to free Gozy's leg and kick the tube away. I roared with laughter for the next ten miles, all the way to the service stop.

We pulled into the services laughing about what had happened, all except Geoff, who being in front, had not seen it at all. We got some food and several strong coffees each as we sat there in a tired daze. Suddenly there was an angry shout at the till, "Don't get me no bloody milk for my coffee then Frozzie you bastard". Looking over we saw One Ball, his foot tipped over to one side, he was struggling to walk. He had what looked like a wing of rubber sticking out of the side of his boot. One heel had melted on the bike's exhaust into a wing-like shape which stuck out from his boot by a couple of inches. He was in a foul mood. The bike had blown another halogen headlamp bulb. He dropped the milk for his coffee on the floor and stamped on it. When we came out it was daylight. Somewhat now refreshed we refuelled and continued our journey. The food and strong coffee, along with these amusing incidents, had certainly woken us up.

In late 1978 and early 1979 there had been a fuel tanker drivers' pay dispute which had led to strikes and shortages. For the '79 TT trip Grizzly in his infinite wisdom had phoned the AA automobile organisation to check on the fuel situation. He was informed that there was plentiful fuel supplies at least on motorways. By this time we had left the Black Horse and were drinking at The Castle Inn in the Bay. The pub landlord was an excellent chap named Miles. For this trip it was decided to all meet at The Castle and leave for the Island from there. We had three couples from the town of Heathfield riding with us, led by a biker known as Wildman. As the pub began to fill up Wildman and his merry band arrived. They brought with them three large

224

heavy duty plastic sacks which they brought into the pub and stood in the fireplace. The fire was unlit at this time. After a while Miles became inquisitive about the contents of the sacks. "Hey, Wildman, what have you got in those sacks?" "Twelve gallons of petrol Miles, all in one gallon cans," replied Wildman. "What the..." Miles exploded, "Get that bloody stuff out of my pub... now!" We all set off with the girls on the backs of the Heathfield bikes, each carrying a sack on their laps. The Heathfield boys would streak ahead and every thirty or forty miles we would come across them refuelling their three bikes with a can or two and throwing the empty cans over the hedge. Then they would come hacking past again only to repeat the same action over and over again until all of their cans were used up.

By this time Bar Steward had moved to Eastcote in West London. As he didn't have a bike at that time he phoned me and asked if I could fix him up with a spare seat for the trip. He said he wanted to find some crumpet on the Island. I laughed and said he wouldn't, as unattached women were in a serious minority on the Isle of Man, as TT racing was a man's sport, but then perhaps, I should have known better. I fixed a ride for him with Ogri's mate Malcolm as he was a safe and steady, no frills rider so on the way to the Island we took a detour to pick him up. We had hardly arrived at Mrs Crowlin's and while we were sitting in the front garden, a young girl walked past with a dog. She was eating a burger. Bar Steward leaned over the wall and said, "Let's have a bit". She laughed and held the burger out to him. He told her he didn't mean the burger. Twenty minutes later she was up in his room and her dog was running around locked in the front garden. This soon set a pattern, as in the ten days that we were on the Island, he was to have several different women in his room. Poor Walrus had the misfortune to share the room with him. He spent half the night saying, "For God's sake Bar Steward get some sleep". One woman said, "He knows what we are doing". Bar Steward replied, "Don't worry about him, he's pissed".

The first few girls were obviously more casual acquaintances as after five days he met a divorcee and spent the rest of the ten day holiday with her. By then Walrus had had enough of sleepless nights. We all went to a bike event at The Palace Lido further along the seafront. While Bar Steward was getting some drinks Walrus stole the room key from Steward's leather jacket pocket. Bar Steward got up to leave and said they would see us back at the hotel later. Walrus was beside himself laughing a he waved the key around, saying that Bar Steward wouldn't be getting any that night. When the event finished we made our way back to the hotel. As we arrived back Bar Steward was leaving with the divorcee. Walrus got the room key and fob out of his pocket and called out to Bar Steward waving the key in the air. Bar Steward reached into his jacket, pulling out a huge bunch of keys, like a jailer's key ring. He called back, "Walrus", jangling the whole bunch of keys at him. He had done a raid on the cleaner's cupboard and he had a key to every room in the hotel on that ring. Walrus was agasp. "You... you... bastard!" Everyone there fell about laughing.

The next morning we decided to put in some laps of the TT circuit. Bar Steward wanted to get in amongst the action to take some photos, so he asked if he could get a ride on the pillion of Ogri's bike. Ogri agreed, he had recently bought a new Suzuki GS1000ET. After a quick lap of the circuit we arrived back in Douglas. Bar Steward was as white as a sheet. His camera was swinging wildly on its strap around his neck and he was gripping onto the grab rail for grim death. We pulled up and he took his helmet off. "Well... I thought I might take a few photos, but not at that fucking speed". Ogri had hit 130 mph across the mountain section. The man was a nervous wreck. That night we went to the Hawaiian Bar on the prom. When we got there they were charging an exorbitant amount to get in, so Bar Steward said, "If we have a whip round to get me in, I will get you all in for free". We all agreed. Bar Steward told us all to wait by a door in an alley. After about five minutes the double doors burst open and we all rushed into the darkened room, scattering amongst the crowds of people already in the bar. As the doors had burst open daylight had flooded into the bar and every bouncer in the venue had made a dash for the open doorway—but they were too late. They caught no one. Once inside we all got our drinks separately and then slowly met up again inside.

Next day Wildman ran into the back of Markie (one of his own Heathfield crew). Wildman's front disc brake acted like a buzz saw and cut an inch long groove into the back of Markie's silencer. That evening we were back at the hotel. Mouth and myself were in Bar Steward and Walrus's room. This was the same room that I had previously, which was directly above the main hotel door and the lounge. Wildman was out on the promenade discussing the damage with Markie. The dinner bell rang. Anne, Wildman's girlfriend rushed out and shouted to him that it was meal time. I told Bar Steward how I had soaked Andy and Carol the year before with water from this very window. Bar Steward filled the metal litter bin with water and we waited for Wildman. As he made his way up the path I told Bar Steward to wait until his foot hit the third step and turn the bin upside down. This he did. All three of us hung out of the third floor window and watched the water go down. Wildman just crested the top step to enter the hotel when the water hit him. It was a direct hit right in the centre of his head. He completely vanished for a second or two under the weight of the water, which fanned outwards as it hit his head. We shut the window quickly and scarpered. Those already in the dining room were startled to see Wildman burst in soaked to the skin and shout to Anne, "Give me the fucking key". Later he came back but had not dried himself. The young waitress served his soup and he sat there scowling at everyone with his hair dripping into his soup, topping up the bowl as fast as he drank it with his spoon. It was one of the funniest things we had seen for a long time, but we were under no illusion that he would be out to get the culprits. From then on you could not get in or out of the hotel without risking a soaking from Bar Steward's window. If you were leaving the hotel you would run down the hall, out of the front door and jump the four steps to the pathway. More often than not the water would hit the ground behind you. Coming in you would keep a keen eye on that open upstairs window before making a sudden dash for it up the steps and throwing yourself through the front doorway. Suddenly... whoosh... down would come the water. On one occasion Mrs Crowlin happened to be near the front door and those in the upstairs window suddenly got a glimpse of an angry glare from a rattled Mrs Crowlin and she stared upward from the main doorway trying to identify the culprits.

In the evening there was a knock on Bar Steward's door. A woman's voice said, "This is Mrs Crowlin, open this door at once. I know you have got a woman in there." Unsure if this was genuine, Bar Steward opened the door just a couple of inches to peer out, jumping back suddenly as a jet of tomato ketchup almost hit him in the eye. It was Wildman and his girl Anne out for revenge. Next day Bar Steward went to the joke shop and bought some stink bombs, planning a revenge attack on Wildman on our last night on the Island. Earlier in the week Markie's girlfriend had written a note asking Grasscut to meet her secretly and in private. She had pushed the note under his door. Grasscut ignored the note, but kept it.

Out on our last night we were down in Douglas town when we

decided to go to The Cave night club. The Cave was at the other end of the promenade nearest to Oncan, so we decided to get on a horse tram which run regularly along Douglas seafront. A tram was just leaving so we ran and got on it, that is all except Gibbo who was lagging slightly behind the rest of us. The tram set off, the Shire horse trotting away up front. Gibbo was running behind trying to catch up, with us all yelling encouragement. He was soon out of breath and had just about given up when the horse tram stopped at the next stop. Gibbo put on a spurt again, intent on making a two hundred yard dash to catch us up. He almost caught up when the tram set off again. He ran almost the length of the promenade that night in pursuit of that tram. The night club was full of bikers. To this day I clearly remember the whole of the dance floor being packed with bikers all shoulder rocking to *Sultans of Swing* by Dire Straits including ourselves, the dancers all being in perfect timing. Later, a young Irishman came over and asked when the fight was to begin. We asked, what fight? He said that the Heathfield girls had told him that we had been picking on their boyfriends and they needed help against the rest of us. I told Wildman what was going on and he exploded. All of us guys went over and confronted them, telling them they had been duped, we were all friends, so fuck off. There was a lot of bad feeling as we made our way back to Crowlins that night as we tried to understand what was going on. Grasscut took the note to Wildman, who passed it on to Markie. Markie and his girlfriend had a big fight in their room over it. Wildman accosted Anne about her part in the fiasco and a domestic incident broke out between them too. Bar Steward, in his room with the divorcee, heard all the commotion and thought an attack on Wildman had commenced, so he grabbed his stink bombs and rushed downstairs. He burst into Wildman's room scattering the stink bombs in the middle of their argument. Wildman grabbed him and they grappled with each other. Anne yelled, "Fuck off, fuck off". She picked up a crash helmet and whacked Bar Steward across his bare back with it as hard as she could. Wildman spun round and sent her flying. Suddenly Mr. Crowlin was in the doorway in his pink pyjamas demanding to know what was going on. Finally, all went quiet and we all settled down to get some sleep. We were leaving tomorrow.

In the morning I went out to my bike and checked how much fuel was in the tank. I decided to put in a couple of final laps of the TT circuit to burn off some of the excess fuel. Each time we had been out on the circuit I had been pleasantly surprised that not a lot had got past us. I contributed this to the fact that in Dilly, Fred, Den and the others we had good teachers or perhaps nobody wanted to make a real race of it. This day was different. I was hurtling across the mountain across the tank when four or five bikes got past me. They then slowed down, waving me past and off we went again. They got past me again. It was then that I noticed their registration plates were both MAN and MN. They were Isle of Man registration plates and so they were residents here. After a few more games of cat and mouse they all waved to me and turned off into the streets of Douglas. I arrived back at our hotel just as Wildman and his Heathfield friends pulled up from the opposite direction.Wildman took his lid off. "Well we are all fuelled up and ready to go". I was astounded, "You what?" "Us, we have just fuelled up. We are just going to load our gear on our bikes". "They will take all that fuel from you on the dock. They will pump your tank out. Don't you remember on the way here. They pumped any excess from the bike tanks and gave us all a 'Tanks Pumped Out' sticker". Wildman was adamant, "They won't get our fuel". I assured him that they would. We got our bikes loaded for the off. The Heathfield crew appeared. Each girl was carrying a full carrier bag in each hand. "I'd like to see them take it now", said Wildman confidently. We all mounted up as one big group and rode down joining the queue at the ferry terminal. The queue moved forward. A handful of us were waved forward to board the ferry, the rest being held back at the entrance to a loading shed by an employee with a walkie-talkie radio. We rode onto the ferry, parked the bikes and made our way to the top deck. We hung over the rail to watch the rest loading. Suddenly there was a terrific roar. Wildman stormed along the dock at speed and onto the ferry. Anne was running behind screaming abuse at him as she ran along the quay in her tight green Kawasaki leathers and knee length high heeled boots, her long blonde hair blowing out behind her. We on the top deck started yelling abuse at her and wolf whistling, "Go on, go on, run you bitch". Anne was angry, looking up as she ran she screamed, "Just fuck off you wankers", she stuck her fingers up at us. Later we found out what had happened. Determined that the Steam Packet Company would not get any of their fuel the Heathfield group had raided all the hotel bins for every container they could find to put fuel in. They had washed out all the containers and filled them up with petrol, which they then put in plastic carrier bags. Some of our group were held up on the dock, with the Heathfield group in front due to load. Those behind noticed drops of fuel dripping from the bottom of the carrier bags. Some of the containers they used were plastic and the petrol had melted them. As they dissolved the bag bottoms fell out. All the glass containers smashed to pieces all over the dock. The walkie-talkie man yelled "What's that?" Wildman shouted, "Bloody petrol, what do you think it is?" He had given the bike a handful of throttle and cleared off at high speed leaving Anne to chase behind. Walkie-talkie man had gone into overdrive on his radio. "There's petrol on the dock... petrol on the dock... severe fire risk... petrol on the dock!" With perhaps ten gallons of spilled fuel on the quayside, panic ensued, "Severe fire risk... put that bloody cigarette out". After a major clear up involving several fire extinguishers, the rest were finally permitted to load. They had certainly managed to cause a stir.

The ferry left port with us queued outside the bar waiting for it to open. After a while at sea we got a round in. Mouth started ribbing Wildman about the petrol on the dock fiasco. Wildman, somewhat agitated did no more than dip his fingers in his pint of beer and splashed beer in Mouth's face. Mouth had just bought a ham sandwich and he retaliated instantly. He threw the sandwich at Wildman. Now ham sandwiches are not particularly well known for their aerodynamic qualities, and this one was no different. It broke up in mid air. One slice of bread went to the left and the other to the right, while the slice of ham carried straight on over Wildman's shoulder. Behind Wildman was a huge Scotsman with long curly black hair down to his shoulders and a big bushy beard. He was stretched out fast asleep and snoring in a wooden armchair. He was the sort of Scot you could imagine tossing a caber in the Highland Games. He was a fine, tough physical looking specimen. With a plop the ham landed across Scotsman's beard just below his mouth. "Arrghh..." with an enormous bellow like an enraged bull he awakened and staggered in a daze to his feet, where he stood glowering around the room at everyone, the slice of ham still hanging, clinging to his beard. Everyone was sniggering and looking away, trying not to laugh. Eventually, not able to find the culprit, he snatched the ham from his beard. He threw it to the ground and returned to his armchair. "That was your fault Wildman", said Mouth, slightly peeved oer the loss of his sandwich.

CHAPTER TWENTY-SIX

Thrills and spills

ONE sunny summer's evening we rode out to a nearby pub called The Rose Cottage Inn. For a few weeks now Sprogg's younger brother Steve had been turning up at The Black Horse with a mate in his mate's car. We had ridden to The Rose Cottage on our bikes and they arrived later by car. Being a fine evening we were all sitting outside on the grass in the beer garden. Several families and some local people were there also taking in the evening sunshine. After a while Funky decided he was going to leave. He fired up his bike but instead of just riding away he made a right turn heading further up the lane which was a dead end, then he turned around and put a flyer past the pub on his way out. Later, Walrus was leaving and he did the same. As he was turning around up the lane Steve's mate became physically excited. Walrus had started his run when Steve's mate suddenly shouted, "Let's jump out in front of him". Before anyone could stop him he did just that. Those present could not believe their eyes and ears. He leapt out into the road in front of Walrus sticking his fingers up at him as he hurtled towards the pub. Walrus could not have avoided him. There was a sudden violent thud. The impact spun him around like a top, then he hit the deck. Walrus's bike went into a violent speed wobble which used up the whole width of the road to get the bike back under control. We ducked as an unidentified object flew through the air skimming over our heads, spinning wildly like a helicopter blade before it disappeared. Steve's mate was laying in the road bleeding from the impact as well as contact with the road surface, but he was conscious. A shocked Walrus returned. He asked what had happened. We told him that this crazy bastard had jumped out in front of him, and that he, Walrus, had collided with him. Everyone rushed to the fallen man's aid. As we helped him up, battered and bruised, he blurted out, "Oh, I am an idiot". I told him, "You bloody well are". One of the shocked onlookers in the pub garden called out, "That will teach you all not to mess about". We shrugged our shoulders, we felt we could not be held responsible for the actions of one total moron with a death wish. The casualty's left leg was already swelling up and was showing signs of severe bruising, as were his ribs. There was blood on his lips. Unsure if he had internal injuries someone drove him hastily to hospital, but, one of his shoes could not be found. After he was whisked away we discussed the event. No one could believe he could have been so stupid. Someone, I cannot now remembe who stated, "Well, we can't understand why the hell he did it, but he sure as hell deserves fifty points for the entertainment factor". Everyone laughed heartily; he became known as "Fifty Points" from then on. A sequel to this event occurred the following spring when I happened to drop in to The Rose Cottage again. On entering I ordered a pint of beer. The landlord said nothing but simply turned away. He came back and placed a white but mouldy green trainer on the bar in front of me. He looked me up and down, but said nothing, as if waiting for a reaction. I looked at the shoe and then at him. A few seconds passed in silence, then he asked in a somewhat aggravated voice, "Do you know where I found that?" I told him I had no idea, he came back with, "Up in my bloody guttering, that's where! Right above the pub door where all the water was overflowing onto my customers every time it rained hard". He gestured to the pub door, then continued, "I had to get my ladders out to get it down". He scowled at me, poured me a pint of beer and threw the shoe in the bin. I drank my beer and left. That bloke never did have much of a sense of humour.

Luck was not on Walrus's side that season. On a windy and stormy day he was riding along the coast road to Eastbourne. Conditions were atrocious, the wind being so strong that he had to lay into it along the straight to maintain a straight line. He came across roadworks with the usual safety rope around it with warning streamers attached, blowing about in the wind. The rope was held in place by metal stakes driven into the road surface. This was the normal set up in the 1970s in pre-Health and Safety days. A length of rope had come free and was blowing around in the strong breeze. As Walrus rode past a savage gust of wind blew. The rope snaked out like a bullwhip, whipping twice around his neck, dragging him off the back of his motorcycle. It could have easily broken his neck. The tension on the rope pulled the metal holding stake clean out of the ground. The bike continued on its way riderless for some distance before crashing further along the road. A while later Walrus took Daffodil the florist out for a spin on the back of his Norton Commando, but they slid off on a bend, breaking Daff's arm. As she was dating Grasscut at that time Grass was not at all impressed—but another riderless motorcycle incident, this time involving Grasscut, was soon to follow, but in the meantime here is another amusing incident involving another Norton Commando.

Freshers had bought himself a Paul Dunstall café racer Norton Commando. It really looked the business with its clip-on handlebars, big aluminium racing petrol tank and seat, rearset footrests and upswept megaphone silencers. He let me take it for a blast. I saw over 120mph on the clock on the A22. It was the fastest I had ever been on a motorcycle at that time and the first time that I had seen 120mph on the clock. On a warm sunny afternoon a group of us went into town and parked in a car park.

When we left we rode up to the barrier and one person paid. As the barrier went up there was a terrific roar as we all took off, that is all except Freshers who had been a little too slow getting the Norton into gear. As we all streaked away I looked back to see Freshers dragging his bike from under the barrier with the attendant out of his kiosk and yelling at him. Later we heard from Freshers that the attendant had rushed from his kiosk shouting, "You thought you were a clever bunch of bastards did you? Well, now you can pay for them all". He made Freshers pay for everyone... serves him right for being too slow getting away. Later, Length bought a raced up Norton Commando resplendent, as it was, with it's bright yellow paintwork. It really looked the nuts and so became known as the "Flying Banana".

On a summer Saturday a few of the lads decided to head for the beach at Eastbourne, on this occasion passing through Willingdon. Worm was leading, with Grass following, the rest of the group being behind. As they arrived at The Triangle there was a group of blonde attractive Norwegian or Swedish foreign students waiting for a bus at the bus stop on the left-hand side. The Triangle is so named because it is a double road junction of that shape of which the main A22 stretch to Eastbourne makes up the longest side. Grass was looking across, eyeing up the girl students. When he looked back the traffic had slowed dramatically. He was almost upon Worm and could not stop in time to avoid him. The handlebar of Grass's bike hit Worm firmly in the back, catapulting Worm's bike forward and sending Worm flying from the machine. Worm was sliding down the road on his backside watching his Suzuki continuing up the centre of the road as straight as a die between two lanes of opposing traffic. He was struggling to get to his feet before he had even stopped sliding in order to pursue the wayward motorcycle. Leaping up, he chased after his bike. The bike was losing speed now and was veering to the right. There was a Citroen 2CV coming down the hill and the Suzuki was on a head-on collision course with it. The Citroen driver panicked, stamping on his brakes he slewed hard left, turning into Gorringe Valley Road to avoid the riderless bike. The motorcycle, having lost momentum, flopped to the right and followed him in. The bike engine then stalled and the Suzuki fell over to the left with its footrest over the kerb where it came to a rest almost upright. A gasping Worm arrived on foot, having pursued his bike up the centre of the road between two lines of traffic for around a hundred yards or more. The Citroen driver was amazed, "Good God, I could not believe what I was seeing. First a riderless bike coming at me head on so I swerved in here and it followed me. Now its just sitting there propped up on the kerb". The others arrived in total disbelief. The bike was completely undamaged, not coming into contact with anything, not even the road surface. There was much laughter and merriment in "the cheeks" that night as Worm and Grass recounted the afternoon's events to a lively audience. With further reference to The Triangle and on hearing about this impending book, I have received the following amusing dialogue from someone, now a respectable businessman and member of society who wishes to remain anonymous, other than by his initials of DJP.

A memory from the vaults

WITH very fond memories I walked away from motorbikes in 1978. I had enormous luck on several occasions and survived many accidents with little more than a bruises and grazes. Having just got engaged I realised I had too much to live for. I owed it to my fiancee to get out of biking while I was ahead. After all my father-in-law to be had just paid the deposit on our wedding reception.

A little earlier I had pulled out from Willingdon Triangle onto the A22. An Austin Maxi was indicating left and started to turn off the main road into the one I was leaving. I then looked left to check that the A22 was clear, and pulled out. I had failed to spot that there was a Mini tucked right up the rear of the Maxi. It ploughed into my bike, its headlamp just missing my knee. Later, Kiddie delivered me home badly bruised. He reassured my distraught mother with the immortal words, *"Don't worry luv, you're not a man until you have been down the road on your arse a few times"*. My mother seemed to derive great comfort from this.

Anyway this memory tells the story of flying through the air yards above the road.

One evening I was drinking with friends in a pub way out in the sticks. Tony had taken me there as a pillion on his Suzuki. Tony had made a single pint last all evening. He said that was all he wanted as he had a nasty headache that a couple of Aspirin was not shifting. When it came time to leave I noticed that Tony did not seem to be himself and looked pissed even though I knew he had only had one pint.

We left the pub in the darkness at great speed with mates trailing behind. As always to minimise wind resistance, I was tucked close to Tony with my head down. I did not see that we were heading into a tight left-hand bend far too fast to get around it. I vaguely remember us leaning to the left before the rear wheel hit the grass at the edge of the road.

Some say adrenalin causes it, but in an accident situation time momentarily freezes. What developed next seemed to happen in slow motion. One second I was sitting on the bike, the next I was flying through the air backwards. Unusually, flying through the air backwards nine feet above the ground was something I was well used to having been Sussex Youth Pole Vault Champion (I still have the medal to prove it).

In the few seconds you were in the air when vaulting you had to manoeuvre your body to get over the bar, while always preparing for your landing. Winning the medal at Withdean Stadium in Brighton, I had the benefit of landing in four feet of foam rubber. I would not have that beneath me this time. However, miraculously, the saving angels were there to catch me.

238

Flying backwards at great speed I hit shrubbery... thick hedge. I remember well the sound of branches breaking as I flew through it. Like the parachute on a drag car the hedge slowed me down. Falling out of it I was delivered gently on my backside into the grass of the field beyond.

Without a single bruise I picked myself up and tried to find my way back through the hedge in the darkness but without success. It was some time before I found a gap. By the time I got to the road our mates had arrived and had started to search for Tony. On arriving they had spotted the bike but without its two passengers. We found Tony some distance ahead in a ditch, bruised but no bones broken, the bike being the main casualty.

My dad was up when we got home. "A good evening?" he enquired. "Oh just a quiet evening in a country pub", I replied. I shared a room with my brother in those days and told him the tale. It was then that I realised I had a bit of a burn on my ankle, possibly where it was on the exhaust for a second, but otherwise I was fine. Once again, how lucky I was. In addition to giving up biking I also stopped pole vaulting, but in both cases those fond memories will be with me forever.   DJP

One morning I was working on a milk round. I was covering a round as a holiday relief, driving an electric milk float out in the countryside near the village of Chalvington. I was approaching a tight right-hand bend when a young police motorcyclist hurtled around the corner from the opposite direction on a Honda CB200. In an instant my motorcycling experience told me he was going much too fast. He would not make the corner and was on a collision course to shoot across the road and hit me head on. I stood hard on the brake pedal and slewed the vehicle as far left as I could, bumping along the grass. Seeing me, he grabbed a handful of front brake, locking the front wheel. He shot across the front of the milk float and across the grass verge, missing me by only eighteen inches or so. His locked front wheel dropped neatly into the roadside ditch stopping the bike's slide in an instant and in doing so kicked the rear of the bike up into the air. The last I saw of the cop was the black arse of his police uniform as it disappeared over the five feet high hedge into a field. This cop had been riding as the lead bike on a police training course. A second trainee managed to pull up in time. He had the instructor riding behind, following him on a police Commando. I was beside myself, I roared with laughter. I jumped out and asked if I should call the police? The other trainee was trying hard not to laugh but the instructor remained ashen faced. He was not at all amused. A few minutes later the cop who had crashed reappeared. He had been unable to find a gap in the hedge, so had to walk further down and climb over a gate to escape from the field. I was just about to leave when the instructor accosted me, "Hang on a minute, I will need your name and address as a witness as we have to put in a report to verify any damage to our machines". Still chuckling I went on my way. It was one of the funniest things I had seen in ages.

That weekend we were out for a run around the countryside as usual. After a quick blast across Pevensey Marshes we took the road from Windmill Hill towards Heathfield. A few up front were setting a fast pace as usual. This was a road we had often ridden before. Approaching a left-hand bend Spud suddenly shot past me and another couple of bikes ahead at great speed. I was amazed as this bend was deceptive. On the face of it the bend looked more of a curve than it was. As if to bite the unwary it suddenly tightened up dramatically into a major bend. Surely Spud had remembered this... but apparently not. He had committed himself. Suddenly Spud realised his big mistake, he sat up, straightened his line and braked like crazy. On the tightest part of the bend there was a field gate on the other side of the road which fortunately for him was left open. Tractors had obviously been in and out of the field harvesting the hay crop so there were two dusty, dried out tyre tracks across the green verge, leading into the field. Spud shot straight across the road hitting one of these tracks and with both wheels locked he threw up a lot of dust. A family had driven into the field and set up a picnic just inside the gate. Their car was parked inside to the left of the gate. The family all jumped to their feet as Spud flew between them. He tore across their picnic mat and picnic taking it all with him under his locked wheels, before he disappeared from our view in the dust cloud. Without further ado Spud spun the bike around in the field and rode out again back across the picnic. With a quick glance left and right he gunned the bike onto the road, leaving behind an array of angry faces glaring after him from the dust storm as it subsided. Nearing Rushlake Green we came across another group of riders. It was our cousin Mauler out for a ride with his mates. They joined us and a tear-up ensued. Further on we came across a procession being directed by police. A policeman made a dash for his vehicle to give chase, but it was a no hoper, our lead being too great, but just in case we did a quick dash to the farm run by our uncle, where we hid in the collecting yard. Here Mauler's mate Pete made a confession. He hadn't got any insurance he said as he was riding a 500cc Triumph on only a provisional licence. On the way home we were approaching the dairy where I worked. I was aware that roadworks had been carried out on the bend just before the dairy and there was a ramp in the road surface there. Andy was leading on our approach and I knew he was going too fast, so I tried to get past to warn him of the danger. Unfortunately, he thought I was racing him and so increased his speed even further. He tore into the bend, hit the ramp, took off and went flying down the road on his backside. What an exciting and eventful afternoon it had been.

At that time a number of us played darts for The Black Horse darts team. On this particular evening we were playing a match against The Yew Tree Inn, who were playing at home. We rode over to The Yew Tree on our motorcycles and as Hoot the photographer also played darts for The Black Horse he rode over with us. Hoot was a steady rider. It was a good social evening and I guess Hoot had too much to drink because as we donned our gear to leave Hoot announced loudly, "Right, let's see how quick you boys can really ride". This statement was like waving a red flag to a bull, so we all set off at a fast rate in the direction of "the cheeks". Unfortunately Hoot never arrived, someone travelling that road found him and his bike where he had left the road and somersaulted into a ditch. This was to be the death knell for his motorcycling career as his damaged Honda was soon sold off in favour of another car. His brief foray into the motorcycling world was prematurely over.

It was a very foggy night when we came out after an evening at the pub. Bar Steward and girlfriend Linda left first, setting off home into the gloom, the fog being so thick you could hardly see your hand in front of your face. With his visor steamed up, Steward flicked it open. Chugging along in the dense fog with such poor visibility he started singing at the top of his voice. Linda joined in. Eventually they arrived at Steward's house, rode down the drive and parked the bike. Just as they walked to the door a police car pulled up outside on the road. Somewhere along the road they must have passed a parked up police car. "Excuse me sir, were you singing?" called out the cop. "Us singing," replied Steward, laughing, "you must be joking... goodnight," as they walked into the house. "That was a close call," said Steward shutting the door behind them.

Late on a Sunday evening a couple from our group arrived at The Black Horse. The girl seemed pretty fed up, complaining to the other girls present about her boyfriend's behaviour that evening. This is the basis of what she said. With her parents away for the evening she had cooked her boyfriend a lovely meal after which the couple retired to the bedroom for a mammoth love making session. Hardly had they finished when her boyfriend looked at his watch, jumping to his feet with a matter of urgency he blurted out, "Fuck me, is that the time? If you get your knickers on quick girl we can make "the cheeks" for a quick one before closing time'. Such was the magnetic pull of the place.

One of our young cousins who had the nickname of Chip had recently taken up schoolboy motocross. With not much else happening that afternoon Geoff and myself had ridden over to Billingshurst to watch the racing and to give him some encouragement. After the meeting we set off home together on our bikes. With its twists and turns, up and downhill slopes the A272, when empty, would be a good road for motorcyclists, but on this Sunday afternoon it was not. We had been following a line of cars, unable to overtake, when we arrived at a length of straight. We instantly checked behind, indicated and gunned our bikes to overtake. On starting our manoeuvre a Range Rover at the rear of the line of traffic suddenly swerved to overtake without looking or indicating. It almost collided with my machine. It was a crazy situation as there was not a long enough straight for a car to overtake the other cars. I hit the horn button hard and the driver swerved back in to the left. So violent was the manoeuvring that the Range Rover went up on two wheels. I quickly hurtled through the gap. At this point the car driver over-corrected, swerving to the right. The Range Rover flipped. Rolling over a hedge it came to rest in a field. I looked around, Geoff was nowhere to be seen. I screeched to a halt and parked my bike by the roadside. I ran back to the flattened hedge looking for Geoff. Everything went strangely quiet, the line of traffic having now disappeared into the distance. Unsure of what I might find I climbed through the hedge, afraid that the Range Rover might have rolled over Geoff. In truth, in order to avoid the Range Rover Geoff had also gone through the hedge. I found Geoff and his bike in the field, Geoff was just picking himself up, shocked but uninjured. We ran to the Range Rover which had come to rest upside-down in the field, its V8 engine still running, its bonnet open, the engine filling the bonnet with leaking petrol. There was no time to lose. I was afraid the car would burst into flames at any moment. The lady driver was hanging upside-down in her harness hunched forward with the roof crushed down against her head. I squirmed through the driver's open window. I switched off the cars ignition and released her seatbelt. She still had trouble getting free, wriggling out between the seat, steering wheel and the crushed in roof. She had a child, a young girl with her, hanging upside-down in the child's seat in the back. Geoff crawled in, released the child and carried her to safety. The girl asked her mum why they were in a field. At that point there was a shout from the hedgerow. It was my uncle along with my cousins Karen and Chip. They had seen my parked bike, the skid marks and the flattened down hedge. The lady was in a state of complete shock. Geoff's bike was promptly repaired and Geoff received a very nice letter from her husband full of thanks for what we had done for his wife and child "in very trying circumstances that day". In reality we were lucky, it could have been a hell of a lot worse.

Not long after there was another hellish crash. We had met at a pub in Polegate and set off to a pub out towards Lewes. There were about fifteen bikes in total. We left the pub, Mouth was out in front. He was on a flyer with girlfriend Sue riding pillion. I was in second place with Andy behind me, his brother Mawanga next, riding hard on Fred's ex-race-prepared Suzuki Super Six. He was tucked flat down on the tank and right on the tail of Andy's Honda. The rest of the pack were behind us. Approaching a left-hand bend a Hillman Hunter suddenly pulled out of a pub car park right in front of us. Christ, it was tight! In desperation I threw my Honda hard left in an attempt to avoid the back end of the car. I had to use the car park entrance to avoid him, then crank hard right to get back onto the road as the car park tarmac expired. Andy quickly did the same, sticking to my line like glue. There was a terrific bang, I spun around. I have a vivid action snapshot memory to this day. Mawanga and his Suzuki came somersaulting completely over the car, the bike disintegrating in mid-air, parts flying off it. They both hit the tarmac over fifty feet further on, the bike kicking up a shower of sparks as it landed and skidded down the road. Then everything happened at once. The rest of the pack pulled up. A group appeared from the garage opposite and began calling out across the road, "Now you're for it". Another shouted, "I have called the police and the ambulance". Within seconds cars were trying to squeeze out of the pub car park to escape before the police arrived, clearly most would have probably failed a breath test. Gozy's girlfriend was a nurse; she had been riding on Gozy's pillion. She rushed to Mawanga's aid, tending him until the ambulance arrived. Meanwhile Mouth had continued on, unaware of the disaster that had occurred behind him. Suddenly, he pulled up and turned around. Sue asked why. Mouth had had a premonition. "Mawanga has had an accident," he said, returning to find the carnage that had unfolded. He had been strangely correct.

Riding a smaller capacity machine Mawanga had been slip-streaming his brother for extra speed. Tucked as he was, right up the exhaust pipe of his brother's machine, he was so close to Andy that he was a huge blind spot to him. The first instant that Mawanga saw the Hillman was when Andy had suddenly veered hard left through the car park entrance to avoid it. By then he stood no chance of missing the car. He smashed headlong into the rear wheel and wing with both him and the bike being catapulted clean over the car. Mawanga had been extremely lucky. Apart from cuts and bruises he broke his collar bone and one of his wrists. Fred's ex-race bike CJK 96D was no more, but its legend would live on in the memories of time. The road was closed for a while as the ambulance recovered Mawanga and whisked him away whilst the Hillman was removed from the scene. Mawanga was summoned to court for his actions. In evidence it was stated that the collision was so severe that the car's back axle was shifted seventeen inches, allowing the prop shaft to be pulled clean out of the gearbox leaving a large pool of gearbox oil over the road surface. The magistrates, of course, did not look down favourably on this young tearaway, and so dished out the usual harsh penalties; but then, perhaps you could say it was all part of the risks taken as part of an outlaw way of life on the edge of society.

CHAPTER TWENTY-SEVEN

Fights and conquests

IT WAS decided to take a summer weekend trip to the West Country. A number of us loaded our bikes with the usual camping gear, setting off in the direction of Lulworth Cove. Initially Geoff was leading as he was familiar with the route. Geoff flew over what appeared at first glance to be only a slight hump of a hump back bridge... but the other side was a larger drop followed by a left-hand bend. Geoff took off and landed perfectly, lining himself up nicely for the corner, but Spud who was following was caught unawares by the large drop. He and his fully loaded Yamaha landed heavily, the bike breaking into a weave on landing. The bike's handlebars could not have been tight enough as the bars swivelled around with the landing impact. Both Spud's and wife Sue's feet came off the footrests. Having just landed heavily and now sporting a set of dropped handlebars they hurtled into the left-hand bend, somehow managing to scrape around it unscathed. Grass was next. He flew over the bridge, landing perfectly and taking the corner in the same fashion as Geoff had before him.

The rest of the run down was uneventful until we came to make a left-hand turn near Bovington army camp and just up the road from Clouds Hill, the former cottage home of the famous T. E. Lawrence, otherwise known as Lawrence of Arabia. Two hundred yards from Lawrence's cottage in a small roadside car park lies a memorial stone marking a spot on the road where Lawrence met his sad demise, crashing his beloved Brough Superior. He was to die six days later in the army camp hospital without ever regaining consciousness. We came over a rise, the left turn being almost directly following. The first two of us made the turn but Wildman, who was riding with us that day, almost overshot the turning. He stopped in the centre of the road, he just put the bike on full lock to try to get around when Geoff came over the brow at around seventy mph, missing him and his girlfriend Ann by less than two feet. That could have been one hell of a nasty prang.

After a ride down to Swanage we headed back to the Lulworth area where we rode into the Cove and took up residence in the bar of a pub for the evening, where we had a good time. Later, in the dark, we found a remote field to pitch our tents. It was then that Wildman confessed he had not brought a tent with him. He preferred to travel light he said, unencumbered by the weight of a tent, hoping that they could bunk with someone else. The rest were not at all keen on that idea, so it fell to Geoff and myself, who were perhaps a little more sympathetic to their self-induced plight, to squeeze four people into our two man tent. It was a tight squeeze and I was awakened in the morning by Ann's voice... "Take that fucking hat off Pixie". I had fallen asleep with my hat on and she thought it looked like a pixie hat. Glancing over I saw Geoff wedged against the side of the tent with Ann's elbow pressed tightly up under his nose. "For fuck's sake" muttered Geoff, stirring, but still in a sleepy daze. For my part I was firmly squashed between Wildman and the other side of the tent. The strange thing about Ann was that she was deeply religious, attending church at least once a week and yet she could swear like a trooper in a most common voice and also had quite a temper to boot. She was a very attractive girl with long blonde hair and a sleek, curvy figure. Her and Wildman lived in a caravan together in a club car park.

Up and about in the morning I was nursing a nasty hangover. There was some excitement occurring around the bikes. I wandered over. Both Spud's and Grasscut's bikes had small flies in their speedo and rev counter clocks and they were trying to figure out how they managed to get in there. For all intents and purposes the clocks appeared to be sealed units except for where the lighting bulbs were tightly pushed into their rubber bungs which sealed any gaps. It was a mystery indeed.

We broke camp, packed up the bikes and rode back down to the café in Lulworth Cove for breakfast. En route Spud was riding very erratically. He kept revving the bike hard then shutting it down suddenly. He would then snatch the throttle open again and take off. It led to some very jerky riding and all the time he was looking down at the bike's clocks. Suddenly a car in front stopped and he almost ran into the back of it. At the Cove he explained that one of the flies was riding around on the tip of the rev counter needle like it was on a roundabout. Each time he changed gear and the revs fell the fly would hang on as the revs increased again. It was really annoying him so to try to flick the fly from the end of the needle became an obsession. Nursing my hangover I could not face food at that time. As Grass was not hungry either we sat outside the café in the bright sunshine. The place was swarming with wasps, so Grass and I did our best to decimate the wasp population by whipping them out of the air with our silk bike scarves and treading on them. Later the rest came out and took a walk down to the water's edge of the Cove. Feeling more like eating now Grass and I went back in and tucked into a full English breakfast before rejoining the others on the seashore. As we lay there in the sunshine I reflected. It had been a most pleasant and relaxed weekend so far. The rest of the weekend would be no different. I have had a passion for the West Country ever since that trip.

On arriving back home we attended "the cheeks" as normal the following evening. Bear went outside to use the gent's toilets at the rear of the building. Bear was a farmer and a fairly big chap. He was known to be particularly well endowed. Standing at the urinal he was just reading a slogan written on the wall in large capital letters in front of him, "I THOUGHT WANKING WAS A TOWN IN CHINA UNTIL I DISCOVERED SMIRNOFF" when Sprogg came in. Standing next to Bear going about his business Sprogg glanced over and in true Sprogg fashion he ribbed Bear, "Christ Bear you're well hung... how the hell did you get one like that..? do you rub chicken shit on it..? can you get me some..?" Just average Sprogg banter.

Bollocks arrived at the pub and informed everyone present that his faithful Bonneville had to go. It was now burning a bit of oil so he had cleaned and polished the bike and taken it up to Grabbers to get a price on trading it in for a new Suzuki 550. Grabber had given him a price and informed him that the new bike would be ready for collection that Saturday.

On the given day Bollocks duly set off with Pus riding pillion to pick up the new steed. Bollocks decided to give the Bonnie one last caning and all went well until about a mile from the motor-cycle dealership when there was a loud bang and the motor expired. "Oh shit", yelled Bollocks at the top of his voice in exasperation. They dismounted and pushed the dead motorcycle until they reached the final bend. Peering around the corner to make sure the coast was clear they ran for the final hundred yards with the bike and parked it on its centre stand outside.

Going into the dealers as if nothing had happened they found the salesman and completed the necessary paperwork. Bollocks took delivery of the gleaming new motorcycle. Just as they were putting on their riding gear to leave the owner himself came out with an inventory and a customer. Flicking through the pages he cast a hand over the still warm Bonneville. "Ah yes, this one is a recent acquisition. It's so new in fact that its not even on our inventory." "Hurry," said Bollocks to Pus with some urgency, "Let's fuck off quick before he tries to kick it over", and they made good their escape.

Once again, however, Bollocks looked like a fish out of water on his new bike, just as he had on the first day that I had met him while riding his highly polished Suzuki T500. His whole animal aura and dress code just did not fit in with the style or type of motorcycle. It just did not suit him. Before long he had sold the new Suzuki on to Walrus.

A week or two later some of us were sitting at a table outside the café opposite Grabbers when an old BSA chopped 650 twin arrived at the café. It obviously had no stand as the rider propped it up against a nearby lamp post where its oil soaked engine proceeded to drip a pool of oil onto the tarmac. A grubby looking girl on the back dismounted as now did the rider who was of a similar appearance, once he was satisfied his bike was reasonably secure against the post. We were joking amongst ourselves as the couple walked by. "What did you say about me?" the rider suddenly snapped, spinning around. "We didn't say anything about you, we were just laughing amongst ourselves, so fuck off." The couple approached menacingly, "Cos if I thought you were taking the piss out of me I would have to sort you all out," he said confronting us. "Oh yeah, dream on pal." I told him, "Who the hell do you think you are?" Clearly this guy had some form of inferiority complex. While the guy's attention was distracted by me Grass picked up a metal chair and positioned himself directly behind the guy. At the slightest nod from myself Grass would have brought the iron chair crashing down upon his skull, but fortunately this mouth-almighty eventually decided to back off. Grass reluctantly put the chair down. As a final gesture the rider's ropey old bird turned and punched Grass in the face. Grass just laughed it off, just shrugging as it was more of a slap than an actual punch and with no real power behind it. "Sod off you bitch." The couple remounted their battered old chopper and rode away leaving a haze of oily smelling smoke behind them. We were not sorry to see them go. We continued on eating.

A horse and rider passed by on the other side of the road. Bog Wright threw back his head and neighed like a horse. It clearly startled the horse which took off suddenly up the road, crabbing sideways with the lady rider hanging on, trying hard to control it. This was a surprising reaction as this was Bog's party piece. When riding along on his Suzuki he would flip open his visor, throw his head back and neigh—and horses in the fields would answer him.

We rode out to Lydden Circuit in Kent for one of the bigger race meetings of the season. Some of our friends and local riders were racing there. Smed was also there. He was the Travelling Marshal whose task was to ride around after each race to make sure that the track was clear before the start of the next race. Smed had already caused something of a stir colliding with the ACU Steward's car which had come out of the pits onto the track. As the car and bike collided he was thrown over the vehicle in front of all the trackside spectators. His Kawasaki Z1 900 was a write-off. To his surprise his insurance company (Norwich Union) paid out in full as he was not racing or pacemaking at the time. He was able to get another new similar bike.

On the way home from the circuit the usual dust-up occurred, this time with Mac on his Kawasaki Z1, with Ogri, who at that time was riding his Yamaha XS750, and myself on my Honda CB500/4. My smaller, more agile bike, was quicker through the corners, while Mac's Z1 had me on the straights and Ogri struggled to stay with us on his XS750. He didn't keep that bike for long, the extra power needed to power the bike's shaft drive meant that it was no faster than my 500/4 and was less agile. He soon traded it in for a Suzuki GS1000E. We had an amazing race back across the Romney Marsh with its long open straights intermingled with tight bends in a zig-zag like fashion where you haired down one straight or streaked out of a certain corner and you could see another bike ahead or behind you on another straight or corner riding hard to make up ground on you or you on him.

On a run with Kiddie later on, he misjudged the second bend on a tight double, shot across the road and hit a large metal gate which is the entrance gate to an old World War II airfield at Deanland. Luckily for him the gate was not latched properly and it swung open with a loud d-o-n-g as he hit it—so he was able to spin around, give the bike some throttle and continue the chase.

On Saturday night we were riding along the coast road from the Bay to Eastbourne heading for the Wimpy when a car full of drunken idiots came hurtling alongside us hanging onto the car's horn and ran me off the road outside a pub. We had been riding along at the speed limit not bothering anyone on this warm, sunny evening. One of them leapt out and attacked me as I leapt off my bike. These guys were clearly intoxicated. We exchanged blows. I punched him several times and was just thinking I was getting the better of him when someone jumped on my back from behind. I instantly thought this was another assailant and so threw him off after a struggle. The rest of our group were otherwise occupied with the others. Unfortunately, it was a police officer. They had been driving along the road when they had come across us fighting. As the driver brought the police car to a halt the passenger had leapt from the car onto my back. The drunken car driver ran into the pub. Initially the cops put me into the back of their car, but after listening to the protests and evidence from the rest of the group they released me and went into the pub after the car driver and occupants. This was typical. Apart from the culture wars between Mods, Skinheads and ourselves we did not go looking for trouble. Our aim was just to go out and above all to have as much fun as possible, but trouble would sometimes find us and we would have to fight, as in this case, with a group of pissheads who wanted to try their luck against us. With our superior numbers our opponents usually came off worse. Generally speaking the assailants would make their move first, but on some occasions if you are sure that trouble was imminent it was perhaps advisable to get in there first, as he who strikes the first blow and makes it count, is fifty per cent more likely to win the fight.

An example of this occurred a short time later. A biker known as Mechanic, as that was his profession, who rode with us on occasions, was riding with a friend on their motorcycles through town. They were stuck in stationary traffic at red traffic lights when a group of Skinheads came into view. With a shout of "Bloody Greasers, have 'em", they ran at the stationary bikers. Mechanic had done a bit of motorcross and enduro riding in his time but had done a bit of martial arts training too. Being vulnerable whilst astride his bike he leapt off and ran a couple of paces forward at the lead Skinhead hitting him on the jaw and knocked the Skinhead clean out. The others fled. The lights changed and the two bikers jumped on their bikes and rode away. A little later Mechanic got to thinking that he may have really hurt the Skinhead, so they rode around the town to check—but at a distance. An ambulance was loading up the injured Skinhead. The other Skinheads spotted the bikes and pointed them out to the police. Mechanic had broken the Skinhead's jaw. Returning to the scene of the crime was clearly not a wise move and Mechanic was taken to court and fined for his actions.

Returning briefly to village hall functions and discos. We often hit the dance floor in large numbers. Status Quo was one of our favourite bands at that time, as were the Rolling Stones and Black Sabbath with their track *Paranoid*. There was much biker shoulder rock dancing done to such records during these events. There were some tracks which were not suitable for shoulder rocking, so Worm, Walrus and Grass invented a new dance. They tried their new dance out to *Rockaria* by ELO. *Down Down* by Status Quo was a tune that started off at a reasonable pace but got faster and faster until all the dancers could not keep up with it, but it worked fine with their new dance. From then on when we hit the discos the dance floor would be full of guys and girls all trying to copy and keep up with all them doing their new dance. One of our parties fell on Weasel's birthday. It was customary on such occasions to give the birthday boy the bumps, which we did then he was debagged and his trousers were thrown out of the fire escape. Frenchie, as usual, was doing the disco. He was up on the stage with his equipment playing record tracks when Weasel suddenly appeared behind him minus his trousers. He grabbed the distracted Frenchie from behind, got him in a headlock and after a long struggle managed to remove his jeans. Weasel then put on Frenchie's jeans. Frenchie continued playing his disco for the next five or six tracks in his underwear before eventually making a request over the air, "Can someone return Weasel's trousers so I can have mine back please".

We all had different girlfriends over the years and liked to pull the birds if we could, but some guys were decidedly better than others at pulling the girls. The truck would often serve as a portable love nest but to a biker the ultimate acclaim was to make it with your girl over your motorcycle. To those of us that did it was like a badge of honour, that is if you made sure your bike was securely parked on its centre stand on good solid ground first.

Unlike Steward, who found himself hopping up and down on one leg trying to finish before the bike fell over after one side of the stand dug into the ground. I know of one older Rocker who called his daughter Bonnie after she was conceived over the seat of his Triumph Bonneville. Said Mickey, "My wife wasn't very pleased because she laddered her stockings... but then she wasn't my wife at that time." On one occasion Douglas was screwing a girl in the back of the truck outside a village hall disco when she suddenly cried, "Oh my God, they are looking in the windows". Doug looked up at the windscreen but could see nothing. Then he looked over his shoulder and there were Bollocks and Sprogg gesturing at him and urging him on through the back windows. Bar Steward met a girl from Hatfield who was staying with her friend locally. He visited her in Hatfield a few times then one night we ran into her friend in a local bar in town. She asked us if Steward was being faithful to her good friend. "Of course he is," we all assured her. Ten minutes later Steward came in as pissed as a fart, says, "Hello", and starts kissing her. Next thing we knew they went out and she became yet another "love nest" conquest in the back of the truck. So much for loyalty to her friend.

One morning our mother was waylaid by a local policeman in the street, "Why would you ever let your boys have motor-cycles?" he asked her, somewhat agitated. "My son wants a motor scooter, but I have told him he is not having one". After a few moments of thought our mother asked if he believed that his son should be in control of his own destiny? "Well, of course" replied the policeman. Our mother told him straight, "Well, we looked at it this way, we would much rather they are out riding their own motorcycles, where they are in control, than be on the back of someone else and they would have no control over what happens. If you try to stop them they will do it anyway or just ride on the back of others. Now they are old enough to do what they want to and we could not stop them, even if we wanted to". Finally, a few months later the policeman's son got his scooter.

CHAPTER TWENTY-EIGHT

Sidecar submarine

BAR STEWARD had moved away to Eastcote but would often hold parties at his maisonette above the main street which generally became pretty wild affairs. Steward's parties became legendary and absolutely everyone wanted an invite, which usually led to a whole convoy of different vehicles heading northwards towards the smoke (London area). One such party was in full swing when a group of young Skinheads came along shouting abuse up at those of us up on the balcony above the street. Mayo went down to confront them. Steward snatched a pint of beer out of Brian's hand. "Look at that prick", he stated, tipping the whole pint over Mayo's head from above as he stood up to the Skinheads. Mayo came storming back upstairs soaked, demanding to know who did it. Brian had disappeared for a refill. Steward told Mayo it was Brian the Sheep who was the culprit. Mayo replied that Brian may be a quiet bloke but he could also be a "nasty piece of work". Often a group of single, divorced or separated women from the local Gingerbread Club would turn up at these parties and a fair amount of banter would ensue between us and them, especially when the alcohol was flowing. One particular woman baited us relentlessly... "You're all wankers, I can see it in your eyes." She had been addressing her remarks mainly in the direction of Weasel, whose answer is perhaps best not repeated fully here—although he did follow it up with, "Who the hell would have you all the time there are dogs on the street?" She continued, "You boys... you are just all talk." Suddenly with a defiant grin she stepped out of her shoes, took off her knickers and tights in the hallway where she stood. "Come on then," she gestured, beckoning accordingly. One of the guys stepped up to the challenge, took her in the bathroom and sorted her out to fulfil her desire. While this was happening Brian the Sheep, muttering "Bloody old tart", scooped up her clothes and tossed them over the balcony and into the street. Her friend came looking for her so we told her she was busy in the bathroom.

Before settling down that night we had a drunken rolled up newspaper fight. Afterwards we were in our sleeping bags in the lounge with our girlfriends. Length was lying in his sleeping bag with his girl Moggs at his side. He was laying on his back with his hands behind his head. A large bulge was clearly visible inside his sleeping bag. Looking across the room he proudly announced, "Hey Sue, what do you think about that then?" "What... that's not real, you've got something there," she ridiculed him. "Not real, aye?" Length flew out of his sleeping bag stark naked and chased her around the room thrusting himself at her. She screamed like mad as she ran, after which, excitement over, we all finally turned in for the night. The next morning as we rode away the woman's knickers and tights from the night before were still hanging in a tree above the main street for all to see.

On the way home Mayo's Triumph 500 café racer developed a leak in its alloy petrol tank from around one of its mounting lugs, fractured due to engine vibration. We stopped at the Happy Eater at Felbridge. While most of us sat in the café eating breakfast, Mayo removed his fuel tank from the bike. He propped it up against a wall on its back-end to stop the fuel leaking out. Raiding the restaurant rockery, he removed a large rock while all the time chewing gum as he worked. Then he pulled on the lug to open the split as much as possible before pushing the chewing gum into the split. He then bashed the lug back into place with the rock using it as a hammer, then refitted the tank, returning the rock from whence it came. A real bodge indeed—but it was a temporary repair which eventually got him home.

That evening some of us stopped by a local pub in a favourite village. On entering we found there was a new landlord who was not at all pleased to see us. "You lot can clear off, I won't have bikers in here". We protested that we always drank there, but he was having none of it. "Not now you don't, so sod off". This bastard clearly needed teaching a lesson for treating us like that. DJP was always messing around with explosive devices, smoke bombs, even stink bombs and he always had a ready supply of such offensive items. So with myself at the wheel of the truck as getaway driver DJP took one of his smoke generators from the packet. These were smoke bombs which emitted an obnoxious concoction of gasses, which once ignited and thrust down a mole hole rid your land of moles. DJP ran back over to the pub and up the alleyway, he ignited a bomb and tossed it into the gent's toilet. Back in the truck we drove away. Ten minutes later we did a drive-by through the village and back to the pub. The pompous landlord was outside with a couple of customers coughing and spluttering with a bucket of water. Rough justice we thought, so now we were even, let that be a lesson to the bastard. A spin off from this incident was that no mole problems have been reported in the area since.

A few weeks on we were on our way to visit a village disco when we stopped at another country pub. There was a large basket of logs next to the open fire, but there was little life in the fire. DJP and his brother JP were known to be not so hardy when it came to cold weather. Sitting almost over the fire they kept putting more and more logs on, but to little avail, the fire continued to just smoulder. Eventually they had placed the entire contents of the log basket on the fire, when w-h-o-o-f the whole lot suddenly flared up. The outraged landlord leapt over the bar with a soda syphon, dashed over and hosed the fire down with soda water. "What bloody idiot did that?" he exclaimed angrily, glaring around for the culprit. That end of the bar had suddenly become strangely empty.

There were five motorcycle dealers in our immediate area, being Park Motorcycles, Eastbourne Motorcycles, Kennards at Seaford and J. W. Groombridge at Cross in Hand; but the one with the most branches was Motcombe Motorcycles. Bob had opened his first branch of Motcombe Motorcycles in the mid 1960s in Eastbourne's Old Town but the business had now grown to encompass three shops. Bob's son worked at the Hailsham branch. He had the nickname of Big Butch. This was his CB radio handle (call sign) as many of us were at that time using illicit CB radio sets that had been smuggled in from abroad. CB radio was illegal then in the UK, the sets being tuned to the 27 AM frequency, which was the same as used for radio-controlled model aircraft. The UK radio waves were regularly monitored and enforced by a section of the General Post Office and its enforcers did their best to track down and prosecute illegal transmitting by way of using DF (direction finding) aerials. This, of course, made it all the more exciting with breakers (operators) constantly keeping on the move to avoid detection and keeping one step ahead of the authorities. It was a constant, but amusing game of cat and mouse.

On opening this, his latest branch, Bob had in his infinite wisdom employed Spud as the motorcycle shop general manager, probably for his managerial experience and almost certainly for Spud to keep an eye on his wayward son. This situation was not practical however as Butch, the owner's son, had no interest at all in complying with Spud's orders or requests. There was an old mechanic who also worked there. He had white hair and went by the nickname of Grandad. Myself in particular had a good working relationship with Butch, Spud and the others at the branch. Butch was a fully competent welder, but Motcombe Motorcycles had no welding gear themselves; so Butch would come round and borrow mine when needed. He would also take away all our waste oil from bike and car oil changes which was used to fuel the workshop waste oil heater during the winter. In return we would buy some sausages, bacon and French bread where several bikers would while away many a cold winter afternoon with a fry up, using a frying pan on the hot plate of the workshop heater. Further, I owned a portable compressor and spray guns with which I would sometimes do minor paint repairs for them to help out. My employment as a milk roundsman meant that I was free most afternoons. If out on a test run, Butch would sometimes drop in at my home for an occasional cup of tea. Motcombe Motorcycles became agents for Cossack and other brands of Russian motorcycles, as well as being a dealer for the major Japanese brands. These Russian machines were basically copies of WW2 German BMW sidecar outfits, both rugged and almost agricultural in build, and they were also fitted with a reverse gear. The sales pitch was that such a machine could do virtually every job on the farm except plough—and for that you needed two. Butch became something of an expert in drifting, wheel spinning in forward and reverse gears, as well as riding with sidecar wheel high in the air but on this occasion he over-cooked it big time.

I was at home on a bitterly cold winter's afternoon when the company works van appeared outside our house towing a Cossack sidecar outfit. I went out and noticed a strong smell of burning clutch or brakes coming from the van. It transpired that during their lunchtime the branch staff had taken two of the machines out for a test run on roads across the local marshes. Butch had taken a Cossack outfit with a regular customer riding as passenger in the sidecar while Grandad followed behind on a Yamaha. Once on the bendy, twisty and narrow lanes across the marsh Butch, it seems, got a little too enthusiastic for his own riding ability. From the explanation given by Grandad from his position behind, it seems that Butch pushed the outfit a little too hard into a left-hand bend. Aided by the inexperience and nervousness of the passenger being reluctant to hang out of the sidecar to get it back down, the sidecar wheel became airborne by about three or four feet. Butch veered away from the sidecar to get the wheel back down but was hampered by the narrowness of the road. His front wheel clipped the verge and instantly sank into the edge of the soggy grass, swerving the outfit hard to the right. With a loud splash the outfit, with its occupants on board, flew into the water-filled dyke bordering the road. Grandad, hardly able to speak now for laughing so much, recalled that as the outfit sank the sidecar passenger leapt to his feet where he slowly disappeared below the bank of the dyke like a captain going down with his sinking ship. The outfit's occupants half splashed, half swam their way back to the bank and dragged themselves out of the murky water.

"Quick, quick", yelled Butch to Grandad, "go back and get the van—and don't forget the tow rope". Grandad sped off, mentally preparing himself for the anger of Spud, the shop manager. While waiting for Grandad to return, Butch and his passenger started to shiver. Ice began to form on their wet clothes. "Christ", complained Butch, breathing on his hands to try to revive them, "it's bloody freezing out here, it was warmer in the water". So they got back in the water, much to the amazement of the odd passing motorist, shocked to see a couple of grown up men up to their necks in the water in the edge of the dyke in winter time. Eventually, Grandad arrived back in the firm's van after incurring the wrath of Spud. Butch had to dive down and by feel managed to attach the tow rope to the front of the bike in the mirk. With Grandad revving the van and dragging and, with the other two pulling and lifting they eventually managed to pull the outfit from the dyke's mud, but not before the van's clutch burnt out. The van's clutch slipped from then on and a new clutch had to be fitted after this incident.

Arriving at my house Butch was in a panic. "Quick, hurry, get a bloody hosepipe and your toolbox, the customer is coming in at four this afternoon to pick it up." I rushed and got the requested items, along with a big bucket of soapy water. Butch took the float chambers off both carburettors and drained them. He took out the air filter whilst I removed the spark plugs. We had to bail the dyke water from the sidecar body. We pushed the outfit down the road in gear to clear the water from inside the motor. Water was spitting out of both the plug holes in the horizontally opposed engine and mud was running out of the ends of the silencers. We heard a croaking noise. Butch pulled the seat pads from the sidecar and a frog jumped out. I washed the seat pads off with the hose then hosed off the rest of the bike and sidecar. Butch gave it a quick wash over with bucket and sponge. I hosed it off again. We bump started it down the road. The motor coughed and fired, then started. It was away.

Butch donned his sodden crash helmet and took off on the outfit in a hurry. The other two gave chase in the van. The rest of this sorry tale goes as follows. They arrived back at the shop to an angry lecture from Spud, after which they all set about cleaning and polishing the outfit with some urgency. Oils and filter were changed. Butch had previously noticed that there were governors fitted in both carburettors to limit the bike's overall performance, so he had snapped them off. The outfit had only come in for a new headlamp dip switch under warranty. The owner came in to collect his steed and thanked them for the work done.

A month later Butch's dad Bob brought a letter over to the shop from the Cossack's owner. It stated how pleased he was with the level of service he had received at the hands of Motcombe Motorcycles. He went on to state that his machine had only come in to have a new dip switch fitted, yet the outfit had been fully washed and polished and a service carried out. The bike now went like the clappers and all free of charge. Completely unaware was he that just a few hours earlier his machine had been resting on the bottom of a dyke. He would definitely recommend them to his friends in the future. Decades went by before Butch felt he could come clean about the incident. After his father had long since retired and the business had closed down, Butch made a full confession and they were eventually able to have a good laugh about the whole dodgy episode.

After the Cossack incident it was decided that the branch would do a display in the small window on the side of the shop. For the display they mounted a Yamaha PW50 child's motocross bike illuminated with coloured lighting, which was to be left on at night. Hindsight may have suggested that perhaps this may not have been the wisest course of actions as after just a few days a member of the local low life community smashed the plate glass window and made off with the new Yamaha mini motocrosser which was never recovered. An angry Butch turned up at the pub threatening what he would like to do to the perpetrator of the crime if he were to ever get hold of him. A week on a Christmas card arrived at the shop. On being opened it bore a matching photo of a Yamaha PW50 cut from a Yamaha sales brochure. Underneath in bold letters it read, "Happy Christmas from PW50. PS. Please leave instruction manual and tool kit by the window on Thursday night".

Kiddie's bike was off the road when one of the regulars at the pub offered him a car. It was a grey Hillman Minx in reasonable condition but somewhat grubby as it had been standing in a barn for a while. There were several months of MoT test still on the car and the owner did not want any payment for the vehicle. Kiddie acquired it believing at least it would get him around until his bike was fixed. He gave the car a thorough clean inside and out and polished the paintwork. The car was soon gleaming and it was now in the same condition in which Kiddie kept his bikes in. Driving around in the car he began calling it his "pride and joy".

Christmas day dawned again and as usual The Black Horse was to be open for just two hours only at lunchtime that day. The vast majority of our band were waiting to enter as soon as the pub doors were open, but for some strange reason Kiddie was absent.

Most of us had decided to go into town on a pub crawl the night before on Christmas Eve. Kiddie did not want to go into town, instead he would tour the normal local country pubs as usual. Kiddie's brother Herb had recently come of age to ride a moped. He had recently been hanging around with Sprogg's younger brother Steve and a local lad who rode a pretty bright red Malaguti sports moped fitted with clip-on handlebars and twin exhausts. We never knew this lad's real name, so he was simply known by all as Malaguti after his moped. Kiddie had agreed to take Herb and his friends along on his Christmas tour of local hostelries.

Back at "the cheeks" on this day the main topic of the conversation was where the hell was Kiddie? He was a creature of habit and would be most unlikely to miss out on a mere two hours of valuable Christmas drinking time. A good hour had passed with much seasonal merriment going on in the pub, when the door suddenly flew back with a crash. "Where is he...? Where's the bastard that shit in my bloody car?" Kiddie was angry. "Who?"

"Malaguti, that's who." One of the girls, startled by this sudden outburst exclaimed, "Malaguti...? Is he foreign?" "He'll wish he was when I get hold of him." I hadn't seen Kiddie so riled since the summer of 1973 when he had burst into the pub in similar fashion shouting, "That's it, the bloody Conservatives are in power and the bastards have introduced VAT and put ten pence on the price of a new visor". On this occasion his mood had not been improved by Madge the pub landlady also announcing that beer had gone up in price by one penny per pint also owing to the new Value Added Tax. Best bitter had gone from 12p to 13p per pint.

Finally after purchasing his first beer Kiddie began to recount his story. He had taken Herb and Malaguti with him on the pub crawl in his car. After a few beers and a couple of whiskies Malaguti was in a sorry state, so was unable to go home. He had come over on his bike so asked if he could sleep in Kiddie's car. Kiddie agreed. There was a severe frost that night. The next morning Kiddie had come out to make his way to "the cheeks" when he thought he saw some dog shit next to his car. On opening the rear door he was horrified to find that Malaguti had defecated all over the back seat. It was a total mess, Kiddie went on exploding with rage once again. "I don't know how the hell he did it as he was wearing jeans tucked into motorcycle boots— but what really pissed me off was that the dirty sod had even wiped his backside on the newspaper that I covered my wind-screen with to keep the frost off and then put it back on the screen." By then the crowd in the pub, already laughing hysteri-cally, burst into hoots of uncontrolled laughter. For his part Malaguti somewhat wisely disappeared from the face of the earth for the next six months. It was on a hot summer's evening in June in the crowded bar that a familiar sheepish voice was heard again. "Err... hello lads." At the bar with his back to the door, Kiddie instantly spun around with a shout, "Ere, that's the bastard that shit in my bloody car". Once again "the cheeks" was in total uproar.

Have a Fag Carl made his way to "the cheeks" for a beer. While making the final turn from the main road towards the pub he hit a large patch of black ice on the road. His motorcycle went into a skid. Bike and rider ended up in the roadside ditch. Carl was pinned down under the sheer weight of his Honda in the ditch. With the bike on top of him he was unable to move. He was a mere fifty yards from the pub, close enough in fact that he could clearly hear the laughter and merriment going on inside. Struggle as he might he could not get free. It was a good twenty minutes before a car came along and the occupants noticed the bike. The car stopped and the passengers freed the unfortunate rider. Carl staggered into the pub, wet through and frozen while all the time cursing the drinkers for not hearing his cries for help and coming to his aid. He certainly got some stick over that one.

New Year's Eve dawned. There was a choice of different events and venues with which to welcome in the new year. We eventually settled on the Golden Martlet, a village pub out in the country-side. The pub had a large hall attached and the New Year's Eve party was being held there. We all met at "the cheeks" before making our way over, *en masse* as usual. When we arrived the party was in full swing and a good evening was had by all, that was until near the end, when there was some sort of altercation going on at the other side of the hall. There seemed to be some sort of problem going on between some loud mouthed idiot and a group of five or six other people. The disturbance was nothing to do with us, so with the party over everyone started to leave. I fired up the truck and the rest climbed aboard. Walrus had borrowed his father's car because of the inclement weather, and he too took some of the group. The crowd outside the pub was too good an opportunity to miss, so with a group of ready spectators I spun the truck around in a drift across the road. As the truck came off the grass verge in a sideways slide across the tarmac it pulled the tubeless tyre away from the rim and a rear tyre went flat.

We limped over the railway bridge and pulled up a fair way down to change the wheel on a straight clear road. I got the jack out along with the wheel brace. Walrus came along and stopped to help. We decided there was enough of us to lift the back corner of the van and not bother to use the lifting jack. I loosened the wheel nuts and removed all but the last two. The group took up position around the back corner and lifted. I took off the last two nuts. I reached for the spare wheel, but as I did so heard a loud revving engine. A Ford Escort estate car came hurtling over the railway bridge, heading straight for us at speed. I yelled a frantic warning to the others to look out. Within a second the car ploughed into us scooping Worm and girlfriend Gill up on his car bonnet from behind and smashing them onto the back of the van. It shot forward, the rear nearside corner dropping onto the road surface as it now had no wheel fitted. The others scattered. We all thought it was an accident, but the truth was much worse. With its engine still racing wildly the Escort reversed back depositing the injured casualties onto the road surface before he tried to drive away.

Myself and the other startled onlookers soon regathered our senses and threw everything we had at the Escort's windscreen to try to stop him escaping. Someone threw the jack, another the jack handle; someone threw a rock and myself the wheel brace but to no avail. All of the items thrown bounced harmlessly off the windscreen. The Escort with its front panel and nearside front wing caved in and one headlight smashed still managed to drive away. Walrus jumped into his car and gave chase. Later he returned with a hysterical young blonde woman on board.

It had been her first date with the offender. Walrus had seen her bale out of the Escort at the end of the road as the car raced away. She blurted out that the offender had mistaken our group for the people that he had the set to with at the party. He had yelled, "There they are, I am going to kill them all". He had then deliberately driven into us at speed, then sped away. The emergency services arrived, an ambulance whisked Worm and Gill away to hospital. An immediate police manhunt was initiated for the hit and run driver. The next morning we had a visit from the police.

While the manhunt was still active the police had realised that they already had the offender in custody. He had broken into his ex-wife's flat at Bexhill, telling her he had to lie low as he had killed someone; but she had another man in her flat and after a fight our offender was arrested and was being held in custody. In court he was jailed for fifteen months for the hit and run attack on Worm and Gill. Worm still suffers with leg pains from his injuries to this day. In a strange way they had been fortunate, their saving grace being that their leg damage was drastically reduced because they were hit from behind and scooped onto the bonnet, rather than hit frontways on which may have led to multiple bone fractures. So much for a happy new year.

CHAPTER TWENTY-NINE

The end of an era

BUTCH was direct and to the point, "Hey Tony, I want you to respray my Escort van." "When and where?" I asked somewhat surprised. "We can do it in the workshop on Sunday when the shop is closed." This was not ideal as although the dealership workshop was large it had no extractor fan facility. Furthermore, my compressor being more of a portable type was fine for bike tanks and side panels, even for a car wing or an odd panel, but would not be up to turning out a good job on a complete vehicle as big as his van. More to the point, there was a fair number of bikes in various states of repair along with other various equipment kicking around the workshop. I expressed my concerns to Butch. "Don't be such a tart!" was his firm reply. "I will do all the prep work on the van and sort the workshop out so it's all ready for you; just turn up with your gear, get your arse in gear and do your stuff." "OK then, if you insist. How about next week?" "You're on", he agreed. Wildman had also asked me if I could respray the frame of his Z1; so I agreed with Butch that Wildman would bring the frame along and I would do both jobs one after the other.

The due day dawned and we all gathered at the shop. Wildman was to one side preparing his frame whilst myself and Butch masked up the van windows, lights, etc. ready for paint. Butch had already stacked the bikes and equipment to one side and covered it all with dust sheets. Wildman had previously been smoking a roll-up cigarette. I mixed up the paint and started spraying. My worst fears were soon realised, as within a short time

271

and after a few passes on the roof and working around the van, it was almost impossible to see across the room. "Bloody hell", Butch yelled through the fog and above the noise of the compressor, "just keep going".

I had just refilled the spray gun with more paint when there was a loud crash. The workshop door burst open and a short fireman fell into the room. He had tripped over the doorstep and the two firemen close behind almost fell over him on entering. It was like watching something out of an old Keystone Cops movie. The Fire Chief shouted for me to switch the compressor off. "We have had reports", he said, "of a strong smell of petroleum spirit. You will have to stop what you are doing". "Fuck that", Butch retorted, "we have to finish the job". At that point matters started to get heated. Spotting Wildman's roll-up still on his lip the Fire Chief yelled across, "Put that bloody cigarette out... one spark and the whole block could go up." Wildman tossed his cigarette on the floor and trod on it. It had been out anyway. Butch was adamant, "We can't stop now, we have to finish the job". The Fire Chief became angry, and glaring at Butch and Wildman he openly chastised them. "You are not doing yourself any good you know working in here without masks on." "We know that, we are not fucking stupid," Butch snapped back. "We will see about that", was the Chief's parting reply, and they left slamming the door behind them. After about ten minutes or so, Butch peered out. "Good, they've gone, come on Tone, finish the bloody job quick". I fired up the compressor and re-started the spraying process.

Hardly any time had passed before the door flew open again and the little fireman was back. As he entered again it occurred to me that his helmet looked far too big for him, and he looked like it may fall over his eyes at any moment. "Bloody hell it's thick in next door", he complained loudly. There was a girl who lived in the flat over the shop next door who had a bit of a loose reputation. "Do you live there then?" asked Butch. "Err, err no... I was just having a bite to eat", he replied uneasily, looking down at the ground and shuffling his feet, "but you've got to stop this right now". "We are almost done", Butch assured him as he left.

Suddenly the shop phone started ringing. It rang and rang. Eventually Butch answered it. It was his father and he was angry. He had just been on the wrong end of an irate call from the Sussex Fire Brigade. "OK dad", Butch assured him, "we will stop now". Butch came back into the workshop just as I finished spraying. "Thank God for that—that was a close thing". "What a bastard", complained Wildman, "what about my frame?" "Fuck you and your frame!" Butch called across the hazy shop whilst inspecting my handiwork... "Well... bit of a shit job, but at least it's all one colour now. Well done". The whole thing had been an amusing, but complete fiasco.

Grizzly bought a new RD400 Yamaha. Apart from his full-time employment he had also taken a part-time job as a barman in the evenings at a local pub for extra income. During this period he became very friendly with the landlord and his wife to the point that when they moved to another pub at Wembley he would sometimes ride up and visit them.

On this occasion he clearly had too much to drink, and on leaving the pub wound the Yamaha up on the A40. The traffic suddenly eased up and Grizzly, caught unprepared, hit a VW Beetle up the rear end straight between the two exhaust pipes. However good fortune did eventually smile on him, as although he was thrown from the bike and completely over the central reservation, he landed directly in front of an empty ambulance on the opposite side of the dual carriageway. The ambulance took instant avoiding action, screeched to a halt, scooped him up and whisked him quickly off to hospital, thus avoiding the clutches of the law with their dreaded breathaliser bag.

The Yamaha suffered considerable front end damage with only 2,000 miles on the clock. The bike sat in our garage for a few months while insurance was sorted out, then Butch purchased the machine and rebuilt it.

Butch was not normally a road rider as motocross was his passion. Along with his buddy Gypsy Joe and our cousin Mauler they raced on the local motocross tracks and we would often ride out to spectate and support them at such events. Now, having bought the Yamaha from Grizzly, Butch came out riding the roads with us. I remember one day in particular when at speed we all approached a narrow bridge just wide enough for a car and a motorcycle to pass each other. There was an elderly pair of pedestrians who wanted to walk across the bridge but the first few bikes raced across. As Butch followed through the gap the old chap became so annoyed that he took a swipe at Butch, trying to whack him hard with his walking stick. "Silly old bastard", ridiculed Butch on reaching our destination.

At that time there was a music festival held annually on nearby farmland. For some unexplained reason Butch was recruited and somehow managed to be put in charge of the fireworks display. Whoever was responsible for such a decision needed their heads tested as such an action was akin to handing an arsonist a gallon of petrol and a box of matches.

As one can imagine as the evening wore on there was a feeling of impending doom amongst some who knew him. The stage on which the bands were performing was of wooden structure but built upon a base of straw bales. Towards the end of the evening Butch ignited the first rocket, but as he did so the rocket launcher fell to the ground. The rocket took off horizontally and just a little over head height. It flew slightly above the heads of the crowd, disappeared under the stage and ignited the straw bales. The band performing at the time were forced to flee, jumping from the burning stage mid song for their own safety and in the process were also doing their best to save their valuable equipment. The music-goers had to form a chain of buckets to try to put the fire out. Unfortunately, Butch had also left the lid off the chest of fireworks and sparks from that first rocket taking off set off the other fireworks all at once. Fireworks were whizzing around in all directions whilst multiple explosions rent the air as revellers scattered. It was total chaos. The whole amusing farce was discussed later in the pub when an outraged girl suddenly blurted out, "Yes, and they ate Henrietta". "Who the hell was Henrietta?" "The farmer's pet sheep; the festival-goers killed her and roasted her on a barbecue spit..." RIP Henrietta.

Dick the Undertaker dropped round from next door to see me. Our neighbour's house had been up for sale for a while now, ever since Dick's wife had been taken by cancer. "Tony", he said sadly, "the house is sold and we are leaving now. It's the end of an era, that's what it is mate, the end of an era". I shook his hand firmly.

We had so much fun with our neighbours ever since they had moved in next door. Dick had entertained us all with his wild antics and his wicked sense of humour. The lovely Jill, his adorable long-suffering wife, had quietly gone along with his crazy ways. They had become honorary members of our group, throwing themselves headlong into our escapades along with Jill's mother and the couple's children, they would all be greatly missed. We were sorry to see them go. Later, on his way home from work, our father was accosted by Dick's other next door neighbour. Being universally known as Old Nosey, she was a curtain twitcher who watched everything that went on in the street from behind her closed curtains. "He's gone then, he's gone," she ranted, "he's an alcoholic you know, an alcoholic."

Our father denied this was the case. "No," he said calmly, "Dick liked a drink but he was certainly not an alcoholic". "Oh yes he was," Nosey replied, "he came into my house to say goodbye to me and my brother, then he took me to one side and said, 'You haven't got a drop of Scotch I could lay my hands on before I go?'." Good old Dick, he had carried on the wind-up with her to the very last. Little did we know then how prophetic Dick's last words to us would be, as within a short time everything we had grown to consider as normality had turned completely on its head.

When it came about it started in a perfectly innocent way. The Black Horse had been our main base of operations for well over a few years now. Our regular trade had spanned the occupancies of several landlords and landladies from Margaret to Madge and Arthur and now on to Doug and his wife Eve. It was felt that like Margaret in previous years, the latest landlord Doug and his wife tolerated us for the large amount of money that we and our friends put over the bar. On first taking over the pub Doug had christened us his "knights of the road", but we felt that in reality, although he desperately needed our trade through the autumn and winter months, he was not so amicable towards us in the spring and summer as the amounts of passing tourists and walkers increased.

One busy summer's evening when the place was packed Mayo accidentally knocked over a full pint of beer which flooded over the table and onto the floor. Jumping up, Mayo rushed to the bar and urgently asked Charles the barman for a cloth to mop up the spillage. Charles could be somewhat pompous, and as he was serving he brushed Mayo away with a frown. "I'm busy" and a sweep of his hand. Being fobbed off in this way Mayo snatched the cloth beer mats from the bar and rushed back to clear up the mess. He soaked up the spilt beer on the table and wrung it back into the glass. He then mopped up the mess on the floor, and in the absence of another available container wrung that into the glass also. Charles hit the roof, exploding at Mayo for his actions. Mayo stood his ground and rightly so. He had asked for help and Charles had refused him, so an argument ensued. Charles called for Doug the landlord who backed Charles. Doug kept muttering feebly on about spore counts on beer glasses. We in turn all argued Mayo's case. At that point Doug's wife Eve appeared and joined in. She was downright abusive and talked down to us like we were dirt on her shoes. We felt that she never really wanted us there in the first place. She threatened to ban us. Sprogg and girlfriend Sally argued with her. Eve and Sally went the rounds so Doug banned us all. We later heard from the village regulars that he soon regretted his actions as his takings dropped dramatically.

A few weeks on a few bikers from another area, unaware of the scenario dropped in at the pub and Doug was shouting his mouth off to them that he was glad that he had banned us. Angered by this I decided to contact the local papers and TV stations. Doug had reporters and interviewers banging on his door. Newspaper photographers took photos of us all outside the pub on our bikes which were repeated in the papers as The Black Horse Incident. Doug was livid. He had got his just deserts. Regrettably though the era of The Black Horse was now over for good.

Some years had passed and I was helping out at another motorcycle shop. The owner had gone abroad on a buying trip. I was in the shop with another member of staff when Dilly walked in. I hadn't seen him for a few years. He greeted me warmly and shook me by the hand. He was interested in a sporty Honda import on a display rack in the shop. He stated that if we could get it registered and serviced up by the next day he would buy it. So we got the bike down and MoT tested and while the other staff members serviced it up I took a bike out of the workshop and sped over to the Brighton vehicle registration office and got it registered. I rode the Honda over to Dilly's Milton Street cottage and he brought me back in his car. I was surprised that he had finally got a car licence now as he was anti-car. Motorcycles had always been his life's passion. On the way back we had a good chat about old times. I never saw him again. His luck finally ran out. He was killed in a horrific crash at East Guldeford near Rye where his motorcycle was in collision with a car travelling in the opposite direction. He had been out riding with Robbo, Stan and others at the time, but at the point of impact the road snakes slightly with crash barriers along both sides of the road. It is possible that the car cut straight across rather than take the curves in the road, as other cars had done so in the past, and the two vehicles collided. The speed of the impact threw Dilly over the barrier and into a field.

Roger "Dilly" Dumbrell had died as he lived his life... at the limit. The grand old man of motorcycling (as we called him), a local legend and the man everyone wanted to beat, the man who had inspired so many of us, had now passed on and left a huge hole in our motorcycling community. He was sorely missed. He was buried in the local village churchyard near where he lived. The sad procession followed his coffin up the steps and past the huge ancient yew tree straining and creaking against its supporting chains into a church packed to capacity with bikers and locals. The vicar sat astonished as in the pulpit one of Dilly's oldest friends stood and recounted some of their exploits and run-ins with the law. Outside again we stood around the open grave with the sun beating down on us. They buried Dilly where *the big fella on the hill could look down upon him*. Geoff put his hand on my shoulder, "You know mate, if you've got to be planted I can't think of a better place," then he continued on, "A while back he said to me, 'You know Geoff, I cannot imagine me as an old man, maybe I'll hit something bloody hard'. Perhaps he had a premonition. Some months later his friends placed a memorial bench bearing his name at Beachy Head above one of his favourite stretches of road. The inscription on the bench reads:

**Think about it logically
You owe it to yourself
The road that winds beneath here
His life, his love, his health.**

Some years later his flint built motorcycle shed and outhouse went up for sale for a quarter of a million pounds with planning permission to be developed into a house.

CHAPTER THIRTY

All that had gone before

BBBRRING... what the hell. That time already? I reached out a weary hand and turned the alarm off in the still dark room. Half asleep I climbed out of bed, washed, dressed and went downstairs. I had a long trip ahead of me today and wanted to make an early start to get as many miles under my belt as possible before too much traffic hit the roads. After a slice of toast and a cup of tea I gathered my bike gear together and went out to the garage, opened the door and wheeled my motorcycle out under a fast lightening sky. Donning my gear I hit the starter button, the motor burst into life instantly, I mounted the bike and chugged slowly out of my drive and down the private close until I reached the main road. Road clear I opened the throttle, accelerated up through the gears and increased speed up to the legal limit. I kept the speed down for a few miles letting the motor warm up to normal running temperature then started to increase speed. Heading along a bendy road I settled down, sweeping through each bend as it came, selecting optimum gear ratios and throttle openings to perfection. It was getting light now even under the trees on this tree-lined road. Odd flashes of mottled sunlight burst intermittently through the overhead canopy. Suddenly I burst out into bright sunlight. A single flip of my right wrist on the throttle grip and over one hundred horses reared... my front wheel lifted effortlessly skyward... my speed increasing over the magic ton (100mph).

What a lovely morning for a bike ride with little traffic at the moment. Whizzing along all thoughts of my route and destination were left trailing far behind in my wake. I was in heaven, enjoying the moment, suspended in my own world. Motorcycles were made for this. A world of the power at your right wrist, a throaty exhaust note, a powerful engine and the warm sun on my face. My only sense of reality being the green landscape of hedges and trees flashing past at ever increasing speed, my angle of lean as I cranked through the corners and the rev counter hitting the red line as the motor cried out for a higher gear.

Slowly, my mind began to drift back to a better time. Nearly fifty years had passed by in what now seemed little more than an instant. Back to those heady days of the village gatherings, discos and parties, The Black Horse, the Sunday afternoon and evening burn ups and the police chases; a free and exciting life, but above all the former characters and the intense comradeship.

There had been many crashes and slide-offs over the years where the main casualties were minor damage to your bike, tears in your jeans, scuffs on your leather jacket and various amounts of flesh and skin left deposited along the tarmac. In general, we had been extremely lucky but we had lost a few along the way, both to motorcycle accidents and in more recent times to natural causes. A neighbouring group lost two killed in three months.

Suddenly I became aware of a being, an almost spiritual presence, an aura, an unusual feeling I was being hemmed in. Within a moment in my mind's eye they were all there, back riding with me once again. There were my two brothers Grizzly and Worm, John, Mick and Eric, the boys from the village days; Kiddie, Den, Snout, Geoff, Johnny and Sprogg. There was Spud, Biddle, Pud, Percy Penis, Bog Wright and Mad Mongol, Dutch, Herman, Andy, Mawanga, One Ball and Frozzie; and there was the two notorious brothers DJP and JP. From the Highlight there was Manure, Robbo, Fred, Stan, Pete, Trev and Smed. There were the boys from the Bay including Grasscut, Bollocks, Walrus and

Pus and local lads Bar Steward, Box, Brian the Sheep, Richard, Bean, Weed... and there was Length, Slime, Mayo, Allen and Have a Fag Carl, Mac, Sondel Steve, Colin and Harry the Dog from the Eastbourne area. There were the Hailsham lads Reg, Gozy, Weasel, Ogri, Malcolm, Mouth and then Mauler and Wildman from Heathfield. There were the girls; Terri, Daff, Gill, Linda, Jayne, Christine, Yvonne, Sally, Pike, Sandra, Pauline, Ann, Moggs, Carol, Louse, the two Sues and so many others.

Finally, there was our first fatal casualty Maz, along with the others now gone before, being Douglas, Blue, the Gibbon brothers (Funky and Gibbo), Freshers, Daffy, Dimwiddy, Snout and last, but not least, Roger "Dilly" Dumbrell. In fact... all those who have lived... and those who died at the limit.

ACKNOWLEDGMENTS

The author wishes to express his sincere gratitude to the following:

DAVE SMEDLEY
NICK GOBLE
SUSAN EVANS
DAVE POTTER
JEFF POTTER
PETER WRIGHT
FELICITY WRIGHT
KEITH HUNNISETT
MICK ROBINSON
FRED HUGGETT
PAUL SAMPLE
Ogri Cartoonist, Bike Magazine

If you have enjoyed this book please recommend it to your friends and others, or on social media.

We would very much appreciate your feedback at
https://bentnosepublications.wordpress.com